THE DIARY OF CHARLES WOOD OF CYFARTHFA IRONWORKS, MERTHYR TYDFIL, 1766–1767

To Rhoda

The Editor and Publisher are greatly indebted to Merthyr Tydfil County Borough Council and the Glamorgan Record Office for generous financial assistance towards the publication of this volume

THE DIARY OF CHARLES WOOD OF CYFARTHFA IRONWORKS, MERTHYR TYDFIL, 1766–1767

Edited by Joseph Gross with an Introduction by Philip Riden

MERTON PRIORY PRESS

First published 2001

Published by
Merton Priory Press Ltd
67 Merthyr Road, Whitchurch
Cardiff CF14 1DD

ISBN 1 898937 48 6

Printed by
Dinfewr Press Ltd
Rawlings Road, Llandybie
Carmarthenshire SA18 3YD

CONTENTS

LIST OF ILLUSTRATIONS

ACKNOWLEDGEMENTS

I wish to express my sincere thanks to Mr John Wood of Norton Summit, Australia, for his kind permission to publish the text of this volume, to Mr Geraint James, Mrs Carolyn Jacobs and the staff of Merthyr Tydfil Libraries, and to Ms Susan Edwards, the Glamorgan Archivist, and her staff, for their invaluable help in making available the text on microfilm and providing photocopies from the film. I am also grateful for my son John for his extensive help in preparing a particularly difficult typescript for the press.

Plate 1 is reproduced by kind permission of Miss Margaret Wood and Messrs Johnson Matthey PLC (through the courtesy of Ms Susan Ashton), Plates 2, 3 and 4 by permission of Mr John Wood, and Plate 5 by permission of the South Wales Record Society. Plate 6 is from a photograph of my own.

I am also indebted to Mr Brian James for help in preparing a number of the footnotes and with the index.

Merthyr Tydfil
April 2001

Joseph Gross

1 A portrait of Charles Wood in later life, in the possession of his descendants in Australia.

INTRODUCTION

The 'Diary of Charles Wood', as the manuscript published here has conveniently come to be called, is in fact a composite volume of writings by an important figure in the eighteenth-century iron industry spanning nearly twenty years towards the end of his life. Besides the daily journal which he kept for about twelve months in 1766–7, while he was supervising the building of what became Cyfarthfa Ironworks at Merthyr Tydfil in South Wales, the book also contains notes from the 1750s and early 1760s concerning Wood's earlier career at Low Mill Forge in Cumberland. As well as providing a unique record of the day-to-day progress of the construction of an early coke-fired blast furnace, the diary also sheds a good deal of light on life in a remote upland parish that was about to be transformed by industrialisation. Although Wood's work has been known to a handful of historians of the iron industry since the 1960s, its full value has not hitherto been appreciated for want of a complete edition of the text, which this volume makes available for the first time.

*

Charles Wood was born in 1702, the seventh of fifteen children of William Wood of Wolverhampton (1671–1730) and his wife Margaret, the daughter of Richard Molyneux of Tettenhall.[1] Towards the end of his life William, whose family had been involved in the metal trades of the West Midlands for several generations, carried out unsuccessful attempts to smelt iron with coke using a reverberatory furnace which he erected at a site near Frizington in Cumberland;[2] he may at an earlier date have been connected with an ironworks at Bellingham in County Durham.[3] The experiments at Frizington were part of a much larger scheme promoted by Wood under the name of the Company of

[1] M.H. Wood, *An interim report on the Wood family genealogy* (Author, 1963) (copy in Society of Genealogists, Family History Tracts, vol. 102), 21.

[2] P. Riden, *A gazetteer of charcoal-fired blast furnaces in use in Great Britain since 1660* (1993), 112.

[3] Ibid., 125.

Ironmasters of Great Britain, which collapsed after his death, so that Charles, who with one of his brothers (William) and a son-in-law (William Buckland) was left all his father's extensive (but essentially worthless) business interests, had to make his own way in the world.[1]

After his father died Charles spent a few years in Jamaica before returning to Cumberland, where in 1735 he married Anne Peel at Harrington, near Whitehaven. The couple went back to Jamaica, where Charles appears to have worked as supervisor of a lead mine and where their first child was born in 1739. They returned in 1741 and settled near Keswick. During his time in Jamaica Wood had acquired some samples of platinum, which he brought back to England and, together with a neighbour, William Brownrigg of Ormathwaite Hall (1712–1800), a medical practitioner and amateur scientist, published the first account of the properties of that metal.[2] The two became more closely connected in 1750, when Charles, following the death of his first wife, married Brownrigg's sister Jemima, the widow of Roger Lyndon, by whom he had six children.[3]

At about the time of his sister's second marriage, Brownrigg also became a partner with Wood and two Whitehaven merchants in the Low Mill Iron Company, which in 1749–50 acquired two leases, one of iron ore and the other of coal, in the manor of Egremont.[4] Wood spent much of the 1750s experimenting at Low Mill with what became known as the potting (or potting and stamping) process of refining pig iron, in which pig was reheated in earthenware pots in a reverberatory furnace, using coal as fuel, as an alternative to the traditional method of producing bar iron using finery and chafery hearths with charcoal. Although cumbersome, potting and stamping was for a time quite widely adopted and in the 1780s, immediately before it was superseded by Henry Cort's puddling process, accounted for about half the output of bar iron in Great

[1] Wood, *Interim Report*, 26–8; M.W. Flinn, 'William Wood and the coke-smelting process', *Transactions of the Newcomen Society*, 34 (1961–2), 55–71; J.M. Treadwell, 'William Wood and the Company of Ironmasters of Great Britain', *Business History*, 16 (1974), 97–112.

[2] D. McDonald, 'The first experiments on platinum. The life and works of Charles Wood', *Platinum Metals Review*, 9 (1965), 21–4; J.V. Beckett, 'Dr William Brownrigg, F.R.S.: physician, chemist and country gentleman', *Notes and Records of the Royal Society of London*, 31 (1977), 260.

[3] Wood, *Interim Report*, 11, 23; McDonald, 'First experiments', 24.

[4] Beckett, 'Dr William Brownrigg', 263–4.

Britain.[1] The earliest entries in the volume published here describe some of Wood's experiments at Low Mill in these years.[2] Other work was carried out at a forge at Wednesbury (Staffs.) operated by Charles's brother John, who in 1761 obtained a patent for making wrought iron in pots. A second patent of 1763, describing a very similar technique, was granted jointly to John and Charles.[3]

In 1754 Charles Wood kept a diary, also included here, of a tour to a number of ironworks in the West Midlands and North of England, taking a particular interest in the use of coke in some of the blast furnaces he visited, including Coalbrookdale, and in the partial adoption of coal at some of the forges.[4] At the time of his visit, the partners at Coalbrookdale, which had been smelting with coke since 1709, had just begun to sell iron to the forgemasters of the Stour valley, whereas until the early 1750s coke-smelted pig had been used, at both Coalbrookdale and the handful of other furnaces which smelted with coke, only for castings. It remains unclear whether, sometime around 1750, the younger Abraham Darby introduced a definite change in blast furnace technique at Coalbrookdale, which made it possible to produce coke-smelted pig suitable for forging, or whether, at a time of rising demand for iron generally, there was a shift in the relative price of coke- and charcoal-smelted pig in favour of the former.[5] What is certain is that during the 1750s about a dozen new furnaces were built on the east Shropshire coalfield, including the Darbys' works at Horsehay, to smelt iron with coke,[6] and that by the end of the decade the new technique was beginning to be introduced elsewhere.

The first region outside Shropshire in which coke-fired blast furnaces producing forge pig as well as castings were established was South Wales, where, on the northern rim of the coalfield, suitable coking coal was available alongside ironstone and also carboniferous limestone, used

[1] G.R. Morton and N. Mutton, 'The transition to Cort's puddling process', *Journal of the Iron and Steel Institute*, 205 (1967), 723–8; R.A. Mott, *Henry Cort. The Great Finer* (1983), 2–8.

[2] Below, 203–16.

[3] Mott, *Henry Cort*, 3–4.

[4] This section of the manuscript was published by C.K. Hyde, 'The iron industry of the West Midlands in 1754: observations from the travel account of Charles Wood', *West Midlands Studies*, 6 (1973), 39–40.

[5] For different views of this debate see C.K. Hyde, *Technological change and the British iron industry, 1700–1870* (1977), ch. 2; B. Trinder, *The Industrial Revolution in Shropshire* (2nd ed., 1981), ch. 4; L. Ince, *The Knight family and the British iron industry (1695–1902)* (1991), ch. 5.

[6] Trinder, *Shropshire*, ch. 4.

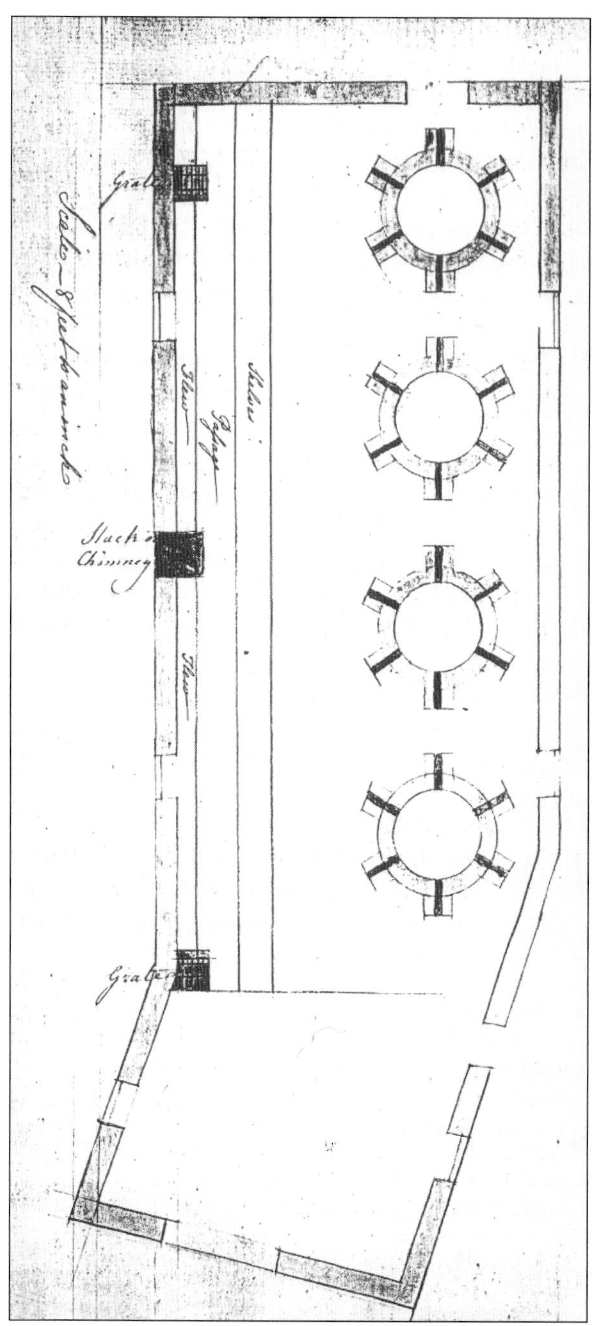

2 Wood's plan of a drying shed for the earthenware pots used in his potting process for refining pig iron, entered in the diary on 19 September 1766.

as a flux in the furnace. Charcoal-fired blast furnaces had been introduced into South Wales in the 1560s by entrepreneurs from the Weald, and the region remained one of the more important centres of the industry during the later phase of charcoal iron-smelting, with a number of new furnaces established in the period 1660–1750.[1] In 1757 John Maybery, who had a charcoal-fired furnace at Brecon and forges elsewhere in Breconshire, built a furnace at Hirwaun, near the head of the Cynon valley, which appears to have been intended to use coke. It is possible Hirwaun also used charcoal in its early years, although when Charles Wood came to South Wales in 1766 it was smelting with coke.[2] In 1759–60 a second new furnace was established at Dowlais, near the head of the Taff valley in the neighbouring parish of Merthyr Tydfil, by a firm headed by Thomas Lewis of New House, Llanishen, near Cardiff, which was undoubtedly coke-fired from the start.[3] A third works was built lower down the Taff valley in Merthyr by a partnership headed by the Cumbrian ironmaster Isaac Wilkinson (1695–1784)[4] and John Guest (1721–87) of Broseley (Salop), which in 1763 obtained a lease of minerals from the Earl of Plymouth. The furnace thus became known as Plymouth and its first proprietors as John White & Co., since White took seven of the twenty shares in the business.[5]

It was against this background of tentative steps by ironmasters, mostly from outside the region, to establish coke-fired blast furnaces in South Wales in the wake of the wider adoption of the process in Shropshire, that William Brownrigg joined Anthony Bacon (1717–86), a successful London merchant and M.P.,[6] in 1765 in taking a lease of minerals under about 4,000 acres in Merthyr from Earl Talbot and Michael Richards of Cardiff for a term of 99 years at a fixed rent of £100 a year, with no provision for royalties, nor any power for the

[1] P. Riden, 'The final phase of charcoal iron-smelting in Great Britain, 1660–1800', *Historical Metallurgy*, 28 (1994), 14–26; idem, *Gazetteer*, ch. 1.

[2] Riden, *Gazetteer*, 19–22; below, 53.

[3] The story of the establishment of the modern iron industry at Merthyr has been told many times, mostly recently by C. Evans, *'The Labyrinth of Flames'. Work and social conflict in early industrial Merthyr Tydfil* (1993), 15–20. Among older accounts of Dowlais, see: J. England, 'The Dowlais iron works, 1759–93', *Morgannwg*, 3 (1959), 41–60; M. Elsas (ed.), *Iron in the making: Dowlais Iron Company letters, 1782–1860* (1960); E. Jones, *A history of GKN*, i (1987).

[4] W.H. Chaloner, 'Isaac Wilkinson, potfounder', in L.S. Pressnell (ed.), *Studies in the Industrial Revolution presented to T.S. Ashton* (1960), 23–51.

[5] Evans, *'The Labyrinth of Flames'*, 15–16; Jones, *GKN*, i. 9.

[6] L.B. Namier, 'Anthony Bacon M.P. An eighteenth-century merchant', *Journal of Economic and Business History*, 2 (1929), 19–70.

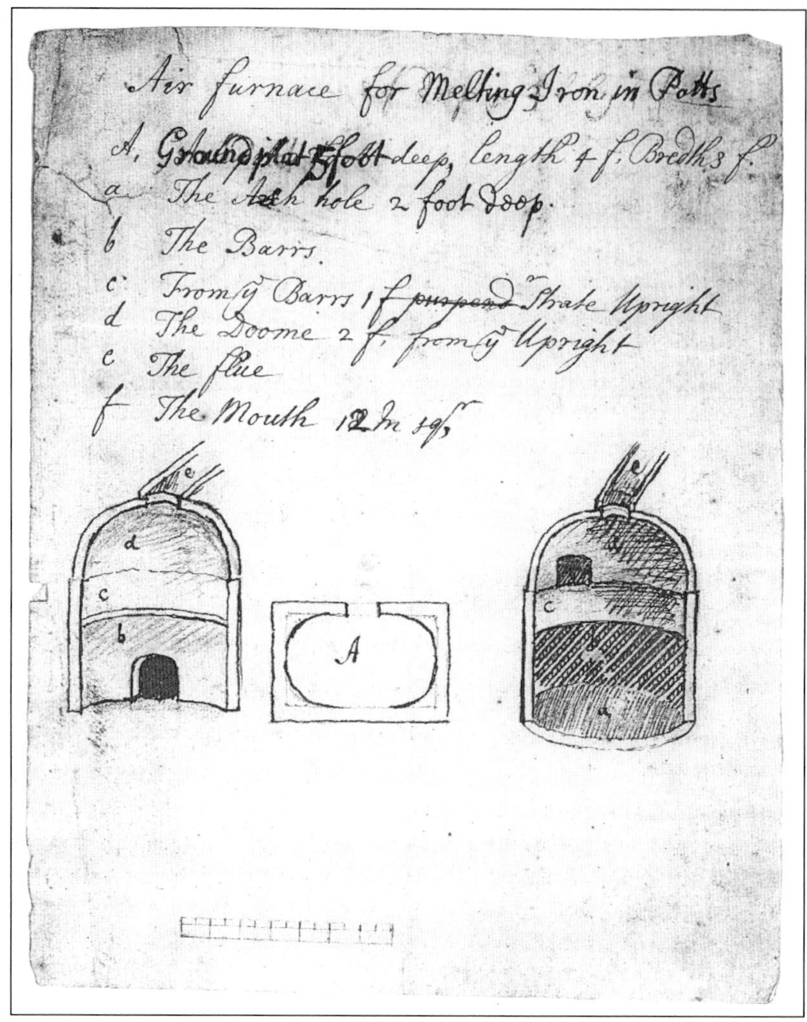

3 Wood's plan and sections of an air furnace for melting iron in pots, entered on a page at the end of the tour diary of 1754. The scale is presumably intended to represent 8 ft.

lessees to erect ironworks. The latter problem was overcome by the purchase or lease of parcels of land from the owners or tenants on which to build the works and construct the watercourses.[1] The partners engaged Brownrigg's brother-in-law, Charles Wood, to supervise the

[1] J.P. Addis, *The Crawshay Dynasty. A study in industrial organisation and development, 1765–1867* (1957), 1–2; J. Lloyd, *The early history of the old South Wales ironworks, 1760–1830* (1906), 48–9.

building of the works and it was for this reason that he came to Merthyr in the spring of 1766 and began to keep a detailed diary.

*

Wood's diary starts with his arrival in Merthyr on 11 April 1766 and continues until the beginning of July, when he spent two weeks in London on business connected with the iron company, all duly recorded in the diary, and George Lyndon, his wife's son by her first marriage, made daily entries noting work done at Merthyr during the same period. After his return, Wood resumed keeping the diary at Merthyr until the end of September 1766. Either then, or a little later, he returned to Low Mill, where he made entries in the book during the first three weeks of January 1767. He returned to Cyfarthfa on 11 April (the exact anniversary of his first arrival) and the diary continues until May that year. The rest of the book has been used for earlier memoranda, including the diary of the tour of 1754.

Diary-keeping was, of course, common enough among a wide range of educated men and women in the eighteenth century and it is quite possible that Wood had kept a journal earlier in his life which has not survived, apart from the fragment of 1754.[1] In the case of his period at Cyfarthfa, however, there was clearly a practical reason for keeping a detailed daily record of work done and this is reflected in the form of the entries. Wood was acting as resident agent for his brother-in-law Brownrigg and his partner Bacon, neither of whom visited South Wales in the period covered by the journal (although Wood's visit to London in July 1766 was mainly to see Bacon), and the diary was presumably used as a basis for making regular progress reports to the two principals, as well as recording negotiations with landowners and other ironmasters, especially the partners at the Plymouth furnace. In addition, the daily lists of workmen and the work undertaken may have been used to calculate the wages due at each fortnightly pay-day.[2]

On the other hand, had the diary been intended purely to supply such information and to make reports to the partners, it need not have included so much other information. Like many diary-writers of the period, Wood begins most entries with a note of the weather each

[1] The outstanding example from South Wales, which overlaps by a few years with Wood's Cyfarthfa diary, is that of William Thomas, of which an abridged edition was published by the South Wales Record Society (R.T.W. Denning (ed.), *The Diary of William Thomas, 1762–1795* (1995)).

[2] See in particular 14 May 1766.

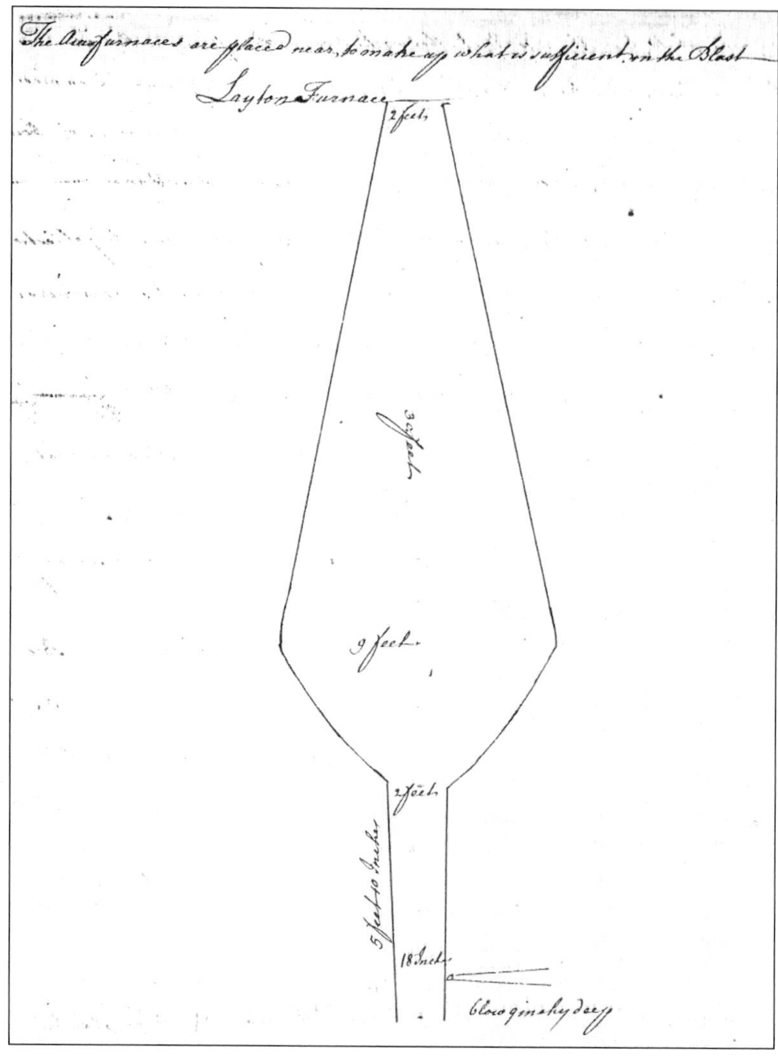

4 Wood's drawing of a section through the blast furnace at Leighton (Salop), which he visited on 16 September 1754.

morning (and often follows this up with additional information about changes during the day, and how bad weather hindered progress). He mentions events in the neighbourhood, such as the Waun Fair,[1] and occasionally further afield, such as the loss of a ship *en route* from

[1] 24 Sept. 1766 is the fullest reference.

Bristol to Cardiff.[1] He also records a variety of domestic matters, including his own health, and how he spent his brief periods of leisure on Sundays. It is these entries that give the diary wider interest beyond the history of the iron industry.

When Wood arrived at Merthyr, a year after the building of the ironworks had begun, he found, as so often in such a situation, that less had been completed than he expected.[2] Thereafter he records progress each day. Cyfarthfa was planned from the start as an integrated works, producing both pig iron in a coke-fired blast furnace and bar iron, using Wood's recently developed potting and stamping process. The enterprise thus differed from Hirwaun, Dowlais and Plymouth, which (like the handful of coke-fired furnaces established in different parts of the country before 1750) were designed merely to produce castings and did not have forges. Since the plant needed for potting and stamping was on a much smaller scale than a blast furnace (and pig iron could be bought in from elsewhere), construction began on the forge first. On 15 May Wood first records contact with the partners at Plymouth furnace which would lead to an agreement by which they would supply Cyfarthfa with pig until the blast furnace there was finished, and also castings until the air furnace was ready.[3] In fact, the Plymouth works was in some difficulties and both Wood and his principals were soon in negotiation for the purchase of the shares in the business held by Wilkinson and Guest.[4] Throughout the summer of 1766 Wood was involved in discussions concerning the work needed to put the Plymouth furnace back into blast and the cost of making pig there.[5] In September a plan was considered, but abandoned, to build a railway, with wooden track, to bring coal and ironstone to the works.[6] By the middle of the same month, Wood was being asked to buy the stock of pig and scrap from Plymouth to enable to company to pay its debts.[7]

All the main structures at Cyfarthfa, including the ancillary buildings and leats as well as the blast furnace itself, were built of local Pennant sandstone, using both 'common mortar', made from carboniferous limestone, available close to the site, and also, for underwater work,

[1] 19 June 1766.

[2] 11 April 1766.

[3] 15 May 1766 and following days.

[4] 28 May, 27 June 1766.

[5] 21 July–31 Aug. 1766.

[6] 30 Aug., 1 Sept. 1766.

[7] 18 Sept. 1766.

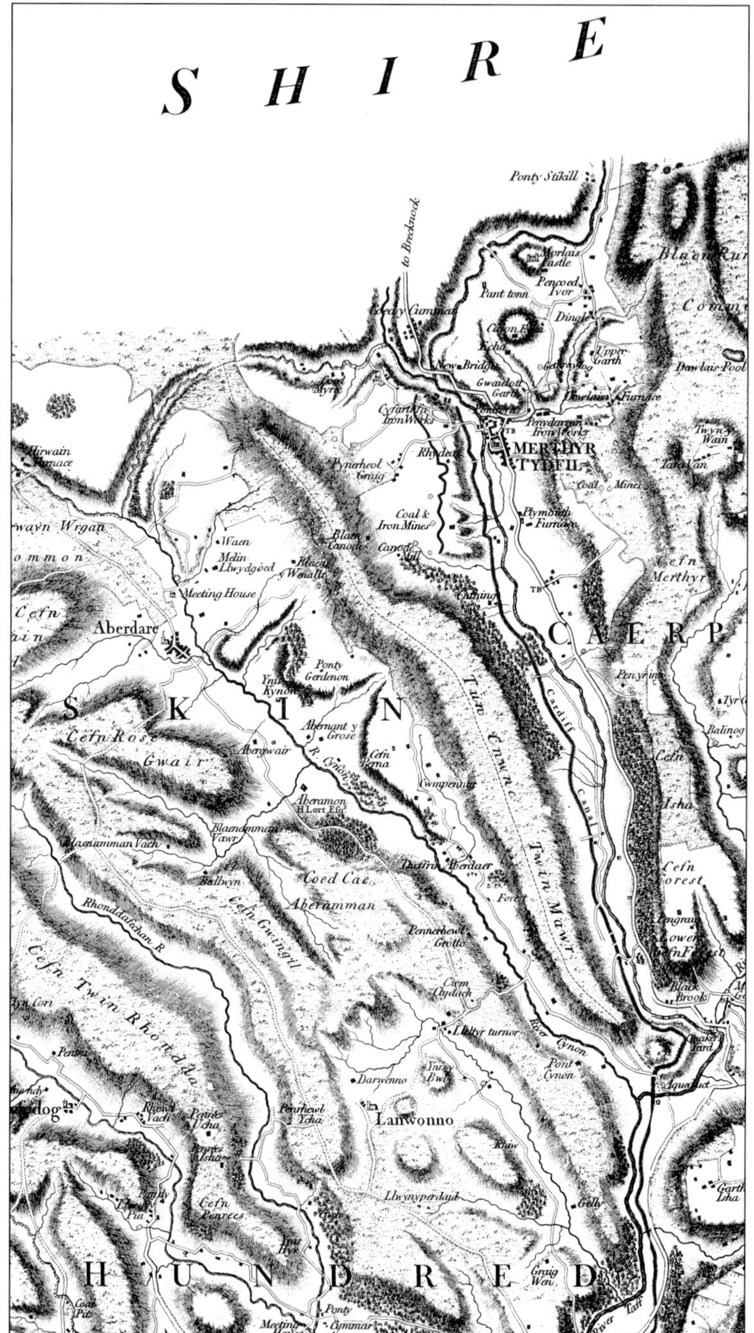

5 An extract from George Yates's map of Glamorgan of 1799, showing Cyfarthfa and the other ironworks in Merthyr Tydfil and at Hirwaun. Scale 1 inch to 2 miles.

hydraulic mortar made from what Wood calls 'Cardiff Lime', made from the Lias found near Cardiff and in the Vale of Glamorgan. The local masons were familiar with the use of both, although Wood complains that their method of working was different from what he was used to in Cumberland; in particular they tended to dress the stone more elaborately than he considered necessary and thus take longer to complete the work.[1]

It is clear from their names that most of the masons and other men, both skilled and unskilled, employed at Cyfarthfa were local. Although by this period the use of *ap* ('son of') had largely disappeared, most if not all of the Welshmen named in the diary were clearly using patronymics, not surnames, and some are given three names in a distinctively Welsh fashion.[2] A few are identified with a single Christian name coupled with a trade, such as Daniel the Hallier; on the other hand, James Mason appears to have been an Englishman with a surname which was coincidentally also the name of his trade. Besides Charles Wood himself, several of the senior men came to Cyfarthfa from Cumberland. His own brother Samuel acted as book-keeper and his stepson George Lyndon took charge on at least one occasion in his absence. In addition, there was Joseph Lucas, one of the leading masons who was in charge of building the blast furnace; William Postlethwaite and George Ford, who seem to have been the two foremen carpenters and patternmakers; Rowley Park; and a potter named Aaron Wedgwood. The range of trades includes, besides those already mentioned, sawyers, a tiler, brickmakers, miners and hauliers.

Only one woman is mentioned as working at Cyfarthfa, David John's daughter Mary, who first appears on 9 June 1766 and is regularly listed thereafter (as Mary David) as a labourer serving one of the masons. On no occasion does Wood make any special comment concerning her.

One of the most interesting figures mentioned in the diary is William Edwards (1719–89), a famous South Wales builder and Dissenting minister.[3] In 1751 Edwards built the forge near Cardiff Castle operated

[1] 9 May 1766.

[2] See, for example, 18 May 1766, when William David's son is called David [son of] William, or the appearance of Edward Thomas John (i.e. Edward the son of Thomas the son of John, not an Englishman named E.T. John) on the previous day. See below, p. 225, for the problem of indexing a text containing a mixture of patronymics and hereditable surnames.

[3] For whom see H.P. Richards, *William Edwards. Architect, Builder, Minister* (1983). Wood first mentions Edwards on 13 May 1766.

by Thomas Lewis of Llanishen[1] and in 1756 completed what remains his best known work, the bridge over the Taff at Pontypridd. On 21 May 1766 Wood was consulting Edwards about the leat that was to carry the water from the Tâf Fawr to the wheel that powered the blowing cylinders serving the blast furnace. Edwards had completed a survey for this by 4 June and produced an estimate for undertaking the work, which Wood was inclined to accept.[2] The leat was then intended to leave the river at Cefn-coed-y-cymer, about half a mile upstream from the works, to which there was a fall of 27 feet. In August a further survey was carried out, as a result of which it was decided to begin work a further 378 yards up the river, which would give an additional fall of 20 feet, and save a great deal of cutting through rock.[3] The total length of what became known as the Tai Mawr Cut would thus be 1,348 yards. Terms were agreed with contractors and work began on 1 September,[4] although it seems to have been suspended when Wood returned to Low Mill. A fresh start was made in April 1767 and Wood refers to various sections of the work, including a length of tunnelling through rock so hard that blasting was required.[5]

At the works the Tâf Fawr was dammed by a weir, which let the water run into a pool. This was narrower at its lower end to increase the flow into the forebay, a solid structure built of dressed stones laid in mortar made of Cardiff lime, on which work was proceeding in April and May 1766.[6] Several sets of penstocks controlled the flow of water from the forebay into races leading to different pieces of plant. Six races can be identified from the diary, namely the clay mill race, two stamper races, the chafery race, and two hammer races, each of which had its own waterwheel.[7] The clay mill housed the rollers and other plant used to prepare the clay for making the pots needed for Wood's potting and stamping process. In the stamper plant, thin cast-iron plates were placed into heavy stamper boxes and broken into small pieces by stampers, cast-iron hammers lifted by cams on a shaft driven by the waterwheel. The pieces were then put into pots for reheating. In the chafery, water-powered bellows heated the hearths at which the refined iron was

1 *Glamorgan County History*, v (1980), 27–8.

2 5 June 1766.

3 26 Aug. 1766.

4 29 Aug., 1 Sept. 1766.

5 13, 14, 30 April, 8 May 1767.

6 11 April, 5 and 28 May 1766.

7 11 April, 5, 12, 22 and 23 May, 6 June 1766.

6 The weir on the Tâf Fawr at which water was led into the leat leading to Cyfarthfa Ironworks, showing masonry walling dating from the building of the works in 1766–7.

reheated and then taken to the hammer house to be worked with hammers, again lifted by cams driven by yet another waterwheel. These six races ended in what Wood called the Great Race (or Grand Race), which eventually discharged the water back into the Taff at a bend in the river below the works. The Great Race, with its six branches, was some 300 yards long and several feet deep; much of it was excavated in solid rock. All the races were arched over in stone and covered with soil and rubble to enable waggons to pass over them.[1]

The first reference to the blast furnace at Cyfarthfa comes towards the end of June 1766, when Isaac Wilkinson visited the works to inspect the site Wood had chosen for the furnace.[2] Wood entered into an agreement on 18 August with three masons to build the furnace, and on 9 September levelling was in progress for the bank behind the furnace, from which it would be charged. The furnace itself was intended to be 50 feet high,[3] rather taller than most of the last generation of charcoal-fired furnaces. By this date Wood had also adopted the plan of using the tail-race from the furnace as a tub-boat canal to carry pig iron to other parts of the works.[4] After Wood's time a much longer canal of the same sort

[1] 10, 12 Aug. 1766.

[2] 22, 25–26 June 1766.

[3] 9 Sept. 1766.

[4] The 'Navigation Cut' is also mentioned on 13 April 1767.

was used to bring coal and ironstone to the blast furnace from pits lower down the valley, which remained in use until the 1830s.[1]

It is clear from memoranda inserted in the volume after the end of the entries for 1766 that Wood intended from the start to use cast-iron blowing cylinders, rather than traditional wood and leather bellows, at Cyfarthfa. As well as making various calculations as to the comparative cost of the two methods of blowing, Wood also talked to Samuel Walker, the Rotherham ironmaster, and John Cookson of Chester-le-Street (Co. Durham), both of whom had coke-fired furnaces used mainly to produce castings,[2] about the advantages of cylinders over bellows.

When Wood returned to Cyfarthfa in April 1767 the blast furnace was under construction.[3] Later that month he was experimenting with different types of coal to see which made the best coke, and obtained figures for the cost of making pig at Dowlais furnace in 1764.[4] He also impressed on the masons the importance of making the blast furnace as strong as possible, and not to use 'cobble stones' (presumably river-washed round stones) for the outer pillars of the stack.[5] More experiments with coal from various seams followed later in the month,[6] when Wood also noted that it was better to use calcined ironstone, rather than raw ore, in the blast furnace.[7] He also decided in favour of a 'gravel road', rather than a railway such as he had considered for Plymouth the previous year, as the best means of bringing coal and ironstone to the furnace.[8]

By 6 May the blast furnace lintels were being cast and a few days later Wood copied down details of the hearth at 'Merthyr furnace'[9] (i.e. Dowlais), presumably as a guide for making the one at Cyfarthfa. The furnace was clearly nearly finished, although not completely so, as the diary ends. Cyfarthfa is conventionally said to have come into operation

[1] C. Hadfield, *The Canals of South Wales and the Border* (1967), 89–90; see also the extract from Yates's map of Glamorgan of 1799 published here.

[2] Riden, *Gazetteer*, 103, 126; A.H. John (ed.), *Minutes relating to Messrs Samuel Walker & Co., Rotherham, iron founders and steel refiners, 1741–1829, and Messrs Walkers, Parker & Co., lead manufacturers, 1788–1893* (1951).

[3] 11 April 1767.

[4] 20 April 1767.

[5] 22 April 1767.

[6] 25, 28 April 1767.

[7] 24 April 1767.

[8] 23 April 1767.

[9] 9 May 1767.

in 1767[1] and the furnace was probably put into blast in the autumn of that year, after raw materials had been accumulated over the summer.

*

Apart from the construction of the ironworks itself, the diary sheds light on various other topics. Building materials were mostly obtained or manufactured close to the site: stone and lime were quarried locally, bricks were made from clay found within the parish of Merthyr Tydfil, and timber was cut in nearby woods. All the buildings at Cyfarthfa were roofed in what Wood calls 'tiles', meaning thin stone flags, which were obtained from a quarry at Aberdare in the adjoining Cynon valley. Both carts and waggons, drawn by oxen as well as horses, and packhorses were used to bring the materials to Cyfarthfa, as were sledges (or carrs) on occasions. Items brought from further afield came by sea to Cardiff, from where they were brought up to Merthyr by waggon.[2] Although there has been a tendency to emphasise the remoteness of the upper Taff valley as a drawback for the location of the new ironworks of the 1750s and 1760s, in fact the main road from Cardiff to Brecon ran through Merthyr, passing very close to Dowlais furnace.[3] The parish was clearly remote compared, say, with the sites chosen close to the western seaboard of Britain for many of the last generation of charcoal-fired furnaces,[4] but it was not as inaccessible as has been claimed. As well as Cardiff, it was also possible to go to and from Newport, which was slightly closer (by sea) to Bristol, and Wood notes approvingly the suggestion by John Bedford, who was then trying to establish a forge at Bassaleg, that Newport might be a better shipping-place for iron from Cyfarthfa than Cardiff.[5] He himself considered that a turnpike road down the Neath valley from near Hirwaun might offer the best access to the coast,[6] albeit at a point much further from Bristol.

The main road from Merthyr to Cardiff was improved, at the ironmasters' initiative, in 1771, when it was turnpiked and partly realigned to run down the valley floor, rather than the high ground to the

[1] P. Riden and J.G. Owen, *British blast furnace statistics, 1790–1980* (1995), 13.

[2] e.g. 27 May 1766.

[3] J. Ogilby, *Britannia* (1675), pl. 64; see also the extract from Yates's map of Glamorgan reproduced here.

[4] See the maps in Riden, *Gazetteer*.

[5] 14 Sept. 1766. For Bedford see P. Riden, *John Bedford and the ironworks at Cefn Cribwr* (1992).

[6] 16 Sept. 1766.

east of the Taff.[1] Although the road from Merthyr down the Neath valley was turnpiked in 1795,[2] the Merthyr ironworks never developed close links with either Newport or Neath and remained linked chiefly to the port of Cardiff, first by road, then by canal and finally by rail.

To keep in touch with his principals in Cumberland and London, Wood relied on the post, not at Cardiff but at Brecon, still the more important administrative centre and also a few miles nearer Merthyr. After a couple of months the postmaster there arranged for Wood to have a private pouch, to which he and Wood would each have a key, and which one of Wood's men would carry between Merthyr and Brecon. This would avoid relying on the local postman, whom Wood described as a 'drinking Man'; he was also convinced that someone was opening his letters and making his business known to others.[3] Wood did not, however, use any of the Brecon attorneys for legal business connected with Cyfarthfa, as many of the other Merthyr ironmasters did.[4] Instead he went to either Bristol, the great hub of the regional economy in the eighteenth century, or London, from where Bacon conducted his affairs. Wood's account of his visit to both places in July 1766 helps to dispell the idea that someone living in a remote spot like Merthyr never travelled any distance and also shows how quickly it was possible, if need be, to get back to South Wales from London at that date. Like most foot passengers he crossed to Bristol not from Cardiff but from the New Passage near Chepstow.[5]

Apart from transport, the other great problem that is always assumed to have faced the first generation of ironmasters in Merthyr was the recruitment and retention of a labour force. Wood's diary deals with the construction, rather than operation, of an ironworks and reveals no insuperable difficulties of this sort. In particular, nowhere does he refer to any obstacles connected with the Welsh language which most of the local men working for him probably spoke. Indeed, he only mentions the language on one occasion, when he notes that only on alternate Sunday afternoons was the service at Merthyr parish church held in English, with

[1] *Glamorgan County History*, v. 426.

[2] Ibid., 431.

[3] 23 June 1766.

[4] The Maybery Collection in the National Library of Wales, a major source for the early history of the Merthyr ironworks and the basis of much of Lloyd's *Early history of the old South Wales ironworks*, is essentially a collection of attorney's clients' papers accumulated by a practitioner who acted for many of the early iron companies.

[5] 1–14 July 1766.

Welsh being used on all other occasions.[1] Much of the work at Cyfarthfa was let as piecework bargains, although some unskilled men were paid by the day and on occasions the mason and other craftsmen were put on daywork. On different occasions, Wood complains of being short of masons or having too many,[2] but this was a common enough problem in large building projects of the period. There is no indication that he ever had to suspend work for lack of men, and only on one occasion was work held up (and then only for a couple of days) by a dispute over wages. The argument was in any case between the masons and their labourers, rather than between the labourers and Wood himself.[3] He did his best to avoid losing men to the militia[4] and seems to have accepted that numbers would fall on the day of the Waun fair or the parish revels.[5]

For both piecework and daywork, wages were paid fortnightly. There was no bank in Glamorgan at this perid—the earliest in the county was established at Merthyr in 1770[6]—and Wood obtained cash about once a month from Thomas Morgan, an attorney at Cowbridge, a small market town in the Vale of Glamorgan twelve miles west of Cardiff. Morgan was steward to Lord Talbot, the Cyfartha Company's landlord, but appears in the diary chiefly as their banker, accepting bills of exchange drawn on Anthony Bacon in return for cash. Either he brought the money to Cyfarthfa or Wood sent a couple of men down to Cowbridge.[7] There is no indication that the works was ever short of cash, nor that Wood was using tokens instead of coin of the realm. On one occasion he decided to postpone the payment of wages for two weeks, but this was to deter men from leaving, not because he was without funds.[8] Equally, there is no evidence for any kind of truck system or that Wood had difficulty obtaining provisions for his men. One of his smiths also had a shop in Merthyr and lost stock worth £50 when a ship was lost between Bristol and Cardiff in June 1766,[9] indicating that, like most South Wales shopkeepers of the period, he dealt with wholesalers in

[1] 25 May 1766.

[2] 26 May, 15 Aug., 12 Sept. 1766.

[3] 27–29 Sept. 1767.

[4] 15 Sept. 1766.

[5] 25 April 1767.

[6] *Glamorgan County History*, v. 367.

[7] 28 May, 26 July, 23 Aug., 8 Sept. 1766.

[8] 23 June 1766.

[9] 19 June 1766.

Bristol. When Wood set up home for himself a few months later and his housekeeper bought an initial supply of meat, he noted that there were markets at Merthyr on Tuesdays and Saturdays.[1] The Waun fair, held outside the village near the road to Abergavenny four times a year, was clearly an important market for both livestock and provisions.[2] In September 1766 Wood agreed to George Ford's suggestion that a pair of grindstones might be fixed up and driven from the chafery waterwheel, so that the company could grind all the corn its men needed. This would save them from falling into debt, and the company from having to advance their wages, which would otherwise be the case, apparently because the men were being forced to pay an excessive price for flour.[3]

As well as the minerals and the site for the ironworks, Wood also leased several farms in Merthyr[4] and in July 1766 took the tithes of Gellideg hamlet, the part of Merthyr parish in which his company's estate lay, for a term of eleven years.[5] The main value of the farms was presumably to provide grazing for the horses and oxen, but Wood also used the farmhouses to accommodate his chief assistants. In May 1766, for example, two men were detailed to move William Postlethwaite's belongings into Llwyncelyn.[6] Others followed a month later, having previously been put up at an alehouse, which they did not like.[7] Wood himself, and some others, initially lodged in rooms at the works.[8] In September that year he considered making Llwyncelyn suitable for his wife to join him there but instead decided to use the house as offices.[9] By this date some of the workmen were also living in tenements at the works.[10] No thought appears to have been given to erecting cottages for workmen, as many of the South Wales ironmasters later did;[11] indeed, Wood specifically observes that the building of 'apartments' over the forge would save the expense of separate houses and enable the men to live close to their work, to both their own benefit and that of their

[1] 31 Aug. 1766.

[2] The fullest account is on 24 Sept. 1766.

[3] 15 Sept. 1766.

[4] See the terriers of three farms following the entry for 17 Sept. 1766.

[5] 17 July 1766.

[6] 14 May 1766.

[7] 28 June 1766.

[8] 20 May 1766.

[9] 7 Sept. 1766.

[10] 5 Sept. 1766.

[11] J.B. Lowe, *Welsh industrial workers' housing, 1775–1875* (1977).

masters.[1]

Wood's wife did not join him at Cyfarthfa until after the period covered by the diary, which thus contains sidelights as to how he and his colleagues, on their own in a strange district some distance from any town, spent their free time. Since building work went on six days a week from six in the morning until dark, they had only to occupy themselves on Sundays. Like many others in a similar position, Wood seems to have gone into the office on Sunday mornings to catch up with paperwork, stopping shortly after midday to have dinner at the Anchor & Crown, either alone or with his assistants. He appears to have attended church only occasionally, at least partly because so few services were held in English.[2] He was, however, on tea-drinking terms with the rector of Merthyr, and also spent quite a lot of time calling socially on the partners or agents at the two ironworks already in existence in the parish. In fact, there seems to have been little to do on Sunday afternoons apart from looking round Dowlais or Plymouth. Polite society in Merthyr in the 1760s was evidently so small that even the local Excise officer was included in Wood's circle.[3] Conversely, increasing numbers were visiting Cyfarthfa on Sundays to inspect the progress of the works: on one occasion Wood found eighteen people looking round the unfinished cast-house and decided to post a watchman there.[4]

*

Charles Wood stayed in Merthyr as the managing agent at Cyfarthfa until his death in October 1774. His wife Jemima, who was executrix and sole beneficiary of her husband's will,[5] lived on as a widow in the parish for another 25 years until her own death in November 1799. Both were buried in St Tydfil's churchyard, from where their remains were transferred to Cefn Coed cemetery in 1911.[6] Of their six children the youngest was a daughter named Ann, whose own daughter Mary married William Howitt; both became well-known popular writers. Many years later Mary Howitt preserved some memories of her mother relating to Charles Wood. He was said to have deeply detested slavery, which he

1 16 June 1766.

2 25 May 1766.

3 10 Aug. 1766.

4 29 June 1766.

5 Wood, *Interim Report*, 28.

6 *Merthyr Express*, 27 May 1911.

had seen at first hand in Jamaica, and during the War of Independence supported George Washington and the Americans.[1] Of his sons, William (b. 1757) became a clerk at Cyfarthfa and later worked for both the Penydarren and Dowlais companies; his stepson George Lyndon also worked for all three. William Wood's son, another William, became a manager with the British Iron Company, the first joint-stock business in the iron trade to be established after the repeal of the Bubble Act in 1825.[2]

The ironworks at Cyfarthfa expanded enormously after Wood's time. Control of the business passed after Bacon's death in 1786 to Richard Crawshay (1739–1810) and remained in the hands of his descendants until the late nineteenth century, when the business shared in the rapid decline of the Merthyr iron industry. Smelting at Cyfarthfa ceased in 1902 and the works became derelict. The site escaped the general destruction of remains of the South Wales iron industry which took place in the third quarter of the twentieth century and has since been scheduled as an ancient monument, although what survives at the site today appears to date entirely from the nineteenth century. All that remains of the building work supervised by Charles Wood in 1766–7 is a portion of walling flanking the leat leading from the Tâf Fawr at Cefn-coed-y-cymer.[3]

[1] M. Howitt, *Autobiography* (1889), 8–9; A. Lee, *Laurels and Rosemary. The Life of William and Mary Howitt* (1955), 12–14.

[2] Evans, *'The Labyrinth of Flames'*, 58–9.

[3] See Plate 6.

A NOTE ON EDITING

The manuscript volume on which this edition is based has remained in the possession of the Wood family since Charles Wood's death and is now the property of Mr John Wood of Pine Hill, Woods Hill Road, Norton Summit, South Australia, Australia 5136. Mr Wood is the son of the late Air Commodore Francis John Powell Wood RAAF, who died in 1988. During the period in which the volume was in Air Cdre Wood's possession it was microfilmed, apparently at the request of the late Prof. M.W. Flinn of Edinburgh University, who used material from the volume in a number of publications. Flinn made the microfilm available to others, including R.A. Mott and C.K. Hyde, both of whom drew on the text for their own work on the iron industry.

At some point a copy of the microfilm was obtained by the Glamorgan Record Office in Cardiff, which Dr Chris Evans used for his study of the Merthyr Tydfil iron industry. More recently, the editor of this volume, who had long taken a keen interest in the industrial history of Merthyr, was able to obtain photocopies from the microfilm from which the text printed here was prepared. It has not been possible to check the transcript against the original manuscript, although Mr Wood has kindly made available better quality reproductions of the three drawings in the volume than could be obtained from the microfilm.

The text as presented here is basically a literal transcript of what Wood wrote, although as anyone who has edited either informal eighteenth-century prose or accounting records of the same period will appreciate, it is virtually impossible to produce an intelligible published work if this principle is applied strictly. In some places in the narrative sections the punctuation has been silently rationalised and some abbreviations and contractions expanded. In the tabular sections every effort has been made to reproduce on the printed page the complexities of the original layout, although here again some tidying up has been done to make the text easier to follow. A few misdated entries or words that are clear in the manuscript but appear from the sense to be wrong have been commented on in footnotes. Other notes identify people, places and events mentioned by Wood, or gloss some of the technical terms he uses.

AN ACCOUNT OF THE MATERIAL TRANSACTIONS AT CYFARTHFA IN THE PARISH OF MERTHYR TYDVIL COMMENCING APRIL 11TH 1766 PER CHARLES WOOD NO 1

The measures of Lands in the Parish of Merthyr Tidvil within the hundred of Carphilly in the County of Glamorgan

A 23 feet square is one yard
48 yards is one Cover
4 covers is one acre.

23 × 23 = 529 × 48 = 25392 × 4 = 101568 ÷ 9 = 11285 ÷ = 2a, 1c, 13p, 5yd, 3ft English Statute Acres.[1]

Came to Merthyr Tidvill April 11th 1766 and found the preparations for our several buildings not so forward as was expected. The grand race from the river was brought up about equel in length in a dead Level agreeable to orders but about 22 yards began by John Ford above the other part of the Arch (it was well finished) is higher than the dead level and (as there is a hard rock at the bottom, which was blasted, at the lower part of this race) it is uncertain whether it can be taken away unless the arching and walls are taken up.

The outer wall from the floodgates, to the turn of the river, was finished in a workmanlike but very expensive manner. The inner wall to form the Pool was brought down which is about 20 feet of the place where the forebay is to be. The Arch over the Clay Mill race was made within about 20 yards of the house and part of a race for the Stampers, which was all that was material done. Since which the Clay Mill race is completed. The Clay Mill building is about 8 feet buildt above the floor, as also the flourishing house, the foundations of both is about 8 feet below the floor, laid upon the rock. The stack for two flourishing furnaces, is about four foot above the floor laid upon the rock.

May 9th. A strong wall buildt on each side the Clay Mill Arch to prevent the weight of the Stack pressing too much upon it, as one pillar

[1] Below, p. 198 for a later reference to customary measures in Glamorgan.

extends no farther than the centre of it. The foundations of the forebay is began with large and small Cobbles, about six foot square, the remaining 3 foot as it is proposed that the whole breadth at bottom should be 9 feet. The mortar used in this forebay, is a great deal, as farr as I can calculate. 4 load to a Perch is to be laid, about a foot next the water in Cardiff Lime and the remaining 2 feet in Common Mortar. This Cardiff Lime costs in Cardiff 6d a horse Load, which is about 2 Winchester bushels and carriage 2s a load. This Lime is slacked with a very small quantity of water, in respect to what is used in Common Mortar the proportion of a clean sand to mix with it, is 2 parts Lime, & one of Sand, well mixed and tempered and to be used the same day it is mixed. The common Lime is but weak in binding and their usual method in making it up into Mortar is equal parts, Sand and Lime, but as there is used, double the quantity in building here than with us, in order to lessen the expense in this article it is ordered that 2 parts of Sand to one of Lime. As the Masons in this country say, it is necessary to use more in their Walls to bed the stone well. As it does not bind, therefore by mixing 2 parts Sand the Mortar is as good for beding as when one part is used & will make it go, one third further.

The Masons here make buildings that look well to appearances with Cobblestones, but they are Scabbled in a tedious expensive method to form them fitter for beding and appear well which occasions their building, more expensive than with Quarry stones but from some distance and requires a larger quantity of Mortar. Their being so much accustomed, to Scabble Cobbles it is a difficult Task to bring them off it even with good flat Quarry Stones.

A Bargain was let unto Thomas Clifton, to remove all the Earth out of the Pool to wheel the Earth to fill up the Wall next the river & the inner wall next the Pool and the remainder over the outer wall into the river that the first flood may carry it away fortwith, And in order to encourage him to keep, such a Labourer that he should employ close to work & that the bargain might be finished in as little time as could be done, he was promised that if he should prove that he did not earn 2s a day for himself, 1s for his son Thomas and eight pence for his son John per day it should be made up to him.

A bargain lett unto Thomas David who took in others to sink a slope line to the rock at yards and then carry it to the rock to the forebay from the high rock next the Smithy on one side, to the rock at the Stamper race on the other side & to leave all the stone, fit for building on the ground cleared & the Earth to carry by three horse and cart to be allowed him to the hollow along the riverside and to be finished in three weeks for £9-10. The three weeks end this day but it appears to me that it will take two weeks more, this is for the forge. The men work well and deserve their wages, if the bargain does not allow it them.

Isaac Bates had framed the Wear in the most expensive axtravigant manner, I ever see and not in the least more wilful — had he proceeded in the manner I ordered him (it was calculated by himself to me that) 23 Ton of timber would have been quite sufficient. But instead of observing the direction left him by CW he has used between 60 and 70 Ton & not got completed in the plan so began by him. Sam Wood says, he told him, upon blaming him for being so extravigant, & not observing my order, that he was determined not to mind what the Master said, he would go his own way, that he might not be blamed.

He fell and got brought to Cyfarthfa such Trees as are of little use has made Arms for the Furnace wheel which are not fitt to be made use of and if he had had a design for it seems pretty evident, by his work, and behaviour to have lost by the lump or week or month.

Sunday, 11 May. [*No entry*]

Monday 12th May. Several of the Masons working viz. Morgan Jenkins, Walter Williams, David John, Wm. John, Jo. Reith, Morgan Evan.

Harry William and Thomas Edwards turned the Arch over one of the pits in the flourishing house next the Clay Mill and part of another. Edward Thomas, William Edwards junior and Joseph Lucas were about the Stack, the stone being hard of the Millstone kind & taff, require a deal of Scabbling which makes such work go on but slow laid only into courses to the covering over the two pillars; four masons were Scabbling Cobbles for completing the side pool wall to be laid in Cardiff Lime now daily expected; two of the 4 Masons were taken off in the afternoon about four o'clock to Arch 6 foot of the grand race that was walled — the remainder about 36 yards being to be done by Edward Thomas & Harry Wm p. bargain at 5/6d the yard in length, to be 1 foot wide in the clear within, 6 feet being that too narrow, the stone Lime and Sand to be laid near their work and they make it up & find Labour to serve them.

George Jo. and his men with Postlethwaite are employed in making ready the Penstock for the Clay Mill & Stamper to fix in the fireclay and side wall in the pool. Two Sawyers sawing Sills for Clay Mill framing. The carriage fetched home 7 poles cut for Scaffolding for the Stack.

Mr White one of the partners of the Plymouth Furnace with Mr. Powell the Rector of this Parish[1] came here after Dinner, to see the work & sat in the Counting House (it raining) some time.

This day two Labourers set on to clear the Clay Mill floor down to the rock. The reason that this Lime that we have does not bind so well as in Cumberland (the stone before burnt seems as good) in my opinion is their putting too much of it in their walls for I believe where it is laid thin it drys and hardens soon, but where it is in heaps and thick it is long in drying and when in a moist place will still be longer.

Tuesday, May 13th. It rains. Absent David John, John Richard, Edward Jo., Wm John, Thomas Lloyd, Walter Wm, Richard John, Morgan Evan Jenkins, Morgan Evans, Masons. There is a new Mason come Thos. Samuel. This being the Wain Fair[2] several Labourers absent.

Harry Wm and Thomas Edwards upon the Arch over one of the Ash pits. Going slowly speaking has no effect to alter their method.

Joseph Lucas & Wm Edwards at the Stack.

Hopkin David and John Gabriel are upon the Arch in the Grand race 6 foot in length to prepare it for the bargain. Set work Edward Thos. John half an hour past seven o'clock morning. The Masons left off it rains hard & all left off work except 2 Labourers upon bargain.

George Ford has two men & Wm Postlethwaite are upon the Clay Mill Frame. This day came 7 loads of Cardiff Lime for the Forebay by William Richard carrier from Wm James Limeburner. This 7 load here is 8 load paid for at the kiln and measures 32 baskets, each basket containing 8 quarts of Sand. I ordered it to be placed in a close, compact heap & covered with 16 baskets of clean drift sand riddled through an iron riddle of about a quarter of an inch mash by thus closing it up with damp Sand it falls in a day or two, and when it is used, as much is to be made up with the addition of no more water, then will serve to make it, by well working into the consistence of good tempered mortar as it is used the same day. So much as remains overnight is tempered will not be so strong when wet again as at the first.

[1] The Revd Gervase Powell (1723–95), was rector of Merthyr Tydfil from 1764 until his death and also prebendary of Llandaff. He succeeded to the Llanharan estate in 1770.

[2] The Waun fair at Dowlais, held four times a year, is said to have been established in the Middle Ages and became one of the most important fairs in Wales, attracting many people. The main business was dealing in horses, sheep and cattle; it was also a hiring fair. It is mentioned in the Dowlais lease of 1748 (Lloyd, *Early History*, 47).

This William Edwards[1] informs me, from a long experience, he has had in the use of this lime. This mortar applied to the beding of flatt & well scabbled stones will swell, & resist any water and is excellent in all water work but care must be taken that the joints of the stones are true and fit each other to save mortar at this place, otherwise the expense will be heavy as the carriage is near 4 times the price of the Lime.

Two smiths have worked all this day not withstanding the Wane Fair. The Carriage brought a parcel of Scaffolding Poles.

Wednesday, May 14th. Received last night a letter from Mr. Bacon, Mr. Jones of Bristol and Isaac Wilkinson. A finer day. There are several Masons absent viz. David John, Hopkin David, Edward Tho. John, John Gabriel, Thomas Lloyd, Richard John Morgan, Evan Jenkin Morgan. At work Tho. Edward, David Lewis, John Richard, Harry Wm, Thomas Samuel came at 12 o'clock. Walter Wm & William John. There is but 7 Masons at work whch make part of the Labourers idle as employed about work not so immediately wanted. Thomas Samuel and John Richard are employed to finish the six foot of the Grand Arch, Harry Williams and Thomas Edwards have finished the Arch above the Ash pit, and are now with Walter Williams and William John upon the Gavel end of the flourishing house above the Ash pit. Joseph Lucas & David Edwards are upon the Stack.

About ten o'clock this morning, I went with Samuel Wood, George Lyndon, George Ford and William Postlethwaite to Llewenkelly farm house[2] and Samuel Wood took out the key from the out Door & gave it to William Postlethwaite and part of his goods were brought in & the remainder to be brought this day and he had possession given him by Thomas Rees his daughter Mary for the Lords Earl Talbot and Michael Richards Esq. & his said daughter promised to remove their Thomas Rees goods as soon as they could.

Ordered John Morgan & David Wm to assist Wm Postlethwaite in removing his goods to Llewenkelly farm house. Sent by David William upon the horse George Lyndon's bedstead & another for George Ford and Joseph Lucas & one made for Chas Wood, to Llewenkelly.

[1] William Edwards (1719–89), stonemason, builder of the Pontypridd bridge (1756) and other bridges. Also a dissenting minister, at Groeswen, near Caerphilly. H.P. Richards, *William Edwards: architect, builder, minister* (Cowbridge, 1983).

[2] Llwyncelyn, one of three farms (Rhyd-y-car and Cwm Glo or Cwm-y-glo being the others) leased by the Cyfarthfa Company from the joint owners of the Llancaiach Estate, Earl Talbot and Michael Richards of Cardiff (see pp. 156–9 for details of the farms). The three farms, together with Tai-mawr and Wern, also mentioned by Wood, were all on the western side of the Taff, in the hamlet of Gelli-deg in Merthyr parish.

The Carriage brought Scaffolding poles gate pole & 6 Stamper shafts. 3 horses brought Three tons of stone & removed Postlethwaites goods to Llewenkelly.

On Monday last the 12th John Morgan went to Landissant fair[1] to purchase Oxen and Bullocks with 2 Cows for Milk for the family but did not buy any they being too dear. He is gone to Aper to David Evans, near Caerfilly, to see four Bullocks & some Cows in order to purchase this 14thday.

George Ford and his two men are about the penstocks, trough and frame of Clay Mill & William Postlethwaite removing his goods to Llewenkelly.

Sent by Rowley Park to Mr. John White the following note viz. if Mr. White is at Leisure now or would appoint any other time & place where we may have a little conversation together Mr. Wood would wait on him & make some proposal that may be of mutual advantage to both companys. And Mr. White sent by the same hand the following answer in writing:

Mr. White's Compliments to Mr. Charles Wood and desires the favour of his Company to Breakfast tomorrow morning at Mr. Thomas Guests, when he will listen to any Proposal Mr. Wood will make. Merthyr 14th May 1766.

Thursday May 15th. Breakfasted with Mr. White, at Mr. Thomas Guest and gave him the underwritten Proposal viz. Anthony Bacon & Co. propose agreeing with John White & Co. for metal in grain of good quality to the amount of 500, 1000 or 2000 Tons delivered at the works of the said Anthony Bacon & Co. at the rate of £4 5s p. Ton long weight, to be paid for every six months, after delivering of one hundred tons. That the said John White & Co. shall make for the said Anthony Bacon & Co. whatever cast uses, they may have occasion for, at their works now Erecting at Cyfartrhfa in the Parish of Merthyr Tidvil at the rate of £5 per Ton long weight, to be paid for at the delivery of every 20 Tons by bill drawn by that Company's Agent on Anthony Bacon, payable Six months after date. By such agreement the many advantages of which it will be productive, is obvious — First it will free John White & Co. from the great uncertainty of procuring Carriage to Cardiff, as well as Sale of the metal when at Market. It will lessen your Capital near

[1] Llantrisant fair was held on 12 May. J.B. Davies, *The freemen and ancient borough of Llantrisant* (Llantrisant, 1989), 54.

one third, of what it will be necessary to carry your work on: The value of your metal will come in at certain stated periods, to answer the demands that will issue from your works and prevent any future calls from the several Proprietors; And as Interest is the strongest tye to unite persons in the same business this will be productive of that End.

All of which is offered for your Consideration.

Mr. White read the proposals over and over & gave them to Thomas Guest for his perusal, & then told me he would consider them call upon me in the Evening & give me his answer about 10 o'clock.

A cloudy day, but no rain got, thou' very like be some has been a very fine day. Masons employed in the fore bay were Walter William, Harry William, David Edwards, Richard John & William John. Upon the Gavel end of the flourishing house Thomas Lloyd and Thomas Samuel. The Labourers upon the bargain in clearing the Clay Mill floor to the rock are good ones and work well. Richard Evan & Jonathan Grosvenor.

The Labourer upon the bargain of clearing for the forge floor work well & deserve the preference when wanted. George Ford, his two men and Wm Postlethwaite upon the Clay Mill frame & Penstock. One of the Sawyers Evan Williams made a sledge for fetching brick from Penwane. Morgan Jenkins the other Sawyer not here this day.

Let the digging of the foundation of the mixing room to Lewis Thomas at 3d per solid yard he works well & seem as if he wd earn 15 or 16d p. day. This day began to lay the fore part of the forebay in Cardiff Lime the Masons are of various opinion relating the certainty of it holding water, some doubt it as Walter Wm. & he says he laid a forebay at Blincanny Mill[1] with this Lime & took great pains with it but it did not answer. But Wm Edward who has the greatest experience of it in water work told me if it was properly used it would certainly do and I think him to be a sober mind & honest Man, & to be relied upon.

8 loads of Cardiff Lime dd Cardiff from the kiln at 6d	4s
Carriage of 7 Load which is what is paid	14
A Man has to heat & prepare at 3 days	3
	21

In riddling there is found stone unburnt & useless a full Load wch must be an imposition and allowance might to be made. The 8 Load of

[1] Presumably Blaencanaid Mill, shown on Yates's map of Glamorgan to the south of Cwm-y-glo.

Lime will serve 7 perches of Wall in length. The cost of this Lime p. perch will be 3s. The forebay where this Lime is used is

	51 perch		
The side Wall will be	22 perch	perch	s
The Hamr Hatchbay	61 perch	134 @	3 p. Perch £20.2.0

The Carriage with 5 horses & two men brought pole of Alder for Stampershaft.

Three horses with two Men brought 24 Stone from Llewenkelly. John Morgan returned from Aper with four bullen purchased from David Evan at £20 which Thomas Morgan pays & is to be accounted in the next London bill.

Let unto David John Mason, who has brought 2 Masons with him from Neath, the finishing of the flourishing house from the Level of the doors to their intended height him finding Labour & to mix up Mortar and serve him with the same and stones (which are to be laid near their work by us) at 14d per perch. This building has so far as has been done, what by Scabbling & the slow method in laying I reckon has cost us 3d per perch, therefore it was high time to reform.

Mr. White called upon me about 7 o'clock & told me he would send me an answer in writing tomorrow.

Friday, May 16th. A fine warm morning. Received 15 load of Cardiff Lime from the kiln of Wm James by William Richard Carrier to be paid for the Carriage of 13 Load.

Tryed an experiment to know wether Cardiff Lime will take water and answer the end proposed in the back of the stone that were laid in the Cardiff Lime was laid loose Cobble the vacancies filled with smaller stone, higher than the course of the front stone laid in that Mortar. Then there was run several pail full of hutchins mixed with sand & made thin, which filled all interstices in so much that the water appeared clear at top and as the water was higher than the joints of the stone if the Cardiff lime would admit any water it would certainly have appeared thro' these joints but as it did not, I conclude it will answer the end proposed by using it. The stone laid in this Mortar are naturally of a flat surface well adapted for such work.

Some timber is brought home that was feln by order of Isaac Bates & the felling & squaring paid, which is wrotten at the bottom as are several other pieces and of little use, therefore they should be represented to the Lord, that an allowance may be made, as C. Woods agreement with Mr. Morgan & Zacharias Phillips was that any here that proved unsound after felling is not to be paid for. And it can not be imagined that the Lords will desire Mr. Bacon & Co. to pay for Timber that will be useless to them thro the carelessness, or worse of a Servant.

About 6 o'clock received of the hand of Mr. Whites Servant, the answer to C. Woods foregoing proposal, in writing, of which the following is a copy vizt.

Mr. John White on behalf of himself and Compy has duly considered the proposal made him by Mr. Charles Wood on the part of Anthony Bacon Esq. & Co. and agrees with him in opinion, that friendly Intercourse between the two Companys, will tend to their mutual advantage. Mr. White is sorry that the Cos. Agent Thos. Guest received such Treatment from Mr. Samuel Wood in regard to the carriage of Timber and also the mine contracted to be delivered to this company. And tho' Mr. White is willing to submit that difference to the judgment of Mr. Bacon whose honour he does not at all doubt, Yet he thinks that Mr. Wood has full power and Authority to settle and adjust the same if he thinks fit.

1st. Mr. White thinks Mr. Bacon and Comp. should employ a person to granulize the metal which would prevent disputes in respect of granulizing, or the quality of the metal.

2nd. Mr. White & Comp. think Mr. Bacon sho'd pay £4 5s p. ton at the furnace clear of all deductions and pay at the end of every three months after the Iron is delivered by a bill payable one month after date.

3. Mr. White & Comp will deliver at Cyfarthfa all open Sand castings that may be wanted at that work only, at the rate of & £5 15s per Ton short weight (i.e.) 112 lb to each Cwt and 20 Cwts to the Ton. Anthony Bacon & Co. finding & providing Patterns for the same, provided that same be cast at such times the furnaces are in Blast.

4. Mr. Bacon & Co. should engage to furnish themselves with castings from Plymouth Co. only.

These proposals are not intended to be binding, or conclusive upon either Co. tho' they are reduced into writing. Wrapped up letter wise and directed to Mr. Charles Wood at Cyfarthfa.

The Carriage and 5 horses draged Timber from the Vilage from the place Tho. Guest bro't it with 2 Men. Two men and three horses bro't 26 Stones from Llewenkelly for the furnace Stacks.

Henry Williams, Walter Williams, Thomas Lloyd, Richard John & Thomas Samuel Masons were upon the forebay. David Edwards & John Richard were preparing stone to led well in Cardiff lime, four labourers attending them.

David John and his two men, Masons, were upon their bargain finishing the flourishing house @ 14d per perch. Evan William Sawyer making Carrs on drags for bringing brick from the mountain.

George Ford and his two Men with Postlethwaite upon the Clay Mill frame.

The dimensions of the Clay Mill frame for the rollers, 2 groundsills 12 In by 15 In laid upon the bottom Sill of wheel frame 6 feet from out to outside of the Mortise 4 Staples on upright pins fixed in the Sill 6ft 3 high & a foot Square 2 Top pieces or Caps 10 inches by 13 inches & 6 ft long fm out to, outside of Mounting 4 Cross brace, morticed thro the Staples 4 ft 3 in. long & 5 inches two Topsills 4 ft 3 Inches long & 10 by 12 inches sq. The same on the other side of the wheelcase.

Saturday May 17th. Fine weather. One of the stamper race that next the forge brought up three foot deep & about 8 feet in length into the Pool. Either this is ignorance, or worse. This mistake occasioned us a deal of trouble & expense in boxing it to the rock and then filling it, part with flat stones laid in Cardiff Lime & Cobbles.

Richard Lewis and Jon. Grovener finished their bargain in taking out the Earth to the rock in Clay Mill and began after breakfast to clear the same of stones upon wages in order to fix the wheel frame & Penstock. Six o'clock the Penstock for Stamper and Clay Mill are fixed in their proper places.

Walter William, Harry William & William John, & Thomas Samuel Masons were upon the forebay. David Edward & John Richard were preparing stones for forebay, 4 Labourers attended them. The Carriage with 2 men & 5 horses brought Alder poles for Scaffolding. Three horses with 2 men brought from Llewenkelly 25 stones. Geo. Ford & Men, fixing Penstock in their places.

Evan William Lewis, Sawyer, was sent by Geo. Ford into the wood to look for proper timber that is fallen for Roofing Clay Mill & flourishing house.

Purchased three Cows from David Rees for £13 he said they were as good Milkers as any in the County also purchased the Copper that is set in the Malthouse for £2 2s which Sam Wood paid & took his receit for same.

Since the setting of the buildings by the perch & allowing the Masons to work over hours, The work goes on briskly. The flourishing furnaces & Stack, cannot be proceeded with any further, until Brick are burnt & fetched from the Mountain. And there are Carrs on draggs making for that purpose, the best method of carriage until a road is made for Carts which require more time than wè have at present from our other work.

Edward Thomas John, a good mason & a good workman, has been absent most of this week he has been sinking, as I am informed therefore not to be depended upon.

Wrote to Mr. Bacon to be sent tomorrow by especial Messenger. This evening Saml. Wood, Rowland Park, George Ford, Jos. Lucas, George Lyndon & myself drank to all our wives & friends in Milk Punch and soon after each went to their Lodgings. Aaron Wedgwood Potter and 2 Labourers have been seeking and getting Clay for Potts for one month past. He says there is plenty of various kinds. Bricks are moulded of every sort and numbers of mixtures, to find the most usefull method for service as it is found by experience that mixtures produce best bricks.

Sunday May 18th. Sent Wm. David's Son, David Wm. to Brecon with a letter for Mr. Bacon & to bring 4 setts of Scaffolding rope for Mr. Mound. Four o'clock evening rain came on. Dined in the Vilage at Edward Morgans and every weekday I have breakfast and Dinner bro't me with the men, to our room over the Smith shop.

Monday May 19th. A cold wind and hail and rain. The Clay Mill Wheel frame is fixed upon the Rock, taking up out a vein of mine & got about 2 cwt.

Harry William,Walter William, Thomas Samuel & Richard John were upon the forebay, Richard Lloyd & David Edward prepared stones for the front of the forebay. Masons & 4 Labourers, Edward Thomas John & Harry Williams Son serve him in rebuilding the Arch with brick in the Smiths hearth which fell. 3 horses & 2 men fetching a turn of brick from the kiln for the Arch before mentioned. David John and his men upon their bargain in finishing the flourishing house and Clay Mill.

The Carriage bro't Scaffolding poles Alder, 2 men. Three horses & 2 men brought 19 stone from Llewenkelly & then Load of Brick from Mountain.

David John and his men upon bargain working until 8 o'clock. Harry William, David Edwards & Thomas Samuel work at the Ash pits (upon bargain). After Six upon bargain. This shows the advantage of letting bargain & allowing the Masons to work after their day's work is over, to encourage them and we have our work done more expeditiously which is what we want & desire.

Mr. Terry the Plymouth Company Agent & some others came often, to see how we proceed this, in my opinion cannot proceed merely out of curiosity, therefore I conclude, that Company have a design to prevent our fixing our Wear and making sure of the water and this suspition arises from a report in the vilage that they have such intention, as well as from what Tho. Guest hinted to my Brother Samuel & I have from these conclusions wrote to Mr. Bacon this day my thoughts in this affair desiring his presence and advice before I begin fixing the frame of the Wear. If this was completed I should not be under any fear of miscarrying in any other part of this undertaking, but I own myself uneasie and under some apprehension of opposition, in this particular.

This day I agreed with Richard Rees to raise 1500 dozen Mine or Iron stone upon the following conditions vizt. To pay him £5 for bringing up a Level, to carry off the water, made use of the Waste of the Soil etc. at 2/6 p. dozen and one guinea in every hundred dozen which will make it 2s 9d 32/100 p. dozen and promised him that if we were ready with our furnace by the time he had raised the quantity of Mine, that he should have one of the Collerys to work but the terms were not mentioned.

Philip of the Wern came and brought Lewis Williams with him to interpret for him, he desired liberty to carry Lime or coal. I agreed he should do either or carry Tile from Aberdare at the price we gave other & was to receive directions from Evan the Tyler, where to fetch these from, that no mistake might happen.

Sent William David's Son to Brecon, with Letters for the Post, one to A. Bacon from C.W. & one from Sam Wood one for Mr. Potter under Mr. Bacon free cover; one from Geo. Lyndon to his Mother, one to Jos. Lucas with a bill for £11 at Carlton & one to George Ford with bill for £12 12s at Egremont. He is to set forward by 3 o'clock tomorrow morning, & wait the Post running in.

Tuesday May 20th. Six o'clock morning a cold N.E.Wind & cloudy turned to Snow.

Edward Thomas John began his bargain Walling & Arching part of the Grand Race, to be 8 ft wide within, in the clear, is 37 yards in length to meet that part that is finished by Jo. Ford.

Measured one length or 14 ft in length of the digging for the aforesaid 8 ft wide Arch which is 9 ft in depth to the rock, the rock 22 inches. Wide 14 ft 3 inches.

Begun to lay the remainder of the forebay to the first Hutch of the forge over or upon the wall laid in the race brought up into the pool, as before taken notice of, is left a conduit of about 4 inches square to take the water off that arises from a spring in the pool, or from the river thro' the joints of the rock which is to be stopt up close, when the forebay is finished.

John Morgan returned from Llandaff fair[1] & purchased there two oxen for the Carriage for £13 these two with four Bullens, bought at Aper before mentioned & 5 or 6 horses we hope will bring up any piece of Timber we have feln in our Libertys.

Daniel Williams the Waggoner or what they call here the Hallier, is gone home sick therefore I have ordered Jonathan Grovener, who says he has often drove a Team to go with John Morgan to Cardiff to fetch the Casks of Nails & what Iron they can bring besides, they are to set forward early in the Morning being Wednesday.

Sett the two Sawyers to make Yokes for the oxen of Beech fell for that purpose.

William Edward returned this day from viewing Mr. Kymers Navigation in Carmarthenshire[2] within about 3½ Miles of the Sea, a Canal is cutt for bringing down Coal for shipping wide enough for two boats to pass each other, and three bridges are to be erected over the Canal at those different places for carriages, as the Canal cuts the high road, the Coal lys near the surface, of a hard kind, called stone coal, & Wm tells me that there is plenty of Mine & Ironstone & a furnace near, that did blow with charcoal, but now out, the men of that work agreed all the Ironstone, but neglected the coal, & now the wood is exhausted the furnace is useless.[3] William has given in his proposals, for Erecting these bridges, which if agreed to he leaves us with our leave.

William Walter Collier, with three more, have been bringing up a Level to a five foot band of coal near the Brick kiln for its one as will save more than gr. Expense—in bringing up in the carriage to supply the kiln wth coal, & it is said to be as good as any for Air furnaces, if so it will be of great use as it is a better road and nearer than per Wain. Two labourers are employed to get and fetch Sand, out of the cut, near the Lime. for the grand race two more are employed to make mortar & to carry Mortar to Masons upon day wages. Six Labourers are employed to

[1] Held on Whitmonday.

[2] Thomas Kymer obtained an Act in 1766 to make a canal from Kidwelly quay to Pwllyllygoed near Carway, which is said to have been opened in 1769 (C. Hadfield, *The Canals of South Wales and the Border* (1977 ed.), 30; W.H. Morris, 'The canals of the Gwendraeth valley. Part I', *Carmarthenshire Antiquary*, vi (1970), 53–8), although Wood's entry suggests that it may have been completed rather sooner.

[3] The furnace at Ponthenri, near Kidwelly, operated in its later years by Robert Morgan of Carmarthen, last sold pig iron to the Knights' forges in the Stour valley in 1763; from that year they took pig from Morgan's other furnace at Carmarthen instead (P. Riden, *A Gazetteer of charcoal-fired blast furnaces in use in Great Britain since 1660* (2nd. ed., 1993), 29–30). The diary entry thus confirms a date of closure for Ponthenri in the early 1760s.

bring Stone from the Quarry to the Masons on bargain & day work. Two more are employed to mix up & Four for Cardiff Lime and one to carry it. Two are employed to fetch sizable stones, scabbled fit for laying the forebay in Cardiff Lime. One to fetch Cobble to fill up the forebay wall.

Harry Williams, Walter Wm, Richard Lloyd & Wm John, Masons, are upon the forebay. David Edwards preparing & sizing Stone for ditto & William Edwards overseer. This day set up my Bed in the room next to the Office & fixed two more in the Garret, for George Lyndon, George Ford & Joseph Lucas. Received a letter off David William (send this morning with letters to the Post Office in Brecon) from Mr. Bacon only, no other letters nor Newspaper.

Wednesday May 21st. A fine moderate day, warm & a change from yesterday, of several degrees. 12 o'clock this morning we fixed the Sills & frame for one pair of rollers upon the rock & filled it up with Stones & Gravel four foot & nailed slabs against the inside of the frame for the wheel.

Harry Williams, Walter Williams, Richard Lloyd, William John & John Gabriel were upon the forebay. David Edward sorting and preparing Courses of stones for it. Wm Edwards overseer and scabbled to quoin stone. All Masons & two Labourers serving Cobbles, 4 ditto fetching stone for Course one fetching Mortar. One tempering, two making & two fetching sand. Two at load of Lime tempering & one serving with ditto.

Three horses with 2 men fetching Coal for Workmen. Walter William has taken the lining the Arch up to the Wheel frame which is about 4 yards in length he fetched & Scabbled stone & Mortar & carry other parts to complete it for 10s and work at it in his own time before and after his days work. Harry William and David Edwards work upon their bargain in Morning & Evening, before and after working hours. This afternoon William Edwards went with George Ford, Joseph Lucas, Sam Wood, George Lyndon & C. Wood, to show us the place, he proposed to take the water in, from Tavour branch of the river[1] which is a very convenient one, one side belongs to Lord Talbot and Michael Richard Esq. the other side to Mr. Gwin.[2] We viewed a place much nearer our work, but as the opposite side belongs to Lord Plymouth and not to be easily obtained, the charge of making the Wear & the fall only 12 feet

[1] i.e. the Tâf Fawr, rather than the Tâf Fechan.

[2] Probably Roderick Gwynne (*c.* 1695–1777) of Buckland (Brecs.) and Glanbrân (Carms.). He was the father of Thynne Howe Gwynne who granted a lease to the Cyfarthfa Company (Lloyd, *Early History*, 50, where no date is given). See pedigree in J. Bradney, *History of Monmouthshire*, i. 409.

the other place is by much to be preferred and there will be upward of 26 ft fall & William Edwards offers to bring the water, sufficient for an overshott wheel & insure it for Seven years for £300 which in my opinion should be accepted as it will be the least expense.

I think the water will be brought from the lower place to obtain 12 feet fall only. And William Edwards will undertake to bring it by the time we can have a furnace ready for using it. There is not any land where the aquaeduct is to come through, belonging to any other person but our Lords, and the damage but trifling to the Tenants in possession.

This day we received 16 load of Cardiff Lime from the burner, but 14 from the Carrier.

Thursday May 22nd. A fine warm morning. A new mason took on named Richard Pritchard a young man, to be paid as he is found to deserve.

Set two men, to lade out the water, in the Stamper race, in order to prepare the remaining part, unfinished, to be walled and arched up, to the forebay upon taking out this water it is found that the Clay Mill race is drove up six inches higher than the Stamper nothwithstanding C. Wood ordered them to be all upon a dead level, from the beginning of the Grand race, which was laid, three feet higher than the river, was, at the time it was began and that was all that was to be allowed, to the foot of the wheel.

Received an invitation with my brother from Mr. Thomas Price one of the partners of the Dowlais Furnace,[1] to Dine with him at the furnace, sent our Compliments, & that we would wait upon him.

Agreed to give David John 3s p. yard in length for walling and Arching the stamper race, the wall to be 22 inches high from the rock, the Arch 5 foot wide in the clear it is ordered to make ready 12 feet at a time & when Arched, the rubbish is to be thrown on the top of it, in clearing a length of 12 feet more, & so on until finished.

Returned from Dining with Mr Thomas Price at Dowlais Furnace where I bespoke eight half hundred, one quarter, one fourteen, and one Seven pound weights, the price he could not inform me, as Mr. Webb the manager was not there. The pigs they now make are of a good grey, but not so much so, as when they have more water & cooler, some they broke to show me that was a very open bright, grey, they put each sort by themselves some a light white, others a Motley, others white with a

[1] Thomas Price J.P., of Watford, near Caerphilly (1712–83). There are several secondary sources in Welsh for his life, mainly to do with his religious connections, e.g. Gomer M. Roberts, *Hanes Methodistiaeth Galfinaidd Cymru*, i (Caernarfon, 1973), 234–5.

Core in the heart of the pig, but the greatest quantity as they informed me, was a good grey grain. There charge is 7 cwt 14 lb of stone and 2 cwt 0 qut 14 lb of Lime stone, they have a good blast with three Tubs one raising after the other alternately, & where there is water sufficient to give stroke enough, they are by much preferable to any Leather Bellows & require less water in proportion of their blast,[1] come home before six.

At the forebay and side wall in the pool William Edwards, David Edwards, Harry William, Walter William, Thomas Lloyd, William John, John Gabriel & Richard Pritchard. Two Labourers serving cobble, four fetching stones to lay in Cardiff Lime, two at Cardiff Lime, one tempering Common Mortar, one making up & two fetching sand & one carrying Mortar. Two Labourers fetching stone from the Quarry to the hurry,[2] one to put them upon it, one to take them from the foot, and four to carry to the Masons in Bargain. George Ford, his two men & Wm. Postlethwaite Carpenter upon the other Stamper Penstock two Sawyers in sawing planks for ditto. William David, Smith went to fix an Iron hoop in the Brick kiln & this evening fire was sett to it.

Mr. Thomas Price informed me that it was reported that the Plymouth Company would endeavour to prevent our fixing our Wear on Ld Plymouth side of the river and that they wd make a cut through part of Lewis John's Land part of the field we had taken from him & Erect a Corn Miln in order to deprive us of the Water. How far this can be legaly put in execution I am not a judge. The Waggon was left upon the Common the horse not being able to draw it out of a soft part of the road up to the Axle tree therefore Jon Grovenor bro't the horse home & is to take two yoke of Oxen in the morning to bring it home. John Morgan stay't to watch the Iron & Nails etc.

Came four load of Lime from a kiln taken of Mr Philip Charles for 3 year this the 2d year Rees the Cobler and partner burning 4 load.

Friday May 23rd. A fine warm morning. Captain Charles Hugh[3] breakfasted with us in our Office with Thomas Williams from Cardiff who brought me a letter from Isaac Wilkinson relating the Cylinder

[1] The Dowlais furnace had adopted cylinder blowing, with large pistons driven by a waterwheel through a crankshaft, in preference to the traditional leather bellows.

[2] A hurry was a shoot or slope used in mines and quarries to transfer minerals from one level to a lower one.

[3] Neither this man, nor the Captain Samuel Hughes mentioned later, has been firmly identified, but they probably belonged to a prominent family of that name then resident at Brecon, which originated at Trostre, near Usk: Bradney, *History of Monmouthshire*, iii. 88.

Bellows. The Captain informed me that he had seen Mr. Bacon, who told him he expected to be here in July. Thomas Williams, with William Edwards informed that there is a race or trough to convey the water to the Corn Miln in Cardiff had occasion to be taken up for some alteration the stone where the Limestone before burnt & were laid in the Mortar and they believed had been laid 150 or 200 years before, the stone, by the strong current of the water were worn, an inch & half or near two inches & left the Mortar standing full and not in the least wasted & harder and more difficult to break than the stone itself, from which it was burnt and that part, that was continually under water & not exposed to the open air was by much the strongest, therefore was not any doubt of its answering the end we propose for using it.

Fixed the other stamper penstock about 10 in the morning. Edward Thomas John & Thomas Samuel began laying the foundation for the mixing room the bargain taken by Harry William at 1s per perch 12ft high & 2d per perch more for every scaffold, it is necessary to erect for raising it higher.

Sent David Lewis to fetch the weight from Dowlais furnace. This day 9 load of lime is sent from our kiln taken of Mr. Philip Charles and burnt by Rees the Cobler and his partner upon bargain. The Waggon came about 2 o'clock and brought 6 casks of nail, 2 gudgeons, 1 scale beam, 1 grate, 2 bearings, 6 strong flatt barrs, and 11 sq. barrs.

At the forebay William Edwards, David Edwards, Harry Williams, Walter Williams, Thomas Lloyd, William John, John Gabriel and Richard Pritchard, Masons. Two Labourers to serve with Cobbles, two to fetch Scabbled stone for front, four to fetch Quarry stone, two at Cardiff Lime one to serve with Lime, two fetching sand, one Tempering, one mixing & one carrying mortar.

George Ford, his 2 men with William Postlethwaite upon Penstock for Chafery & Stampers in the forge. Received from Dowlais Company 8 half hundred, 1 qu, 1 of 14 & one of 7 lb of cast iron adjusted.

Saturday May 24th. A cloudy morning with rain until near eleven o'clock then broke up & proved a fine warm day.

Mr. Morgan came breakfasted with us with Captain Hughes. Put down and fixed the other frame for Clay Mill. David John began his bargain in making the side walls & Arch for first stamper race, 5 feet wide in the clear and at 3s per yard in Length.

Received 16 Load of Cardiff lime from the burner and to the carrier 14 load.

Wrote to Mr. Bacon, Wilkinson & my wife & sent by Captain Hughes to Brecon with the fortnight pay bill from Sam. At the forebay

Harry William, Walter William, William John, John Gabriel, Thomas Lloyd, David Edward & William Edward Masons. Thomas Pritchard being a poor hand was paid but 1s. p. day therefore left us. Two labourers serving stone, four with hand barrow to fetch Quarry stone, two to fetch them to the hurry, one to thro' them down, & one to take them from the foot of the hurry, two at Cardiff Lime, one serving it, one mixing Common Lime and sand, one tempering, two fetching Sand and one carrying Mortar.

This day several men left Thomas Clifton who is upon the bargain of taking the Earth in the Pool their names as under written vizt. Isaac Williams, Richard Lewis, John Isaac & Thomas Davies, it is said they are gone to Dowlais Furnace.

David Lewis with three horses went four times with Sand and brought brick back.

The Waggon and horse at home. John Morgan with horse & Cart mending road and preparing for fixing a Gate at the entrance to the old road.

Two Sawyers sawing for Sundry uses.

Past five all left work as they began at 5 this morning the Labourers & Masons etc have an hour for breakfast and one hour at dinner. It now rains & like to be showers very fine weather for the land which looks well & promising plenty of grass.

Thomas David has finished his bargain in taking the earth to the rock for the forge floor they were to have £9 10s but as they worked well and their days work came to more than the £9 10s, I thought it right to allow each 1s per day and paid them.

To Walther Rhys	16¼	days @ 1s p day	£0 16 3
John Edwards	24¼	do	1 4 3
Thomas David	27¼	do	1 7 3
Richard Evan	27¼	do	1 7 3
Thomas William	19½	do	- 19 6
William Williams	25¼	do	1 5 3
Lewis Thomas	14¾	do	- 14 9
William Moses	21	do	1 1 0
William David	10	do	- 10 0
Evan Thomas	16¼	do	- 16 3
	201¾		£10. 1.9

I showed Mr. Morgan[1] Lord Talbot Stewart the rotten load Timber that Isaac Bates had feln & brought home, some by Mr. Guest at 15s per Ton which he expects and he thought it very reasonable that we should have an allowance or other Timber for it. I also showed him some Alder that we cut for Scaffolding poles, which we could not do without, & for which we would pay for agreeable to Article in our Lease, after the rate of Cordwood at the time it was feln which he approved.

Wrote to Mr. Bacon & sent the charge for Cylinders for the 6" Diameter.

				cwt	q	lb		£	s	d
3 Cylinders when bored is supposed to weigh				61	3	8. @	26	77	5	5
3 bottoms	19	1	4							
3 pistons	19	1	4	36	2	8. @	14	26	10	0
Two cranks				56	-	-. @	18	50	8	0
								154	3	5

A cylinder of 5 feet diameter will make it more

	cwt	q	lb		£	s	d
One will weigh 23 0 16 for 3 will be	69	1	20. @	25	86	15	6
3 bottoms & pistons all the same	40	-	-. @	14	28	0	0
2 cranks	56	-	-. @	18	50	8	0
					165	3	6

Sunday May 25th. The river fuller of water from rain that fell in the night. A hazy morning with a misty rain staid within until after 10 o'clock when Sam Wood came to me from the Vilage took a walk round the work, met Mr. Terry Agent of Plymouth Company, entered into discussion about water wheels & furnace bellows his opinion relating to bellows, was that instead of having two large ones, which requires a powerful wheel to blow them as they ought he wld have three, that should blow alternately with a Crank, which would answer better, in a blast, take a less wheel & might be made to Cam oftener, without straining the wheel & or Gear, more smooth and easie & answer all the purposes much better than two large ones. He had another thought which was to have a weight upon the breech of each bellow sufficient to press them down, as quick as should be found necessary, & lifted up by a Crank & wheel which would take off great part of the weight in the

[1] Thomas Morgan of Cilfynydd (d. 1788), attorney in practice at Cowbridge, and steward of Earl Talbot's estate. William Thomas refers to him in his diary in several times in this capacity. The pedigree in G.T. Clark, *Limbus Patrum* (1886), 335, is very inaccurate; ancestor of the Morgans of Marlborough Grange, Llanblethian.

paces and prepare of the bellows by the wheel in the old way as a large pair of bellows with pace will require 20 cwt or 30 cwt or 40 cwt wt in a pace to raise the bellows which must be lifted by the wheel as well as press the bellows down to force out the air.

These thoughts seem to me to be just ones & the Crank in particular I think would be an improvement in blowing the Common bellows as it would take off the great weight in the paces which securing a greater power then would be necessary without it.

How far the method he proposes to blow with weight on the breech and the wheel with a Crank, applied to the raising them, will answer experience to those who will make it, will show. But upon the whole I think his thought ingenious & rational.

Went into the office & staid until about half past 12 o'clock, then locked the door & went to the Anchor & Crown, Edward Morgan in the Vilage & dined with my brother Samuel, Rowley Park & George Lyndon. George Ford & Joseph Lucas did not come until we had done. They had been at the Brick kiln which was out. Josh observed that they had not covered the top courses with old brick ends which was necessary to keep the flame down that the top might be burnt as well as other parts which is a just observation and what ought to have been done the consequence of this neglect will be seen when they draw her.

Half past two came to the office again, alone, George Lyndon, George Ford & Josh Lucas went to Church, Prayers and Sermon every other Sunday in the afternoon being in English at all other times in Welsh. It began to rain as I came up and continues to do past four o'clock.

George Lyndon, Ford & Lucas, are just now came to the rock. Walked about the work until near 7 then went in & sait talking over affairs untill about half past nine & then to bed.

Monday May 26th. A close morning with small rain, like dew, a deal of rain fell in the night. Gave Wm. Edwards direction for springing an Arch & making a Wall to each end over the first hammer hutch to have passage from the Stamping house into the forge for carrying pots ready filled for shingling as it would be very inconvenient to pass the Furnace & hammer when at work as they will be almost continually. The arch to be sprang from the rock, & the rock under the Arch to be hollowed deep to admit a free passage for the water by doing this the road or passage will be near level with both floors. The passage, to be 4 foot wide & 8 foot of wall, at each end upon the Arch.

Our Masons leave us weekly, we have new upon day wages, at the forebay no more than William Edwards & his son David, Harry Williams, Walter Williams, John Gabriel & Thomas Lloyd. David John and one of his partners upon the 5 foot arch for the race for the first pair of Stampers, two others of his partners are upon the Clay Mill house. Edward Thomas, John & Thomas Samuel are upon the Mixing Room building. Harry Williams has wrote into Monmouthshire for his Brother, a Mason & as many men as he could procure. David John has likewise wrote for two more Masons. William Postlethwaite has made & fixed Style at the Entrance of the old road, where a Gate is to be fixed, as our grass is eat by our neighbour cattle & sheep. Four labourers removing stone for continuing the side of the hammer hatch two in serving Masons with stones to the fore bay, one serving with common Mortar two mixing Lime and sand, one tempering, one getting Sand, one mending the road where the gate is fixed. Two labourers filling between the frame of the Clay Mill rolls. Two Labourers serving stones, to the Masons of the Clay Mill & two to the mixing room. David Penry and his three partners are upon their bargain on the grand race, two upon Cardiff lime, & one to serve it.

George Ford & his 2 Men upon the Chafery wheel penstock. Wrote to Doctor Brownrigg & enclosed my proposal to the Plymouth Company with their answer. To Mr. Jordan that we could not treat for his work at Mellin Griffiths.[1] Took by my brother to the Postman for Brecon.

Joseph Lucas filling between the Clay Mill frames. Showers of rain often this day. Fine for the Land. Two sawyers sawing for the hammer hutch. John Morgan and John Grosvenor gone with the Waggon to Cardiff for iron that came from Low Mill,[2] and two yoke of Oxen, one to meet him tomorrow upon the Mountain in aid to the horses. Three horses with David Lewis carry Sand to the Brick makers and bring brick back. Three horses with carrs on Draggs, with Lewis Strachan fetch brick from brick kiln the former 4 tonne of sand which is 12 bags and the six horse brought but 1500 brick as the horse run away, the last two and their loads were thrown off.

Zacharias Phillips, Lord Talbot's Woodman, was here I showed him the bad timber we had feln by Isaac Bates & which was given in to Mr. Morgan, Lord Talbot's Stewart and I hope some allowance will be made either in the price or other way allowed to make up our loss but what will be done herein time must show.

[1] The tinplate works in the Taff valley a few miles north of Cardiff, established *c.* 1750: E.L. Chappell, *Historic Melingriffith: an account of Pentrych iron works* (Cardiff, 1940).

[2] See above, Introduction, for Wood's connection with this forge.

Tuesday May 27. half past five a fine warm sunny morning Rowley Parks called the men over at 6 o'clock. Morgan Jenkin & Masons came to work again a good hand & thinks he can stay constantly. Lett the sinking of one of the forge wheel case & race in the rock to Thomas David & his partner, three more, four feet & half deep and five feet wide at 9d p. solid yard.

Fetched the rod and bitts for boring of pipes from Lewis Wm John belonging to Thomas Williams of Cardiff he giving us liberty to make use of them.

Joseph Lucas took David John & his three partners, Masons, to assist him at the Stack.

George Ford and his two men have began to prepare Alder wood to bore for pipes to convey water to the boshes in the flourishing house and to the wash for Cinder etc. George Ford and me have measured the Alder that was cut for Scaffolding Poles etc. vizt.

	ft	in	cu.ft
1 piece	26 long	6 girth =	6½
1 do	30 do	4½ do =	4
1 do	24 do	9 do =	13½
1 do	20 do	8 do =	9
1 do	10 do	8 do =	4½
18 each	29 do	4 do =	54
3 each	29 do	4 do =	9
2 do	16 do	7 do =	11
2 do	15 do	7 do =	10
30 pieces measure			121½

These are to be reckoned & paid for etc at the rate of cordwood as per Lease and their measurement is near a Cord.

Went to the mountain to see the bricks drawn from a kiln the first time burnt in, John Edge & Robert Wilson the maker, thought the coal weak, therefore mixed the small coal among the brick in the middle & finding that the Coal was stronger than they expected the brick in the centre of the kiln were run into a loop & made useless which loss may be a service as it will teach them how to manage for the future & avoid the blunder committed they being told that the coal was good and produced a hot fire, what has been got is at the outburst and when it is got more under cover I am of opinion that it will prove an excellent Air furnace Coal; it dips fast and a low Level should be brought up for the geting a large quantity £10 I think will bring one up, to serve several years. This coal is within about fifty yards of the brick kiln. There has been several kinds of fire Clay made into brick to try the quality of it. Some alone and others mixed in various proportions which seem to be good & to appearance better then those made at Low Mill. The sundry mixture were well down by Aaron Wedgwood, on Account of which is as underwritten vizt. There is no judging from the Acct they give, but it appears very clear that that the mixture make the best sort but the furnace must determine by trying them there.

A Piston of 5 ft diameter to find the area multiply half of circumference by half the Diameter vizt.

the diameter 5 ft = 60 in the Circumference 16 ft = 192 in - 96 × 30 = 2880 in ÷ 4 = 720 lb = 6 cwt, 1 q, 20lb.

A bottom the same 6, 1, 20 = 0 t, 12 cwt, 3 q, 12 lb @ 14p p cwt.

A cylinder 6 ft high & 5ft diameter will be equal to a plate of 96 ft × 144 = 13824 sq. inches but as the Cylinder will be but ¾ of an inch thick, it will reduce to 10368 sq. inches, an inch thick & as 4 Cubic inches of cast iron weighs a pound then 10368 ÷ 4 = 2592 lb = 23 cwt, 0 q, 16 lb @ 25s p. cwt.

As a Crank may break, it will be prudent to have a spare one ready to put in in case of such an accident therefore two should be made, each it is suggested will be 28 cwt the two 56 cwt @ 18s p. cwt.

One o'clock just now came Mr. Terry & informed me that the Plymouth Company were willing to cast anything we wanted that could be done in open sand upon the terms proposed which was £5 15s per ton short weight i.e. 112 lb to the hundred & 20 hundred to the ton delivered at Cyfarthfa and if I agree desired the patterns might be made as soon as we could. C.W. agreed to it & promised to get moulds made as soon as he could.

Mr. Terry told me on Sunday last that they the Plymouth Company had put some white pigs in the water to meliorate & after they had laid there in some time, a twelve month or more, they would be sent to Market and might pass for foreign pigs had they the right mark it is common practice to put the wire into Water covered with Mud to meliorate it & take off the red short quality.

The Waggon bro't from Cardiff 3 pair of Tongs 2 pattern Spindles, 1 Grate, 12 riddles, 1 Morris plate, 1 loop for Anvil block, 1 Iron riddle, 18 bunches of hoops & 59 boxes of Iron hoops & flatts.

Wednesday, May 28th. Half past five a Cold Easter Wind; walked about the work most of the men here ready to begin at Six. Received two letters from Mr. Bacon one from Mr. Wilkinson and one from my wife.

Mr. Thomas Morgan, Lord Talbot's Stewart came here about Nine o'clock paid my brother Sam money to make what he received before £250 for which he gave his bill on Mr. Bacon. Mr. Morgan promised to be here again in three weeks with Zacharias Lord Talbot's woodman & stay 2 or 3 days & there they would consider of an allowance for the bad timber. I gave Mr. Morgan a copy of Isaac Wilkinson and Mr. Guest Articles of Co-partnership to draw Articles of Sale for Isaac Wilkinson to CW of his three shares in Plymouth Works.

William Richard brought from Cardiff 9 arms, 5 fore & 9 back plates, 6 broad barrs for arm hoops 6 cams, 2 Stampershanks 20 fire bars 6 rabble heads & 2 tueres wt 25 cwt 1 q 17 lb.

David John & his three men were at the stack with Josh Lucas, William Edwards, his son David, Harry Wm, Walter Williams, Morgan Jenkins, John Gabriel & Thomas Lloyd. Masons were upon the forebay, two labourers serving stone, two serving Mortar & two fetching stone from Quarry. Three Labourers sinking the Stamper race in the rock for 12 ft in length of Walling & Arching for David John bargain two mixing lime with sand, one tempering & 2 carrying Sand. Four labourers sinking one of the hammer races in the rock for bargain at 9d per yard. Two labourers serving Joseph Lucas and his men with brick & mortar for the Stack.

George Ford & his two men about the frame for one hammer hutch. William Postlethwaite making patterns for hammers, Anvil and for Castings pursuant to agreement with Plymouth Company for castings. Two Sawyers sawing Timber for hammer hutch. Edward Thomas John & Thomas Samuel Walling & Arching 14 ft of the grand race 8 ft wide. Two labourers serving stone to them.

Waggon at home three horses fetching brick on their backs and three more the same in carrs with 2 Men bro't 1460 brick & two loads of coal for the Smith Shop.

The forebay goes on but slowly as it is tedious requiring great exactness to prevent any water coming thro' which would make the Stamp house etc. almost useless should it not be made quite water proof. The cold North East Wind has brought rain which put all hands off work at 5 o'clock.

Thursday May 29th. Half past five a cold North East Wind. This morning wrote to Mr. Bacon in answer to his two letters of the 22nd and 24th to Isaac Wilkinson to be sent by John Morgan to Brecon tomorrow the 30th.

Wrote to my wife, Betty Wood and Mr. Potter, the two former under one of Mr. Bacon's franked & sent by Mr. Morgan.

The pattern for bearing bars & for furnace base made, the bearing bar 2 inch $^7/_8$ to the level, the level inch and $^7/_8$ in length, 5 ft 6 inches at each end, to go into the Wall 3 feet ½ for the bars. The bars 3 feet 2 inches long & 2 inch base Square. The pattern for a hammer is finished.

Two o'clock it rains continues until four when Masons left off vizt. William Edwards, his son David, Harry Willm, Walter William, Morgan Jenkin & John Gabriel. The Labourers continue working, rather choosing to be wet then loose a quarter of a day. Thomas Lloyd not here.

In rainy weather the Masons can do little therefore shd not allow them to work but they are not satisfied to loose any time therefore I agree that they shall have liberty to make it up by working over hours.

George Ford and his man David, upon the hammer hutch frame, William Postlethwaite & Joseph, Geo. Ford's other Man upon patterns for bars etc. Two Sawyers upon frame for brick bay. Two men with 6 horse leading brick three in carrs & three in pannier upon their back.

The Waggon horse confined for want of Yoke, for the Oxen to assist in bringing Timber.

Edward Thomas John & Thomas Samuel upon a length of the grand Arch. David John & his partner upon the Stamper Arch.

Friday May 30th. A quarter before Six a cold raw morning uncomfortable weather and many of our Masons absent by sickness. Thomas Lloyd a Mason came this morning work but his Eye was so painfull from a stroke with the splinter of a stone he could not bear the light therefore was obliged to return home & 4 men lye ill we are in great want of Masons.

Sent William Postlethwaite this morning with the patterns underwritten by the Plymouth Furnace to be cast pursuant to agreement with Mr Terry their agent. C.W order to John White & Co. is copyed in the day Book. A hammer Mould, bearg bar mould, furnace bar mould and ledges for washing plates with order for 4 plates each 4 feet square about ¾ of an inch thick these plates are to form a square to mix upon. Nine o'clock it rains and like to continue but not so hard as to oblige Masons and Labourers to leave off.

One o'clock turned out a fine day warmer than it was.

Three o'clock a great shower of rain.

William Postlethwaite returned from Plymouth furnace after waiting to see our hammer cast & brought a piece of the metal a mottle grain which may do for the shingling but would prove too white for drawing.

Near four o'clock Mr. Terry came to desire leave to fetch some Sand for their pig bed & castings, gave them leave. This day my Bror. received a Lr. as did Rowlay Park, advising them that their wives were both ill & desired both return home.

This day laid the Sill in part of the Stamp House Wall for the headstock for one end of Stamper Wheel shaft to lye upon. William Edwards upon the forebay wall alone. The other Masons vizt. David

Edwards upon dam Wall and Walter William, Harry William & Morgan Griffiths in the Quarry, Scabbling Stone for the forebay, those that were Scabbled being worked up. Four labourers carrying stone out of the Quarry, one throwing them down the hurry two raising stone in the Quarry, two carrying stones from the hurry to the rock that David John is about, two carrying stone to the Grand Arch that Edward Thomas John is about. Edward Thomas John and Thomas Samuel at the Grand Arch. David John and 2 of his partners at the Stamp race Arch. Joseph Lucas & one of David Johns partners at the Stack & two labourers to serve them. One Labourer at Cardiff Lime, two mixing Common Mortar & two mixing Sand within 20 yards of Lime. William Edwards has just now desired leave to go home he will return on Monday gave him leave and desired him to endeavour to procure more Masons. George Ford and his Men are upon the Hammer Hutch. Two Sawyers serving for ditto. Past six a fine evening.

This evening Morgan Griffiths began his bargain at the other Arch pit at 10d p. Perch.

The expense of building the kiln for burning of 12 m[1] Brick

Labourers & one Masons wages	£1	18	9
Joseph Lucas 8 days	£1	–	–
Brick, 6 m of the brick burnt in a Clamp by Benjamin Brown softener dresser	£3	–	–
Lime & Stone reckoned at loading	£1	1	3
	£7	–	–

This kiln burns 12 m I thought that it would 14 m, but as there are very few soft or bad ones & it will serve for years I look upon it the cheapest method of burning where quantity are wanted.

Saturday May 31st. Five o'clock rains a little. Looks like a great deal. Masons and part of the Labourers began at five that they might leave off at five as some of them have 5 or 6 miles home. At eight the rain was so hard both Masons and Labourers left off for the day & has continued so to this time & like to continue. The river pretty high & the work from the race full of water which will make it troublesome, with some additional expense to clear it and the work not fit to go upon if some days to do it.

George Ford his two men & Postlethwaite Carpenter are the only men at work, the former at the forge hutch, the latter upon patterns. John

[1] i.e. 1,000.

Morgan with Jonathan Grovenor, Lewis Trehane were halling such piece of Timber that were easily come at into the road they halled seven but the rain prevented them from doing so much as they might and George Ford attending them to mark such pieces as were most wanted. Six horses bo't two turns of Smith Coal from a two feet vein at Cumdee but the rain prevented them going any more. Nine o'clock still rains. We had some Milk punch to drink health to our wives and children. My Bror., Rowland Parker, George Ford, Joseph Lucas, Geo. Lyndon and myself.

Settled my Brother Cash Account & examined it by his Cash book and pay bills & signed it for Anthony Bacon and Company and received in Cash £150 in payment by him since last pay day to be included in the next pay bill £25 12s 1½d, the whole from him £175 12s 1½d.

Sunday, June 1st. Seven o'clock a fine warm morning. A cold has settled in my left ear, it is swell'd very sore.

Wrote to Mr. Bacon, to Doctor Brownrigg & my wife, & sent to Brecon by Samuel Wood, or to any post upon the road. A quarter past eleven my Bro., Rowley Park & George Ford went forward. George Ford was to set them to Warrington & then return with the horse, he is to call at Bringewood Forge abot three miles from Ludlow,[1] to see & take of dimension of their Iron Anvil block & Anvil as it is thought such is the best adapted for Shingling as it will save blocking Scrap and prevent the block over burning. John Morgan went with them, to send them into the nearest road over the Mountain to Hay which will save them 8 mile, being so much nearer then going thro' Brecon.[2]

Continuing a fine warm day. Went down to the Vilage at near one & dined at Edward Morgan, at the Anchor & Crown returned to the rock at half past two, overclouded & very like more rain. Joseph Lucas & George Lyndon went after dinner to Rhyd y car. Seven o'clock continues fair. Captain Samuel Hughes was so kind to bring me letters from Brecon, one from Mr. Bacon, with three newspapers. He read me a letter from Major Alderton informing him that Mr. Bacon desires he would call upon Mr. Parrit about purchasing his shares in the Plymouth works & as the Captain had had some talk when in London with Mr. Parrit he desired him to let him know what had passed which would supply him, the Major, with matter for such a treaty. Upon considering the affair the

[1] One of the forges operated by the Knight family: L. Ince, *The Knight family and the British iron industry, 1692–1902* (1991).

[2] They were evidently directed to a track over the mountain that would take them to Hay via Crickhowell and Talgarth, rather than along the old carriage road from Merthyr to Brecon.

Captain agreed with me that the Major should not wait upon Mr. Parrit, but that this affair should remain & in time they might be had at a more reasonable rate than they could be had now. As my proposal must have given some spirit to that work.

Monday June 2nd. Past six lay in bed this morng my ear being sore. It rains and is quite overcast. Four o'clock rain over but a cold wind. William Edwards & his son David absent. Captain Samuel Hughes dined with us at Cyfarthfa and after walked to his Estate at Aberdare. Desired I would allow our Smith Wm David to make him a Spade to push land, gave orders accordingly. Wrote to Mr. Bacon in answer to his of the 29th ult. to be sent to Brecon by the Merthyr Post Man.

Hopkin David Mason who had been ill came to work. I sent him with Joseph Lucas, at the furnace under cover as it was rain in morning & cold to prevent his having a relapse.

The Plymouth Company fetched one large Cast & four Waggon load of Sand p. leave.

William Postlethwaite finished the hust and bait mould and sent them to Plymouth furnace by their Waggon that came for Sand and ordered four of each to be cast. William Postlethwaite & Josh Samson one of George Fords Men squaring Stamper Shafts. David Millingan the other of George Fords men, was mortizing the hammer hutch Sill. The Sawyers sawing Slabs for hoppers for mixing room, and boards off the thick Stamper Shafts for mending barrows. David John & his partner about the flourishing house. Edward Thomas John about the mixing room both by perch. John Gabriel & Thomas Lloyd Scabbling stone upon the Dam wall. Henry William, Morgan Evan Jenkins & William Jones all Masons Scabbling stone in the Quarry.

Rees David & Howel Rees a Labourer raising stone in Quarry. Four Labourers carrying stone to the hurry one puting them down & one taking them from the foot of it. Two serving David John etc with Quarry stones etc, one serving Joseph Lucas & Hopkin David three preparing an other Length of Stamper race for Arching. Three mixing Lime & carrying Sand one riddling Cardiff Lime & one Lading water out of Stamper race.

My ear very sore I imagine it may come to a head & discharge. Three horses setting my Brother & Rowland Parker. Two with 2 men carrying Clay for fire brick & the remainder with three men halling timber out of the Gully & and Inn ground into the highway for fetching as wanted.

Past six it rains & like to continue.

Tuesday, June 3rd. Seven o'clock rested but poorly my ear very painful & a great deal of rain fell last night the river full and it now rains. Do not think it prudent to go out this day. Nine o'clock (breakfast time) rain continues but not heavy. Altho' it prevents the Masons laying stones in Mortar. William Edwards & his son David are gone up the river, to be more exact in Leveling the water in Tavour trough intended to be brought for our intended furnace.[1] Twelve o'clock rains hard all hands left work.

Thomas Lloyd, Harry Williams, John Gabriel, Morgan Evan Jenkins & William Jenkin, Masons, Scabbling Stones for forebay. This morning Hopkin David, with Joseph Lucas at the furnace. Two Labourers raising stones, four carrying stones from Quarry to hurry, one putting them down, one taking them from the foot, one attending Joseph Lucas & Hopkin, four at the Mortar. Two getting Sand to cover the Lime & two fetching Quarry stones to the Masons. Two striking in the Smith Shop, William Postlthwaite & George Ford & two men squaring stamper shaft. Sawyers sawing board off Stamper shaft. Three o'clock continued to rain very hard.

John Morgan returned from the wood and informed me that they halled pieces of timber yesterday into the highway ready for carriage that these are pieces from 28 to 35 feet long & 20 inches in Girth that he spoke to one of the Tennants thro' whose land we must hall some of the pieces and he told him he desired no more than reasonable damages & would repair it to himself. Mr. Jenkins Farmers sd the same but that these was one of Lord Plymouth Tenants believed would be difficult to argue with. John Morgan very wet, sent him home to change his clothes. William Edward & his son returned from leveling Tavour branch could not compleat it for rain, very wet, sent them home to change their clothes.

Past six. A large flood which carryed away Gravel & Stones, thrown over the outwall from the Pool which was in several heaps as high as the Wall. Also part of the Island.

Last night I found myself much out of order & the pain in my ear occasioned a slight fever. I took two of Andersons pills & some small warm Punch which occasioned a fine healing Sweat and two stools which relieved me, and lessened the pain but this evening I find myself rather worse and a pain in the back of my head as well as in the left ear, but not so violent as it was last night. It is now eight o'clock the rain is ceased and the river falling, all our work where our forge is to be is

[1] i.e. surveying the water level in the Tâf Fawr.

under water which must be laded out, when the river is got into its usual Channel. Mr. Terry called upon me to know if we had anything to bring from Cardiff they had a Waggon to go there tomorrow. I told him we had & that he might have them from Mr. Howels warehouse but being pained in my head forgot to settle the price but I do not imagine he will demand an unreasonable one.

Nine o'clock took a little small warm brandy punch and eat a slice of toasted bread went to bed. Edward Parry returned this evening from seeing his friends in Mongomeryshire being about 3 weeks & one day. He tells me that there fell a great deal of snow on their Mountains which I suppose was on the 20th May last as we had some fall here and a cold N.E. Wind.

Wednesday, June 4th. half past seven, rested pretty well the pain in my ear much abated. It rains & the river is still up. Order'd a Shade to be made for the masons to Scabble under in wet weather for the forebay walls which will be a means of keeping them for as some of them live at a distance thay stay at home upon any appearence of rain, & by that method loose a deal of time to themselves and us but when they have a convenient place to work under we shall be more certian of them & as stones must be scabbled for the forebay there doing it in wet weather is forwarding our work & employing them at those times they could not otherwise work.

Nine o'clock continues raining, only one Mason Morgan Evan Jenkin work at furnace under a shade with Joseph Lucas. 3 o'clock rain cease, but no appearance of clearing up.

William Edwards has finished his survey of the place and distance to bring his water from, to the place where our furnace is intended; and give me his account. The whole distance to the delivery of the water is 960 yards, of which 560 is a hard rock & 400 Soil. It appears to him. The rock on the side of Lord Talbot and Mr. Richards land is formed to convey the water through this landed Cut without the aid of a Weir to be bound on the opposite side, on the Land of Mr. Gwin. We may be certain of 27 feet fall and as this level is taken to deliver the water for the furnace as high as the top of our intended Wear and as the wheel we have nearly ready prepared is 28 feet in diameter it would not be useless as its having only one foot backwater by wade in, cannot affect it, in any degree to hurt or retard its action he will insure the aquaduct water proof i.e. not to loose any on its passage to the delivery upon the wheel. He was desired by C.W. to give in an Estimate of the charge or expense he would undertake the building a Stack only, without Bridge House, Bellows or Casting House 36 feet square and supposing it 50 feet high to be at all the charge of getting & carrying of stone, getting Sand & paying for the Lime upon the same terms as we have it. A. Bacon & Company not to be at any more charge or expense but the price p. Perch to be agreed upon.

No Masons work, but Morgan Evan Jenkins, Harry Williams, a day & John Gabriel ½ day Scabbling stone for forebay under the shade erected for that purpose.

Sawyers Sawing for forge hutch, William Postlethwaite making moulds for stamper box & bottoms, George Fords 2 men mortising the hutch sills.

The Waggon horses at home three horses fetched Coal for the families, 2 Load to Aaron Wedgwood, two to James Mason, three to John Morgan & 2 to Wm Postlethwaite. Timothy Davis brought 4 brick moulds of different sizes for the Air furnaces p. order & direction. He was desired to assist William Postlethwaite to make Moulds for castdings and promised to be here tomorrow morning.

Ordered from Timothy Davis some Yokes for Oxen as many as our new wood vizt Beech, would make.

The labourers here are not worth more than 8d a day compared to with our Labourers at Lowmill and the Masons as the same in Walling therefore in any Estimate double the price should be allowed for all such work in this Country and there is double the quantity of Mortar used here than we use in Cumberland & no more the half the quantity of Sand used to Lime & to lead them out of their old method I find is not to be done.

Thursday June 5th. Half past six, rested well, the pain in my eye gone, but remains tender. A close cool morning, fair but very like more rain. William Edwards upon the forge finish hatch wall next the stamper. Hopkin David with Joseph Lucas, David Edward & John Gabriel & Thomas Lloyd scabbling stone. Harry William & Morgan Evan Jenkins making scaffold for the forebay for one quarter. Nine o'clock Breakfast sett in rain again. David John and his partner upon their bargain and Edward Thomas John & his men upon his bargain but I am afraid they will be obliged to leave off. William Edwards his son David, Harry Williams, Walter William, Morgan Evan Jenkins, John Gabriel and Thomas Lloyd all Masons have Scabbled Stones.

Six Labourers fetching stones to the Scabblers & Masons upon bargain, four at the Lime & Mortar, one serving Jos. Lucas & Hopkin, two raising Stone in Quarry four carrying Stones out of Quarry two at the hurry, one at head four at foot.

William Edwards has given in his proposals for bringing race from the place mentioned in yesterdays observations as under, vizt That he will undertake to convey it in a secure workmanlike manner, not to loose any water in the passage untill it is delivered upon the wheel clear of all other expense to the Company for £300 & our Smith sharpen which Tool he use in the work, he finding Iron & Steel for new laying and steeling them & to complete it by July 1, 1767. He likewise ask for the building stack only, without bellows, bridge or casting house to be 36 feet square & fifty feet high if found necessary clear the foundations for it & compleat the back race for the delivery of its water into the pool (upon a level with the Wear) for the wheel, raise stone & carry them from the present Quarry now cleated and squared if it should happen that the p. Quarry should not produce sufficient for our present designed buildings agreeable to our plan laid down & that Stack then in that case Wm Edwards is to be at the charge of clearing and opening another to make up such deficiency or so much as he may make use of for the aforesaid stack he to find sand to mix with the Lime and make it into Mortar & to pay for the Lime at the rate we now pay. The cast iron lintels for the Arch & the Centre that may be wanted for that purpose to be found by A. B. & Co. The fire brick for the Inner Walls to be laid near the work by the said Company. William Edwards to be at the expense & charge of every other particular relative to the Erecting & finishing the said Stack agreeable of dimension before named & to finish the sane the first day of July 1767 for the sum of of £550. These are Wm Edwards proposals which I think too high but then I consider that it may be prudent to give more, if such a payment will be a means to complete the whole for blowing sooner than would be done were we to undertake it by using men by days wages. We find it very difficult to procure Masons to carry on our present work and if these are not completed before the Stack & the cut is began it will make it more so. William knows most of the Masons in this & the neighbouring County and can procure where we cannot. He will be able to manage them much better than we can and will I find by experience as well as from information execute his work in a workmanlike, substantial manner as he stands partly upon his Credit, from all the works he undertakes, from these considerations it is to be considered whether it will be prudent to give him an extra price, perhaps of £100 more than another would take it for & loose time and have the work slight performed as to require further expense in repairing it by which the greatest loss of all, the binding perhaps a blast. Now my opinion is that the cut in the first place will cost us as much if not more than the £300 to complete it as he proposes, as so many branches being merged on at the same time must be disadvantageous to one of them at least, therefore I think he should be agreed with for that to begin as soon as he can. As to the Stack it may remain for a further consideration as it cannot be made use of untill the water is brought and may be compleated in less than half the time that the cut can be made, for the conveying of the water to it. But upon the whole I think it will cost us more than Wm. asks if we get it done by days wages.

Wrote to Mr. Bacon, Mr. Ellison and my wife sent Wm David Son to Brecon. The team with six oxen & 7 horses & three men halling timber out of the wood into the road. Two horses & one man bro't 600 brick for kiln, two horses & one man halling Clay in a Slade to kiln for fire brick, 16 load each load contains about four horse loads.

William Postlethwaite & Tim Davis's Man making Stamper box bottom Moulds. George Fords two men about the Penstock Chafery. Two Sawyers sawing timber & taking Slabs of he Triangle Poles they being too heavy. It has rained small rain all day not to prevent the Masons Scabbling, tho' it did laying of Stones. The Labourers are put to a variety of work there is no noticing the exact work they do; they should do so much as can be done with benefit of the work, be employed at one particular branch and then their work may be easily known.

A Stack 36 ft sq and 50 ft high contains 1800 perch of walling deduct for the hollow 138/1662 perch wh. Wm Edwards asks £550 which will be a little more than 6s 6d p. perch. Suppose we give 18d p. perch to Masons & lay all materials near work convenient for them & they to find Labour to serve.

mix Lime & Sand viz.

		£	s	d
1662 perch	@ 1/6 p. perch	124	13	0
Quarrying stone	@ 1s p. perch	83	2	0
Carriage ditto	@ 8d do	55	8	0
Lime 3 load p. perch	1/9	145	8	6
Sand 0/3d do	5/2	20	15	6
Cutt race & digging foundation		50	0	0
		£479	7	0

	479	7	0
Wm Edward Wages	54	15	6
	534	2	6

Therefore I am of opinion that Wm Edwards proposal shd be accepted as the above calculation may perhaps prove, and therefore uncertain & there is a risk of not having it done in such a manner as we would have it for reason given to Mr. Bacon and I think by agreeing with Mr. Edwards we shall be at greater certainty as he never slights any building he undertakes as I have been informed and have experienced & the difference of his demand & of calculation above being £15 5s 3d is too trifling in this affair to run any risk to save.

Friday June 6th. Half past Six rested well my eye quite free of pain, but am dull of hearing. A fine morning the Sun appears which it has not done for some time. I am in hopes the weather may take up. Near twelve o'clock continues a fine warm day a clear sky has appearance of fine weather.

The underwritten Masons are upon the forebay, viz. Wm Edwards his son David, Harry William, Morgan Evan Jenkins, John Gabriel, Thomas Lloyd & Walter Wm, come at 9 o'clock Hopkin David with Joseph Lucas at the furnaces. These Masons are upon day wages, David John & his 3 Partners, are upon the flourishing house upon bargain at 14d per perch.

Edward Thomas John & Thomas Samuel began this morning another length of the grand 8 foot race and wall & Arch per 5/6 p. perch bargain, which is too much.

Tim Davis and his men are here, his man was here yesterday & this day assisting Wm. Postlethwaite to make moulds for casting. Tim Davis and one of the Sawyers are making Yokes for the oxen. The other sawyer is gone with John Morgan, Daniel the Waggoner (they call him the Hallier) Lewis Trahan & another to fetch timber. George Fords two men are preparing Clay Mill heads & planks for the first stamper penstock, that the Masons may not be hindered from proceding on the forebay walls. The Carriage, 4 men 6 horses & 3 Yoke of Oxen brought 2 pieces of timber

	L		G		
1 piece	26	-	13	=	30½
1 piece	29	-	15	=	45½

One Man Harry Evan with 2 horses, one in a car, brought 600 brick. David Lewis with 2 horses were loading clay for fire brick. Plymouth Co. Team brought 13 bundles of hoops, 11 cams & three pieces for Arm hoop weighing 11 cwt, 13 q, 19 lb.

Saturday June 6th.[1] Six o'clock. A close morning with small rain. It turned out a fine day, the masons William Edwards & his son David, Walter William, Morgan Evan Jenkins, John Gabriel & Thomas Lloyd Scabbled stone in the morning & were upon forebay, in the afternoon. Harry William not here this day, nor his son William Harry. David John & two of his Men went home yesterday Sick, were upon a length of the Stamper race, Walling & Arching.

Edward Thomas John was absent this day, only Thomas Samuel upon the Grand Arch race, this absence of Edward Thomas is a forfeiture of his work as verbally agreed. William Postlethwaite & Tim Davies Men upon patterns for castings. George Ford's two men upon Chafery Penstock. Two Sawyers fitting & making a large crooked piece of Timber for Shroud for Claymill wheel. Tim Davies went into the wood to choose proper pieces of Timber for roofing. Daniel the Hallier, John Morgan, Lewis Trehan & another with carriage & 6 horses & Six Oxen & brought home 2 pieces for beams contain 80 feet. Two labourers raising stones; Six bearing Stones to hurry, one putting them down & one taking them from the foot, four bringing Stone to Shade for Scabbling. Two serving Masons, one at Lime & One carrying Mortar and one Cardiff Lime.

Hopkin David with Joseph Lucas at the Furnace both Furnaces ready for bearing bars & Door plate to lay fire brick.

Paid by order of Mr. Thomas Guest Wm Thomas for the Carriage of 11 cwt. 3 q. 19 lb of Iron bro't from Cardiff in their Waggon @ 14d p. cwt. £00 13s 10½d.

Harry Evans & his partner have agreed to make five dozen hurdles for Scaffolding Seven feet long & three broad for four shillings per dozen.

Agreed with Thomas David to fetch from the Brick kiln at Penywain every week from this day until the first day of November 3m Brick Common & fire, at 5s p. m to be paid for every fortnight & to lend him a Carr & Slade with a pair of pannier in good order & he engaged to deliver them back in the same condition He engaged also to supply the Brickmaker with Sand as much as they may want from this day during the Season of making for 5s.

The Moulds for the Stamper box, bottom, Stoke hole & Doorplate are finished. The Stamper box is 2 ft 8 in sq within the bottom 2 ft 8 in by 2 ft 2in. The Stamper one foot long & 10 × 8 square. The Stoke hole is in four pieces for the Convenience of casting in open Sand.

[1] *Sic* MS; *recte* 7th.

Wrote to Mr. Watkin Attorney[1] Agent to Mr. Gwin by favour of Captain Hughes to know if the Lease he promised to procure from Mr. Gwin for getting Lime Stone was ready for executing & desired an Answer by the Captain.

William Harry and Edward Thomas John, Masons, drinking all day two good hands but not to be depended upon for any bargain that requires dispatch.

Agreed with Betty Postletwhwaite for the Milk of three Cows from this day to October the 11th the time Cattle are taken out of pasture at 6d per week.

Sunday Morning. [June 8th] Seven o'clock a fine moderate morning looks like showers staid at home until noon. Near five o'clock has been a fine day. Dined at the Vilage, at one after dinner called upon Mr. Guest & Terry, both at the furnace[2] and went down to the furnace met Mr. Guest coming from there & see Casting, the metal was lively the hammer of Mottle grain four cast, well sunk bearing barr cast gave the founder 2/6 he showed the grain of the Pigs some a very open good gray grain other a mottle but an indifferent one will do for our common castings they tell me they make about 12 Ton a week. Their bellows seem to have but a moderate Blast, they drive pretty hard about 25 Cams in a minute as near as I could judge. In returning from the furnace met Mr. Guest and Terry they returned with me to the vilage. Went to Mr. Guests house drank part of a bowl of Punch with him and Mr. Terry. They promised to cast every pattern that we should send of such metal as was suitable upon our informing them which we should chose. By the Cinder they must use a large proportion of Lime to their stone or Mine.

A Stamper Box Bottom is 32 inches by 26 & 7 inches thick. 32 × 26 = 832 × 7 = 5824 ft : 4 =1456 lb = 13 cwt

The Stamper head 12 inches high & 10 × 8 sq
12 × 10 = 120 × 8 = 960 : 4 = 240 lb

The plate for the furnace charging door 30 inches long 2.75 thick & as it has two long ends I call it 9 inches head therefore 30 × 2.75 = 82.5 × 9 =742.5 : 4 = 185 lb.

[1] Also mentioned on p. 131 as 'Mr Penrice Watkins, attorney'. Probably Penoyre Watkins (1721–91) of Brecon, a lawyer who 'accumlated a very considerable property'. Penoyre Watkins's son, George Price Watkins, married in 1787 Elizabeth Bacon, a niece of Anthony Bacon. Theophilus Jones, *History of Brecknockshire* (Glanusk Edition), ii (Brecknock, 1909), 198–201.

[2] i.e. Plymouth Furnace.

Therefore upon this calculation the Stamper will weigh reckoning 4 Cubic inches to a pound Avoirdupois wt

	cwt	q	lb	cwt	q	lb
	25	3	6			
Six of these boxes will weigh			6			
	Error[1]			154	3	8
the bottom 13 cwt × 6 for Six of these				78	-	-
One plate 18.5 lb × 11 = 2035 lb				19	0	19
Stamper heads 240 lb × 12 = 2880				25	2	24
4 bush & 4 bolts supposed to weigh				10	-	-
22 bearing barrs						
120 furnace barrs				40	2	24
4 hammers each 6 cwt				24	-	-
4 plates each 4 ft sq ¾ in thick mixing				15	1	20
4 do for Washing				6	-	-
Plates before the furnace Mouth 3 feet by 2 ft square 1 inch thick four of these						
7, 2, 2, 4 four				404	2	23

	T cwt	q	lb
Brought forward	20 4	2	23
Six boxes each box 23 cwt 2 q 12 lb total	141	2	16
Six bottoms each 13 cwt	78	-	-
Eleven plates each 1 cwt 12 q 17 lb	18	-	19
Fourteen Stamp head each	33	3	-
Four husts & 4 Coits supposed to weigh	11	-	-
Four hammer do	25	-	21
Four mixing plates each 4 feet sq ¾ in thick	15	1	20
Four plates for washing do	6	-	-
Four to lay before the furnace door upon the ground 3 ft × 2 ft	7	2	24
22 bearing bars	19	3	21
120 furnace bars	40	2	24
Two Anvils, one more at 15 cwt each	45	-	-
Two standards	10	-	-

One side of the box is 33 inches by 25. The end is 38 by 25 inches and 2½ inches thick. The bottom 32 by 32 & 4 inches thick viz.
33 × 25 = 825 × 2½ = 2062 Cubic inches : 4 as four Cubic inches weighs a pound Avoirdupois = 513 lb for one side two sides will be 1026

[1] *Sic* MS.

	cwt	q	lb
Two sides will weigh	9	0	18
The end 38 × 25 = 950 × 2.5 = 2375 ÷ 4 =	5	1	6
The bottom 32 × 32 = 1024 × 4 = 4096 ÷ 4	9	0	16
The weight of the whole box	23	2	12

The stamp head mould is altered it is now 12" high & 9 by 10 square.

12 × 10 = 120 × 9 = 1080 ÷ 4 = 270 lb × 14 the number to be cast 3780 lb = 33 cwt 3 q.

An Account of the Castings from Plymouth Furnace p. Computation of bill at a medium

	Computed weight				Weight of bill dd fm furnace				
	T	cwt	q	lb	T	cwt	q	lb	
Stamping box	1	3	2	12	1	5	0	18	@ a medium
bottom	-	13	-	-	-	12	-	22	do
hammer	-	6	1	5	-	6	1	5	do
Anvil	-	15	-	-		14	1	24	do
Stamper head	-	2	-	12	-	2	-	8	"

N.B. Those that are cast exact to the pattern, answer the same quoted weight 4 Cubic inches to the pound weight. Several of the other castings were made much thicker then the pattern in particular 4 plates for mixing upon which were computed at quarter of an inch thick & some of them were an inch full four were computed at 15 cwt 1 q 20 lb but weigh 25 cwt 1 q.

1766				
May 10th	Thos Clifton & his men their wages come to this day inclusive upon their bargain supposing they were upon day wages	£9	8	3
17th	To this day inclusive 36 ¾ days	1	16	9
	Thomas Clifton was paid 1s p. day for 6 days	-	6	-
23rd	Thomas Clifton & men this week	4	8	10
May 10th	Thomas David with his men upon bargain supposing they were upon day wages come to to this day inclusive 122 days work at	6	2	-
17th	ditto to this day inclusive 45 days	2	5	-
23rd	ditto to this day 36 days	1	16	9
24th	ditto	-	7	0
	paid him	10	10	9

BOOK II

AN ACCOUNT OF THE MATERIAL TRANSACTIONS AT CYFARTHFA IN THE PARISH OF MERTHYR TYDVIL CONTINUED FROM ANOTHER BOOK NO I VIZ

1766 Monday June 9th. Six o'clock a close rainy morning. Ordered William Postlethwaite to take the Patterns underwritten to the Plymouth Furnace, to be cast, viz. a Stamper box moulding a bottom of former we calculate will weigh when cast 23 cwt 2 q and the latter 13 cwt. A Mould for a furnace mouth plate 1 cwt 2 q 17 lb. A stoke hole in 4 pieces that it may be moulded in open Sand. The box to be of grey grain. The bottom the harder the metal the better. Wrote to Devonshire & Reeve in Bristol relating an Anvil bought by them for this company it being cracked. I am informed that it is customary to exchange them if they crack within the year & this was sent Nov. 1765 cwt 2 ct 2 q 22 lb @ 38s p. cwt £5 2s 6d. Wrote to Mr. Bacon enclosed the fortnightly pay bill £72 4s 4d & enclosed a letter from Mr. Manston about Scrap Iron to be answered by him as also a letter directed to Miss H.Z.D. Hamill Dublin that was found in a letter from Mr. Bacon to me accidentally got in at the General Posthouse in London as I suppose; therefore for fear of miscarriage I sent it to Mr. Bacon to be sent to the Post Office.

Nine o'clock. It rains hard. The Masons underwritten have been scabbling stones under the shade erected for that purpose viz. William Edwards, Walter William, Harry William, Thomas Lloyd and John Gabriel as they could not work in the Stone & Mortar in wet weather. The coolest summer I have known of many years but an exceeding fine season for grass & corn. Two Labourers raising stone in the Quarry, two carrying them to the hurry, one putting them down and one taking them from the foot. David John, Mason, has lost one of his best hands, gone home very ill. Hopkin David Mason works with Joseph Lucas at the furnace & David John's daughter serves them with Mortar at 6d per day. Twelve o'clock, rain is over a fine day the Masons are upon the forebay walls.

Paid David Richard William for the carriage of several of the Iron Tools that came from Low Mill from Cardiff weight 25 cwt 1 q 17 lb £1 6s 6d allowed 1s 2d for Turnpike.

Six o'clock this afternoon has continued a fine one but cool the Masons continued upon the forebay.

David John finished the Stamper Arch at Dinner then went upon the flourishing house, which is ready for the Beams. Two labourers baling out water to allow three more to clear the said race for another length of walling and Arching, which will be the last, until the two Stamper races meet in this.

One Labourer at Cardiff Lime & three at Common Mortar. Two serving Edward Thomas John & Thomas Samuel at the grand race rock.

William Postlethwaite carpenter at the Clay Mill frame. George Fords two men at the Penstock. Timothy David's men making Moulds for a brick for for furnace door head. Two Sawyers sawing a piece of worked wood for shrouds for Clay Mill Wheel.

George Ford returned from setting my Brother & Rowley Park as far as Warrington. He called at Bridgewood Forge to see Mr. Knights Iron Anvil Block and by the Acct he had from the Men I find it will not do for us.[1] As sometimes the Anvil breaks in the block which is to be cut out & requires so much time in performing, that such an accident with us would be a greater loss than double the value of the block. George saw Mr. Knight & when he heard who he belonged to he was very free, gave him leave to see everything & asked him of my method in making the iron & the quantity we could make in a week, he said Mr. Henry Kendall had told him but he did not believe him & he told George that when we were ready to work here, he would come over and see us and would buy half bloom if we could agree.

David Edward Mason did not begin work untill twelve o'clock for half a day.

Edward Parry wrote to his father to procure two or more Masons in Montgomeryshire and send here as soon as he could. This letter with my two for Mr. Bacon & Devonshire & Reeve, were given by Edwd Parry to John Morgan to give the Postman who goes tomorrow morning for Brecon.

Tuesday June 10th. Half past six o'clock. A cloudy morning like rain.

Nine o'clock continues fair. William Edwards, his son David, Walter Williams, Henry William, Thomas Lloyd, John Gabriel, Morgan Evan Jenkins & William Jenkins upon the forebay.

Edward Thomas John & Thomas Samuel have finished the length of the Grand Arch & began their bargain upon Mixing room. David John & his men scabbling stone for their bargain. Lime is ordered to be

[1] Above, p. 27.

stoped mixing until further order. Ordered the Lime carrier to take to Rhyd y Carr & Lewen Kelly farms three hundred loads & agreed to give them 3½d per load carriage. Showed Timothy Davis, Thomas Farnels offer, to make roofs, Windows, floors etc. and gave him the refusal according to agreement signed by him August 3d 1765 and wait his answer. The Oxen are ordered to plough land and the horse to harrow it for receiving the lime upon it to prepare for Sewing of wheat. Ordered the carriage to fetch Timber for roofs & to continue it every day & after the Oxen & the horse have ploughed & harrowed the Land that they should dragg Timber from the Wood, such Timber as can receive the least damage by dragging.

Lewis Williams John complained of three gaps being made by our Men in halling timber. Agreed to give him 1s to repair it himself.

Two Labourers are set to lade water out of Stamp Race and are obliged to be continued until the upper part is dug and closed for walling & setting the Centres in this manner we have been obliged to proceed which makes it both tedious & expensive. The forebay is the most tedious & expensive piece of work. I have known from the custom of the Welsh Masons have of Scabbling stones to answer Courses which make an appearance indeed but not the least stronger or more usefull. I have used all the methods I could think to alter this & to bring 'em into a more expeditious method, but all to no purpose, if I desire them while they are scabbling to leave off & lay the stone rough & that if I am satisfied with rough work, it should them, yet they pay no regard to what I say & will rather loose their place than leave off an old habit. Therefore I see that there is a necessity to submit to this Extra expense, rather than suffer the work to stand, by losing the Masons and as the performing of this forebay in an effectual method, to prevent water from running through walls into the Stamper house & other parts which would be of worst consequence is absolutely necessary the carrying my method into execution against their inclination & prejudice for their old method, might defeat the care & trouble in what is already done. Therefore I think it the most prudent method, to suffer a larger expense in this particular and to lett this off by bargain. I think would be as imprudent, as there would not be any certainty of their acting the part they ought & we should expect in the execution of it.

Six o'clock has rained all the afternoon, but not so hard as to prevent the Masons work, tho' uncomfortably.

David John & his men began Walling & Arching another length of the stamper race which is the last length.

Cleared for laying the other side of the first hammer hatch & marked it out. Hopkin David left Joseph Lucas & went to the forebay wall. Four labourers were clearing for the other end of the forebay. Four were carrying Stones. One served one end of the forebay Wall & two at the other end. One at Cardiff Lime, two at Common Mortar. A girl served Joseph Lucas with Brick & Mortar. Two in Quarry, One lading water & three at the Stamper Race.

George Ford and his Men at the Claymill frame, William Postlethwaite making hoppers for putting the granulated metal through the Wall into the mixing room Binns, to prevent them the carriers coming in to dirty the floor. Two Sawyers sawing the crooked piece of timber for Shrouds for Clay Mill Wheel.

The Smiths have a book to write down all their work in which weight & price therefore I do not mention them daily here.

The horse dragged two pieces of Timber for roofing, one piece contained 24 feet, the other 22 feet.

Timothy Davis Carpenter brought in his bill for work done in my absence which I thought extravagant, therefore he agreed to refer to George Ford which I accepted.

Thomas David began this day to load brick from the kiln as per agreement & brought upon four horse back 650 in Number @ 5s p.m.[1] A new Mason came in this day and begins working with David John tomorrow morning, vizt. William Lewis. Received two letters from Isaac Wilkinson of the 4th & 7th instsnt.

Wedesday June 11th. A cold cloudy morning up before Six o'clock. The Masons & Labourers waiting the call for six, to begin work.

Nine o'clock Breakfast. Timothy Davis Carpenter has refused taking the roofing of the several buildings & other Carpenters work as offered by Edward Farnell therefore the latter has the executing of the same at the several rates he has sett his name to & which as witnessed April 14th last p. Samuel Wood. Paid Tim Davis the balance of his account £1 18s 4d.

It rains and looks very like to continue. Eleven o'clock rains very hard.

The six Waggon horses brought pieces of Timber by dragging of it for one footing beam, containing 18 feet.

Sett four Labourers to clear the Saw pitt for another pair of Sawyers to saw roofing for flourishing house & Clay Mill.

Six Oxen ploughing & 2 horses harrowing Land for to receive Lime upon it for wheat.

[1] i.e. per thousand.

David Lewis with two horses on the Mountain leading fireclay to the Brick kiln.

George Ford & Tim Davis Man were appointed by Thos. Tim & C. Wood to examine the said Timothy's bill for sundry work for Cyfarthfa Company & have taken off about 8s.

Two sawyers have finished the crooked pieces of Timber for shrouds, but it proves bad, and part will be useless for that purpose which will be a great loss. A great deal of the Timber that has been felled and squared when sawed into the proper uses proves bad therefore has been observed before. The Lords ought to give other timber for it or make an allowance in the price which I hope will be considered & done by Mr. Morgan Lord Talbots Steward and Zachary Philips my Lords Woodman. As I agreed with them that if any proved draged and not fitt for our use we shd be at liberty to refuse it. But by the negligence or worse of Isaac Bates our Carpenter who was confided in to overlook & direct this among other affairs has suffered this loss to the company.

Philip David of the Wern his brother came here this morning to get his Tyle numbered that he brought from the Estate of Mr. Lewis in Aberdair at 10s p.m. but as he thinks the price too little, refuses to fetch any more at that rate. He said he desired to get no more than 1s per day for each horse. Therefore I told him that if he would go with his horse in company with some of ours that I intended to send and load as we loaded ours I would allow 1s per day for each horse including his own labour he said he would try one journey. The number of Tyle that has been already brought to be paid for at 10s p.m. is 3m. 300, as told out, before the said Philips brother by Evan the Tyler.

A loop is proposed to be cast for the Anvil Block 12 inches broad, 2 thick & the diameter three feet eight inches which by calculation will weigh viz Diameter 44 inches × 3 to bring it to above = 132 inches × 12 the breadth = 1584 × 2 the thickness = 3168 inches : 4 as four cubic inches of cast metal weigh one pound = 792 lb.

A box for the block to be two feet square within, four inches thick which when brought to a plate will be 8 ft 8 inches long & 24 inches deep or broad 104 In long × 24 In depth = 2496 In × 4 In the thickness = 9984 : 4. As four Cubic Inches will weigh a pound Avoirdupois = 2496 lb = 22 cwt 1 q 4 lb. A bottom to this box cast to it or loose 24 In Square & 8 inches thick for a Meeze = 24 In × 24 In = 576 In × 8, the thickness = 4608 In : 4 = 1152 lb = 10 cwt 1 q 4 lb + 22 cwt 1 q 4 lb = 32 cwt 2 q 8 lb if cast together in one.

If these can be performed by the Plymouth Company on their part and we can perform our part in fixing them properly in our Block I think they would serve many years without alteration, save a deal in Wood, labour & time & enable us to make more Iron as the shifting the Anvil retards our charges frequently, to the loss of ourselves, as well as the Men.

Past two o'clock continues raining. Weighed No 25 Stone Tyle as sorted by Evan the Tyler as they rise in the quarry as near as he could, which weighed 1 cwt 2 q 12 lb short wt is Long weight 1 cwt 2 q. A horse should bring 50 of them upon his back every load and go twice every day and allow 1s a day for each horse will be exactly 10s p. m[1] the price agreed to be paid but which they think too little.

Agreed with David John Mason to raise the Wall of the Clay Mill next to the Pool from the end next to Thomas Clifton's road about [*Figure omitted*] feet beyond the Stamper Penstock with Cardiff Lime, in a good & substantial manner to raise water, Six feet higher than it now is as measured by Joseph Lucas for one pound eleven shillings & 6d & he to be paid the measurement of the inside wall, two feet thick, at the Common walling price. As all the Masons are employed on the forepart of the forebay & another side of the first hammer hatch. This part of the Clay Mill wall must have remained unfinished for some time had not I lett it in this manner to David John, and this method of letting off p. Bargain Expedites the work greatly.

Six o'clock continuing showery. William Edwards his son David Walter Williams, Harry William, Morgan Evan Jenkin, Thomas Lloyd, William Jenkin, & John Gabriel, Masons were all of them upon the farr part of the forebay & hammer hatch. Four Labourers to attend them, two to serve Cardiff lime & four at the Common Lime. Two at the Quarry raising stone, two carrying stones to the Hurry, one putting them down, one taking them from the foot of the Hurry & six carrying Stones to the Bargainers. George Ford and his two men upon the Clay Mill roller heads. Wm. Postlethwaite upon hoppers for mixing room & Lewis Wm Edwards upon anvil pattern. Two Sawyers sawing slabs for hoppers.

The horses brought another piece of Timber containing 25 feet the pieces brought this day are fit for the beams for buildings. Thomas William David brought upon 5 horses back 1 m. Brick.

David John & his 3 men scabbling stone for his bargain. The Masons Edward Thomas John & Thomas Samuel upon their bargain Mixing Room. Morgan Evan Jenkins & John Gabriel upon their bargain the furnace Ash pit, upon bargain overtime. Walter Williams & Thomas Loyd, upon their bargain, the Clay Mill race in the house over hours.

[1] i.e. per thousand.

David Lewis with two horses loading fireclay to the kiln with 10 turns.

Thursday June 12th. Past six o'clock a Cloudy morning, very like rain. Nine o'clock showers often, which made the Masons work uncomfortable and makes their hands sore. Two Masons have been to offer themselves. Accepted of same they promise to be here next Tuesday.

Half past three o'clock there has been Showers all day, Six horses have brought two pieces of Timber for beams, containing 39 feet. William Edwards, David his Son, Walter William, Harry Williams, John Gabriel, Morgan Evan Jenkins & Thomas Lloyd, Masons are upon the forebay. Edward Thomas John & Thomas Samuel upon their bargain, the mixing room. David John & his three men Scabbling Stones in the quarry for their bargain, the Clay Mill wall. Two Labourers raising Stones in the Quarry viz. Rees David & Howel Rhys. Two serving David John Scabbled Stones, three carrying Stones to the Masons at forebay, Six carrying Cobbles out of the cleared place for the forge to make room for the sinking in the rock for the races. Two getting Sand to mix with Lime for bargains. One making up Cardiff Lime & one serving. One serving Joseph Lucas at the Stack, three at Common Mortar. Two carrying in Brick to flourishing house & two more carrying cobbles, in the whole 22.

George Ford & his two men upon the Clay Mill Wheel Shroud, Wm Postlethwaite upon the hopper for mixing room Boxes. Lewis William Edwards upon Anvil mould & Two sawyers sawing odd pieces of oak for head stocks etc.

The Anvil Mould. The square of the Butt is 16 inches in the medium from the shoulder to the butt 18 inch the shoulder 16 ft tapers to 3½ ditto to the butt length 15 inches, the medium is 12 inches square & 18 high, therefore the question is: The butt a Cube of 16 inch & the neck part, 18 inches high & 12 square 16 in × 16 in = 256 in × 16 = 4096 In : 4 = 1024 lb = 9 cwt 1 q 12 lb. The Neck 18 high × 144 = 2592 : 4 = 648 lb = 5cwt 3 q 4 lb. [*Total*] 15 cwt 0 q 16 lb.

This is a heavy anvil but as it has a broad bed & a long neck I imagine and expect it will be more durable & operate more work than two or three of the common ones; and this will answer to the box mentioned the 11th instant.

The last part of the bricks that were burnt in the first kiln from Robert Wilson & his son in Law, John Edge came in this day the whole amounting to 10 m., 24 Common & 200 fire brick made of various sorts of clay for tryals. Wrote to my wife & sent it under cover to Mr. Potter with a few lines to him.

Six o'clock a very cold wind more than I have felt it since I come here with showers often, very uncomfortable weather for the season.

Robert Wilson & John Edge have burnt another kiln of Common Brick. Ordered the next kiln to be fire Brick.

Friday June 13th. Half past five o'clock, a fine morning but cool. The Masons upon bargain at work until six & the Labourers are waiting the call.

Near 10 o'clock continues a fine day, after breakfast I lett unto six labourers viz. Tho. J. Wm, Wm. John Wm, Jenkin John Wm, Robert Edward Evan, W. & Lewis Thomas, to clear the ground upon which the forge is to be Erected of the cobble & other stones now upon it in the manner following, vizt. those stones that are too heavy to be caryied by two men, upon a hand barrows are to be left upon the place, those that are fitt for Quoins, & good building stones, are to be carryed upon the flatt next the first stamper Arch & the remainder to those that were carryed by those men before this bargain was made, for the sum of two guineas.

Plymouth Company Team brought from Cardiff 13 Cams, the remainder of the Iron that was brought from Lowmill except one square bar of finery Iron & a piece of furnace bar, which is wanting, weighing 6 cwt, 1 q, 12 lb @ 14d p. cwt paid William Thomas, that Company's Hallier or Waggoner 7s 5d in full for the said carriage, as p. his receipt upon the file. Their Waggons carryed a load of Sand back p. leave.

One o'clock, all the men gone to Dinner, continue a fine warm day & I hope for settled warm weather. Four o'clock Received from Plymouth Company p. their Waggon Wm Thomas 4 hammers weighing 25 cwt 21 lb & 22 bearing bars for the furnace at 19 cwt 3 q 21 lb p. their bill of parcels sent with them.

Six o'clock it has been a fine day. I have ordered John Morgan & David Lewis to take three horses to fetch from Brecon three pair of Cart wheels for light carts to fetch Brick & Clay from the Mountain & sent by him a letter to Mr. Potter.

William Edwards & his son David, Walter Williams, Henry William, Thomas Loyd, John Gabriel, Hopkin David, William Jenkin & Morgan Evan Jenkin Masons were upon the forebay.

David John & his three men, Masons, were upon the pool wall & Clay Mill. Edward Thomas John & Thomas Samuel, upon their bargain, the Mixing room. Six Labourers upon their bargain in clearing the forge floor of the cobbles, four Labourers serving Masons with stones, four in the Quarry, four bearing stones from the hurry, one girl serving Joseph Lucas with brick & Mortar, upon the Stack, 2 at Cardiff Lime, & one sieving it, three at the Common Mortar & one serving.

George Ford, his two men & Lewis Wm Edward upon the Chafery Penstock. William Postlethwaite making a pattern for the Standard. Two Sawyers Sawing, staples or upright pieces for 2d hammer hutch. Sent to Plymouth furnace another pattern for the Stokehole the first would not do and a pattern for furnace bush barr to cast a dozen or twelve of each.

David Lewis with 2 horses dragging fire clay lot home to the kiln, the road is bad & deep, the horse cannot do half the work they ought. Agreed with Long Dick & Thomas Clifton to take rock down level with pool floor within the pool and six feet deep on the outside of the forebay agreeable to a measure taken by Edward Parry before they began at 8d per yard for hacking and filling the barrow and C.W. to find two wheelers, but after this was agreed upon Thomas Clifton said he thought it would be better to allow for wheeling and I agreed to it at 2d p. yard which is 10d yard whole. The horse & oxen brought 4 pieces of timber containing 74 feet. It rains at Seven o'clock. Walter William & Thomas Lloyd, Masons have finished their bargain of the Clay Mill race back at over house for 10s. Harry William & David Edwards, are upon their bargain, one of the furnace Ash pit. Morgan Evan Jenkins & John Gabriel, Masons are upon their bargain the other furnace Ashpit. David John & his men work upon their bargain late & Early. George Fords two men & Wm Postlethwaite Carpenter work over hours in making door & window frames. All which bargain pleases the men and me, as it gains them pocket money & expedites the Work. Hopkin David has taken the building of wall under the Clay Mill roll frames at the same rate the ashpits are done for viz. 10d p. Peck. Isaac Wilkinson has sent me word by William David's Son who has been at Bristol that the rolls and wheel would be sent by the first vessel for Cardiff.

	Cwt	q	ft
The four pieces of timber No	20	12	20
	20	13	22
	24	10½	18½
	20	10	14
		feet	74½

N.B. The Labourers here are the slowest in any kind of work even upon bargains I ever know in the general. One Labourer at Lowmill will do as much work in one day as two here. I have often tried both by fair or harsh words to alter their method, but I find it to no purpose. William Edwards told me that they would not leave off their old customs.

Saturday June 14th. Past six o'clock. A cold N.W. windy morning. There has been a great deal of rain last night and it now rains; the Masons cannot wall therefore at Scabbling stone under the shade.

Nine o'clock. Breakfast time, very cold & raining.

Eleven o'clock a strong north west wind with rain. William Edwards and his son David, began at five & left at eleven to go home near Caerfilly to return again on Monday morning. All the Masons began at the same hour, 5, in order to leave off sooner to go home on a Saturday eveng. John Morgan & David Lewis sett out for Brecon at three o'clock this morning to fetch three pair of Cart wheels; he took a letter for Mr. Potter, to put into the Post Office. I gave him two 36s pieces and one guinea,[1] in the whole £4 13s to pay for the wheels. Past twelve o'clock, the rain over & looks better like a fair afternoon. Walter Williams, Henry William, John Gabriel, Hopkin David, Thomas Loyd, William Jenkin & Morgan Evan Jenkin, Masons, all of them were Scabbling stones this morning under the Shade.

The same are at the forebay this afternoon, laying stones.

Five o'clock it has held up fair until now, but very like for rain, all hands left work.

Fixed the Chafery Penstock in the forebay wall which is the last. Four Labourers serving the Masons upon the forebay, Two serving Masons upon bargain, two serving Edward Thomas John who is at another length at the great race. Four at the Common Mortar, one at the Cardiff Lime and one serving that Mortar & four at the Quarry. David John & his three masons upon the Clay Mill wall this afternoon, in the morning Scabbling stone for it. Joseph Lucas at the Stack & David John's daughter serving brick & Mortar.

George Ford & his two men & Lewis Williams Edward on the finishing and fixing the Chafery Penstock. William Postlethwaite upon the pattern for a Standard.

Two Sawyers sawing a piece of timber for Clay Mill flooring beams. Eight horses, 4 Oxen & four men brought 4 pieces of Oak timber containing 66½ ft. David John & his men continue working every night when fair after the others leave off he is a very diligent careful man, was the first who informed me, Custom of the Country, after Wm. Edwards,

[1] The 'six and thirty shilling piece' was a gold coin, like the guinea. Both were withdrawn from circulation in 1816.

& that took the first bargain by the Perch and is ready at any time to sett an example in taking bargains therefore, he ought & is encouraged by me. William Black a forge man, who worked at Low Mill & Keswick came here this day & informed me that Reynold Mitchell a hammer man, who serving his time with Thomas Bewley at Low Mill would be here in a day or two; that he Renold worked at a forge within about three Mile from Hereford. Both of these are ramblers & not to be depended upon. The former I believe to be honest and I wish I could say as much of the latter.

In taking down the rock for the fore hammer hutch there are several veins of fine mine, about an inch thick. Thomas Clifton who raised Mine for the Dale & Ketley Company[1] informs me that this pure Mine is so good that Abraham Darby gave a guinea a dozen for raising it for mixing with the other Mine and that this is very like it.

Thomas David brought of Brick upon two horses, 50 upon each horses back & they are small light ones part of these was from the second burnt kiln and most of these now brought are an inferior fire brick and may serve for the lower part of the fireplace next the bearing barrs & the lower course in the body of the furnace. The Stack bricks made of this clay will serve at end near the top as well as the best clay & for making potts & sundry other uses to save the best kind of Clay.

John Morgan returned from Brecon with three pair of cartwheels. Received from Plymouth Company 4 Stamper bottoms weighing by their bill of parcels 2 T, 11 cwt, 2 q, 6 lb we have not weights to weigh them ourselves.

John Morgan did not bring any letters, only few Newspapers. Eight o'clock. As cold as I well can bear it have kindled a good fire in the Accounting House.

The bottoms to stamp upon by calculation should weigh each 13 cwt & the 4 that are received do weigh 51 cwt, 2 q, 6 lb which is short of the calculation 1 q 22 lb but if they could be cast exactly the size of the pattern it would be the weight but this cannot be expected as some will be a little heavier others lighter by too much, as too little metal running into the Mould these four came as near the calculated weight as one may ever expect to see.

Sunday, June 15th. near eight o'clock a very rainy Morning. A cold whistling wind, like winter.

[1] i.e. Abraham Darby's Coalbrookdale Company of Shropshire, which had also works nearby at Ketley (B. Trinder, *The Industrial Revolution in Shropshire* (2nd ed., 1981), 23.

Past eleven o'clock has rained all this morning & like to continue. George Ford, Joseph Lucas, George Lyndon & Charles Wood breakfasted here about Nine o'clock on Tea & dry Toast as usual. The river is high & if the rain continues much longer there will be a great flood.

Six o'clock. It has rained from the time that I got up to this without interruption & still continues & like to do so. George Ford, Joseph Lucas & George Lyndon went to the Vilage to dinner & brought me part of a Leg of Mutton & Cabbage which I boiled and made a good dinner.

William David called to receive my orders to go to Pontepool for Stamper shank, wheel axle head & rod Iron, the best and toughest Iron being made there of any in these parts,[1] but as it is such rainy weather & the water may very likely be up. I propose sending him untill it is more moderate.

Monday June 16th. Six o'clock, continues raining. Nine o'clock Breakfast. Continues raining. Harry William, Hopkin David, John Gabriel, Thomas Loyd, & William Jenkin, Masons, have been scabbling stones, under the shade. I ordered that not any small thin stones should be scabbled as a large, thick one is nearly as soon done, as a small one and in laying it takes more room, & raises the wall sooner & takes less Cardiff Mortar. The river continues high.

The Labourers work in the rain. Two raising stones in the Quarry, two carrying them to the hurry, one putting them down, one taking them from the foot of the hurry, six carrying them to the Masons to scabble.

David John & his Men are Scabbling Stones for their Bargain, Edward Thomas John & Thomas Samuels upon the great race, Arching for bargain. Two Labourers to serve them with stones, George Ford, his two Men, William Postlethwaite & William Edward Lewis, are upon the forge Hutch frames.

Two Sawyers, Evan William Lewis & Morgan William Jenkin are Sawing Beams & joists for Clay Mill.

The river is high & the road to & on the Mountain so bad and soft that the carriage nor cart can not go to any business therefore the horse & cattle all kept in the house until dry weather.

William Black began this morning to strike for William David & Thomas Williams, Smiths upon his promise to continue untill the furnaces are ready when he will undertake the working of one of them. Near Eleven o'clock, John Edge one of our Brickmakers come from the

[1] Pontypool was an old-established ironmaking centre, with important forges on the Afon Llwyd: Riden, *Gazetteer*, 30–1.

Mountain to inform me that they had six thousand brick spoilt by rain, all washed away except a few Stack bricks.

It rains hard several of the Labourers have quitted their work and wait untill twelve or one after Dinner to see whether it will take up.

Ordered the Smiths to make the Brickmakers, a small axe for them to cut & prepare wood for a shade, round the kiln to dry and keep the bricks as made, from the rain in wett weather. Borrowed an Axe, from Evan Lewis Williams the Sawyer for John Edge untill one can be made for him.

One o'clock continues raining & no appearance of taking up. The Masons have Scabbled stones under the shade & 9 Labourers as mentioned before. Four o'clock it is now fair but looks like more rain.

Six o'clock it has continued fair since four, but dark & cloudy. David Lewis brought eighteen Hurdles for Scaffolding made by Harry Evans & John Williams at 4s per dozen. These hurdles are seven feet long & three broad, are excellent for scaffolding & save Dale[1] boards which must otherwise have been got from Bristol & would have been very expensive with the first cost, freight from thence, to Cardiff & then by Land to Merthyr. In the whole I estimate that hurdles to the amount of £5 will save £30 in dales or other boards. Joseph Lucas is upon the Stack since four o'clock and William Roberts serves him. David Johns daughter went home at 9 o'clock.

Eight o'clock it began to rain again.

In considering the intended method of letting the Top of the Stamper wheels above the floors 3 feet & to be cased, close, with boards to prevent the Water coming through the joints will make it very inconvenient to the family that are to live in them as also loose as much room as may serve one family. I propose therefore that the walls should be raised about 3½ feet higher to allow top of the wheel to run under the beams which will be an additional charge of about eight pound. But by which, there will be gained as much room as will make four appartments for four families whereas in the method before mentioned, it would be pinched for three and by this method the apartments may be continued over the forge to the rock which will make room for eight families and an entrance by a Gallery may be made from the rock to each apartment. The flooring & the roofs will be the same, as it would be for three. By contriving dwellings above the several branches of buildings for the workmen belonging thereto it will save the Erecting of separate Houses for them at much greater expense and the convenience of every workman

[1] i.e. deal.

being near his work will be an ease to them & an advantage to the Masters as I have experienced.

Sent a new Axe made by our Smiths by Aaron Wedgwood, to the Brickmakers, Robert Wilson & John Edge with orders to return that borrowed from Evan Lewis Williams, the Sawyer.

Tuesday, June 17th. Six o'clock there has been a deal of rain this morning and rains small now. The Quarry being full of water, no stones can be got fitt for Scabbling for the forebay wall & therefore to keep the Masons as it is too wet to Wall, I have ordered stones to be scabbled for the Air furnace Stacks, which will expedite that part when we are ready to begin having nine more to build.

Eight o'clock. The rain is over, the Sun appears & looks like a fine day: William Edwards, his son David, Harry Williams, Hopkin David, Morgan Evan Jenkin & Thomas Loyd Scabbled stones for Air furnace stacks. A whistling South Wind denotes more rain.

After Breakfast about half past Nine the Masons began walling upon the forebay. Walter William came near 10 o'clock.

David John & his men began their Bargain the Clay Mill end, next the Pool.

Edward Thomas John & Thos. Samuel, are upon their Bargain, the great race Arch. Two o'clock. Squally weather. Wind and rain, and as cold as March. Cloudy and very like a deal of rain. Uncommon weather for the season.

No thought beginning to put down our Wear while this weather continues.

Near three o'clock rains and blows hard. The Masons are drawn off from the forebay Wall ordered stones to the shade, to be scabbled for Stack pillars.

Six o'clock it has rained all this afternoon and very like to continue. The Masons have continued Scabbling stones under Shade and the Labourers have continued their work, nothwithstanding the heavy rain. Two raising stones at the Quarry, two carrying them to the Hurry, one putting them down, one taking them from the foot, two carrying them near the building for the Masons, two at the Lime, and three at the Stamper race, clearing for the Arch.

George Ford, his two men & William Edward Lewis at the forge hatch and William Postlethwaite making a lathe for turning the Clay Mill Spindles for the rolls. Evan Lewis William & Morgan William Jenkin Sawyers sawing offall pieces of oak for the turning lathe.

The horse and cattle have brought from the Wood 5 pieces of Timber containing ninety one feet.

Nine o'clock it has rained to this time and now ceased, but looks like a deal more.

Estimate of making metal at the Hirwain furnace

2½ dz of Mine at 6d p. dozen	£0	15	-
2 dozen of cokes		14	-
Limestone & sand		2	6
making		6	-
Wear & Tear		6	-
	£2	3	6

Sir,

The above is a true estimate Provided you have the materials on the furnace Bank otherwise there is a further expense.

That attends the Mine Works and Collieries Exclusive of the above.

T. Dorset[1]

[1] Probably Thomas Dorsett, a member of a family who acted as agents to the Charlton family's Apley Castle estate in Shropshire and were also involved in the iron industry in that county (Trinder, *Industrial Revolution in Shropshire*, 30–2, 121–2).

A calculation of the weight of the several castings
ordered from the Plymouth Company
@ £5 15s p. Ton dd at Cyfarthfa vizt

					Weight by calculation				Weight from their bill of parcels			
	cwt	q	lb		T	cwt	q	lb	T	cwt	q	lb
Six Stamper boxes each	23	2	12									
				total	7	1	2	16				
Six Bottoms each	13	-	-	do	3	18	-	-				
Four hammers each	6			do	1	4	-	-	1	5	-	21
22 bearing bars	19			do	-	19	-	-		19	2	21
120 furnace bars				do	2	-	2	24		3	1	15
Three Anvils each	15			do	2	5	-	-	2	3	1	15
Two standars each	5			do	-	10	-	-				
Eleven fur. door plates each	1	2	17	do	-	18	-	19				
14 Stamp heads each	2	0	16	do	1	10	-	-				
4 mixing plates each	1	3	12	do	-	15	1	20				
4 plates for washing				do	-	6	-	-				
4 do before the furnace 3 ft × 2 ft				do	-	7	1	20				
4 bars & 4 coils supposed				do	-		11	-	-	13	-	14
Stoke holes												

Wednesday June 18th. Six o'clock, a rainy morning and I believe has continued all last night as the river is higher. Twelve o'clock continues rain. The Masons are scabbling stone for the pillars for the Air furnace Stacks, under shades vizt. William Edwards & David his son, Walter Williams, Hopkin David, Harry William, Thomas Lloyd & Morgan Evan Jenkin. Four Laboaurers at the Quarry. All the other Labourers gone home.

Near Three o'clock, the rain is over, only showery at times. David John & his men Scabbling Stones for their bargain. Edward Thomas John & Thomas Samuel have been scabbling stones for their bargain but now are gone to the great race arch.

George Ford, his two men & William Postlethwaite upon the Lathe for turning the Clay Mill roll spindles. William Edward Lewis jointing boards for the Wear. Evan Lewis Williams & Morgan William Jenkin Sawyers sawing joists for the dwellings over the Clay Mill.

Agreed with Lodowick Thomas a Sawyer to saw all kind of Sawing at 3/2 p. 100 feet running measure without any other allowance for Master cut or any other claim, whatever before William Edward Lewis, George Ford, Wm Postlethwaite & Georges Men.

No horses nor Cattle could go for timber this day.

David Lewis brought three horse load of Coal for the use of this place and the familys at Rhydycar & Lewenkelly from the pit near the Brick kiln.

Thursday June 19th. Six o'clock. A fair but cloudy morning as the river is much lower & the ground dry I suppose there has not been any rain last night.

In several places in Brecknockshire I am informed that the sheep that are shorn and turned upon the mountain, hundreds are dead by the cold, the weather is now as cold as I have felt it since March, the weather was much warmer in Cumberland when I left it beginning of March than it is now, the Wind being cold and piercing.

William David one of our Smith, informs me that several hundred sheep, have dyed in the Mountain, by cold since their being sheared. Wrote to Mr. Bacon yesterday, and included him a copy of part of Samuel Wood Letter to me from Milnthop. Wrote to my wife, Billy & Molly Wood & Billy Nicholson, all enclosed in one for Mrs. Wood & send to Mr. Bacon requesting his puting them under cover and forwarding to Mrs. Wood.

Nine o'clock. It continues fair but Wind blows cold like more rain. The Masons are upon their several branches of buildings, viz. William Edwards & his son David, Walter William, Harry William, Morgan Evan Jenkin, Hopkin David, Thomas Loyd & William Jenkins upon the forebay Wall per day wages.

David John & his three men upon their bargain, Clay Mill Walling to the Pool. Edward Thomas John & Thomas Samuel upon their bargain the mixing room. The length of great race Arch being finished. Eleven o'clock. Began to rain hard, quite overcast & look like a deal.

The Plymouth Company have sent their Waggon three Anvils but no bill of parcels one of them has a large Lump where the Blocking should be & the hole not thro'. Not Merchantable, the Lump must be cut off.

Edward Farnell Carpenter came this day to perform his agreement for the roofs, floors and other carpenters work upon the Conditions underwritten, & which he signed on April 14th last and witnessed by Samuel Wood viz. Roofing 4s 6d p. square or 100 feet, Doors & Case 1s 6d each, Windows & Window shutters at 8d each light, half Venitian the same price. Flooring 4s p. 100 feet, Partitioning 3s 6d p. 100 feet & Joisting 1s 6d p. 100 feet. Notes that this last joisting is for the ceiling in the Garrets & not the flooring below. There arising a dispute between him & George Ford, about the cross cutting of the timber which we thought belonged to him nothwithstanding it was not particularly mentioned in the agreement he claimed 5 feet in measure for every

Crosscut be it ever so small which we thought unreasonable but to compromise this affair it is agreed that he shall find one Man, & our Company another, and it is so settled.

The horses & cattle have brought three pieces of Timber from the Wood & returned to fetch more if the rain does not prevent them.

Lodowick Thomas & his partner came this morning to saw pursuant to an agreement made yesterday.

The Plymouth Company Waggon loaded back with sand upon their delivery of three Anvils.

One o'clock it has rained since Eleven. Mr. Glover Master of Abergwyddon furnace & forge[1] dined with me he informed me that he had laid claim for Lowmill Co. debt due from Edward Weston. Mrs. Weston his wife having all her husbands Assets & she becoming bankrupt as a Creditor to her, but it was refused by her Assignees, as it was not her own but her husbands Debts, several others being in our situation, the affair was laid before the Lord Chancellor[2] who decreed that all the husbands Bonds should be discharged with interest but as she did not have effect sufficient to answer all other demands upon him, and Mrs Weston the wife having carryed her husbands business on, & contracted several debts, those debts so contracted by her should have preference to her husbands simple debts, so that our demand is entirely lost, there not being more than 10s in the pound. Mr. Glover told me that he was out of blast his bellows being bad & must have new boards.[3] I offered him ours that lye at Cardiff & Bridgewater, he said he would look at them and if he liked them would give me a line or two.

Near five o'clock. The Plymouth Company have sent their Waggon 4 husts & 4 boils, 1 bottom plate, 9 furnace doors plates wt as under

[1] Samuel Glover's furnace and forge stood near the modern village of Abercarn (Mon.) and were powered by the Gwythen brook which here joins the Ebbw (Riden, *Gazetteer*, 12).

[2] i.e. the creditors brought an action in the Court of Chancery to seek clarification of the position.

[3] Abercarn Furnace does not in fact appear to have worked again after this date, although the forge remained in use (Riden, *Gazetteer*, 12).

	T cwt	q	lb
4 husts & 4 boils	13	0	14
1 bottom	12	3	21
9 furn. door plates	16	2	14
3 Anvils	43	1	15
	4 6	0	8

Continues raining. The Masons were Scabbling from Eleven until Six o'clock. Two Labourers raising stone in Quarry four carrying to Hurry, One puting them down one taking them from the foot of the Hurry, four carrying them to Scabbling, two at the Common Mortar & Two carrying Sand to the lime.

The Horse & Cattle brought two more pieces of Timber in the whole 5 pieces today containing 84¾ feet.

George Ford & his two men & Lewis William Edward with Wm. Postlethwaite were upon the Lathe and planks for the Wear. Lodovick Thomas & his partner, Sawyer, sawing beams & joists for floor p. the hundred feet and Evan Lewis William and Morgan William Jenkin Sawyers p. the day, sawing joists.

Morgan Evan Jenkin, a Mason is upon his Bargain one of the Ash pits, this evening after six o'clock. Walter William upon a Wall upon the end of the Clay Mill race Arch. David John & his men continue work upon their bargain untill 8 o'clock at night. This shows industry and merits Encouragement.

I find a pain in my right ear and as the pain & swelling in my left ear some time ago affected my hearing, I am afraid this may do the same & will make me deaf.[1]

Mr Glover informed me that he heard Mr. Priests vessel was lost in venue from Bristol to Cardiff and one woman that stood on board, perished in her, several passangers with the vessel and were saved by the Boat, but with difficulty. It occasioned great loss to numbers, William David, a shopkeeper in the vilage and one of our smiths had goods on board value £50. It is said Sir Edmund Thomas, Member for the County, had plate & other goods to the amount of £2000.[2]

Friday June 20th. Near Seven o'clock. I have taken cold, my right ear swelled & sore. The night, I believe has been without rain, as the

[1] See above, 3 June, for Wood's previous trouble with his ear.

[2] William Thomas (*Diary*, 164) also records the sinking of John Priest's boat in the Bristol Channel returning from Bristol to Cardiff. Sir Edmund Thomas of Wenvoe Bt (1712–67) was M.P. for Glamorgan.

river is lower. But it is a thick misty morning with small rain, such as sometimes turns out a fine day at this season of the year. The appearance of the sun has not been often in this summer.

Ten o'clock, small rain, overcast, but warmer than it has been for some time & but little Wind as the rain does not prevent the Masons working upon the Wall and their several Bargains.

Six o'clock. William Edward, his son David, Walter Williams, Harry William, Hopkin David, Morgan Evan Jenkins, Thomas Loyd & William Jenkin upon the forebay wall upon days wages. David John & his three Men upon their bargain the Clay Mill wall next the pool. Edward Thomas John & Thomas Samuel upon their bargain the mixing room. Two labourers in the quarry raising stones, four Labourers carrying to the Hurry, one puting them down, one taking them from the foot of the hurry, three at the Common Mortar, two at the Cardiff, two serving Masons with stones.

George Ford and one of his men finishing the Lathe, the other with Lewis William Edward preparing boards for the Wear, William Postlethwaite went to Plymouth Furnace to alter the Stamper box pattern.

Evan Lewis William & Morgan William Jenkin, Sawyers sawing for stamper wheel frame, Lodowick Thomas & his partner sawing for wheel frame p. the 100 feet.

The horses & oxen brought 4 pieces of Timber containing 76½ feet.

Saturday June 21st. Half past seven o'clock. My ear very sore but rested better than I expected.

A warm close dry morning, no appearance of rain last night, the river lessens, therefore am in hopes, the weather will take up & settle. Six o'clock this has been a fine warm day. The Masons upon the forebay wall upon day wages, were William Edwards & his son David, Walter William, Harry William, Morgan Evan Jenkin, Thomas Loyd, Hopkin David, William Jenkin, Thomas David & Joshua Thomas, the two last come this day. David John's Men are gone to their familys & himself was idle this day. Edward Thomas John was absent from his work this day & Thomas Samuel was scabbling stones for the great race Arch, another Length.

Two Labourers in the quarry raising stones, two carrying to the Hurry, three serving Masons, three at the Cardiff lime, three at Common Mortar, one serving Joseph Lucas.

George Ford & his men with William Postlethwaite & Lewis Edward William at the Wheel cases the Clay Mill wheel shaft & jointing planks & nailing them to the Penstock upon the forebay wall.

Evan Lewis Williams & Morgan William Jenkins Sawyers upon days wages sawing joists for mixing room floor. Ludowick Thomas & his partner sawing joists per 100 feet 3s 2d.

The horses & cattle brought 3 pieces of Timber containing 61 feet. David Lewis with four horses fetching Tyle from Aberdair & brought 60 upon each of our horse backs.[1] The Country horses will not bring more than 40 saying they cannot carry any more, in order to advance the price therefore I send four horses to show them what might be done & that we would not be imposed upon, & I believe now they will undertake the carriage at the price fixed vizt. 10s p. m.[2] There is not any method of dealing with these people, but by showing them, that you can do without them, & then in time they will be brought to reason.

Edward Farnell & his men are preparing the floor for the Clay Mill mixing room for dwellings for the Workmen.

Sunday June 22. Eight o'clock. My ear not so painful, but very dull of hearing. A warm but close morning, no Sun appears. George Ford & Joseph Lucas went to Lewen kelly, before I was up.

One o'clock, a very fine warm day, staid in the Office all this Morning, wrote to my Brother John Wood except about half an hour, that I took a walk upon the hill & to the quarry.

On Friday I received a letter from Mr. Jones of Bristol, informing me that he had seen my Brother at Wednesbury and that he desired him to inform me that he had made such discovery as would surprize me and desired I would meet him at Bristol in my letter to my brother desired him to come here, if he could not to inform me the discovery he had made.[3]

Three o'clock took a walk, down the side of the quarry to the Holme where the Blast furnace is proposed to be erected, it is a very convenient place, a fine bank for an high one and if there should not be found room sufficient for a bridge house at the back of the stack an Arch may be sprang to the rock upon the Bank and Walls on each side will form a very commodious Bridge house, in my opinion be cheaper than filling it up with rubbish as there must be two walls built to keep up the

[1] In fact thin flags of local sandstone suitable for roofing, not clay tiles. They were brought by packhorse, rather than waggon, a reflection of the state of the roads between Aberdare and Merthyr.

[2] i.e. per thousand.

[3] This presumably refers to some significant progress in the Woods' attempts to perfect the potting and stamping process at their forge at Wednesbury (Staffs.).

rubbish.[1] The bank for coking the Coal will be inconvenient as it must be below the bridge house & an ascent to wheel them to it but by taking in the other field, in a line from the Bridge house [*and*] by filling up the hollow between them, it will make it discend which should be attained if at any expense which will be but once but the labour to wheel uphill will be a continual expense.[2] I think the bank will allow the Stack to be near 50 ft high which in my opinion it aught to be, as the hight will be a means to prevent the cold mine[3] falling down too soon as it often does in low ones before it is sufficiently heated to fuse immediately when it reaches the Tuères which is the occasion of such bad metal being made at several furnaces, the Earthy part, which is the Scoria not being separated from the metalic part. It is not so material having your furnace very wide, as the Mine, Coal etc. fall in a perpendicular pillar, in proportion to the Tunnel those several materials which fill the bulge above the boshes remain for months, sometimes the whole blast. Therefore if there is command of blast, the benefit from a high furnace wil be experienced by those who make use of it.

Nine o'clock. This day has been a warm fine, pleasant one. I find the pain in my ear much abated but nearly lost the sense of hearing. I hope it may proceed from hard wax in my ear but have tried with an Ear picker & cannot find any.

Monday June 23. Near six o'clock a fine warm Morning and looks like settled weather, but few Masons appear this morning only William Edwards, Harry William, Thomas Loyd, William Jenkin, Thomas David & Joshua Thomas, Walter William and Morgan Evan Jenkins came after Seven.

Nine o'clock. Breakfast time a fine warm Morning and as it was full moon last night at 5 I am in hopes we may have settled weather. It is rumoured that several of our Labourers intend to leave us at the next pay day which will be the 4th July and as it will be very inconvenient as we may want them at the laying down of the Wear, and as cutting of the

[1] i.e. Wood envisages an open arch supporting the bridge connecting the furnace bank with the furnace top, along which the raw materials for charging the furnace would be barrowed, rather than a solid embankment, as tended to be the practice in contemporary charcoal-fired furnaces (for surviving examples, see Riden, *Gazetteer*).

[2] A rather convoluted sentence in which Wood argues that capital expenditure to create an area for coking level with the furnace bridge-house and charging ramp would be worthwhile, since it would avoid continual barrowing of coke uphill.

[3] i.e. the iron ore immediately after it has been charged into the furnace, before it has been heated to melting point.

grass for Hay may begin in some places, at that time, therefore in order to be at some certainty at that time, I think it cannot be amiss to postpone the pay day untill it amounts to a month, this may be done without any loss of credit. By communicating this to William Edwards & some of the others, the chief of the Masons that intend remaining at this place for the Season or until the whole buildings are completed. Should we be disappointed of hands, when we begin to lay down our Wear, it may prevent it being done this year.

Six o'clock. This has been a fine warm day, and the work has gone on briskly for the hands we have had. Three Masons & several Labourers etc absent. The Masons upon the forebay wall were William Edwards, Harry William, Walter William, Morgan Evan Jenkins, Thomas Loyd, William Jenkin, Thomas David & Joshua Thomas, day wages. David John & one of his men only upon the Clay Millwall next the Pool. Edward Thomas John & Thomas Samuel upon the wall and Arch on the great race upon Bargain. Six labourers serving the Masons upon days wages with stones, two serving Edward Thomas John with stones at the great race. Two at the Cardiff Mortar, four at the common Mortar, one serving Joseph Lucas upon the Stack, two at the Quarry raising stones, Carrying stones to the hurry, one putting them down the hurry, & one taking them from the foot, besides three in clearing the great race for Walling and arching, & five with Thomas Clifton in taking down the rock for one side of the farr Hammer hatch. George Ford turning the Clay Mill wheel Gudgeons, his two men morticing the Stamper wheel case, William Postlethwaite Squaring & Morticing the Clay Mill wheel shaft & Lewis Edward William jointing planks for the front of the several Penstocks. These are Carpenters. Evan Lewis William, & Morgan William Jenkin Sawyers sawing joists by day & Lodovick Thomas & his partner sawing the same p. 3s 2d for every 100 ft.

Edward Farnel & three Men framing the floor for the Clay Mill and mixing room which are drawn by our horse to near the place for raising this is done by bargain p. agreement.

Six horses, 6 cattle & 3 men in the Carriage brought a piece of Timber 34 feet long & 16 inches girth containing 64 feet in this piece will serve as one for a Drone beam.[1]

Two Smiths & one striker are kept employed in making & mending tools for Masons Labourers & Carpenters, binders for Stock, shoing horses & Cattle, and carriage, etc.

[1] A beam placed as a spring over a helve-, trip- or tilt-hammer to augment the blow (information kindly provided by Mr M.T. Wright, curator of mechanical engineering, Science Museum).

Wrote to Mr. Bacon & sent the last fortnight Accounts. Amounting to £88 14s 1½d. Wrote to Mr. Ellison & enclosed one to my wife, to Mr. Hick, Ian Harris, Brother John & Samuel & give them to Jon. Morgan to deliver the postman.

The Postmaster in Brecon was so kind to tell John Morgan our servant that if we would procure a pouch with a Lock & two keys & leave one with him, he would take care of all letters that come for us & when we sent any to him he would open the pouch with his key, take out what letters we sent and put in those that came to him for us, lock it & return it by the postman.

As the postman is a drinking Man he sometimes loses them and it has been suspected that some of our letters have been taken from him, which must be by his consent, opened & returned, this suspicion, seems just from its being known, what we have wrote which could not be but by this method & by this method proposed, it would prevent any loss, unless he lost the pouch, or any letter being opened by any daringly inquisitive person, and for their prying in our affairs.

Four of our horses with David Lewis brought two tons of Tyles upon their backs from Aberdair quarry. Ordered them up to the Mountain tomorrow to load fire clay to the Brick makers that as many may be made this fine weather as can be done.

I enclosed six letters to the Postmaster in Brecon with a Letter to him desiring he would procure a small pouch with one lock & two keys. Sent the Letter to John Morgan p. Edmund Williams to give the Postman himself. The flooring beams of mixing room are 14 by 7 inches, & the joists are 5 × 3 inches & the beams are Six feet eight inches above the bottom. The floor of the mixing room is foot by [*Blank*] feet.

Tuesday June 24th. Near Six o'clock a fine warm morning, the men ready to begin their work.

George Ford is gone to the Wood, with the Carriage, to see what Timber there is felled and to order these pieces, that are at present wanted to be brought.

Nine o'clock the workmen at breakfast. William Edward & Joshua Thomas, Masons, upon one part of the forebay Wall, Walter William, Thomas Loyd & William Jenkin & Hopkin David upon the other part. Harry William, Morgan Evan Jenkin & Thomas David Scabbling stones for the forebay wall in the quarry. The flooring beams and joists are fixed in the Mixing Room. John Morgan brought the Sill horse[1] one of

[1] i.e. a shaft horse.

the best that we have for me to see a swelling in the Testacle bagg between his hind legs which is supposed to the nature of a rupture, he seemed to be in great pain by his uneasiness, they gave him a pint of sweet oil and turned him into the field to grass.

The Claymill wheel is 18 feet in diameter, the sole [*Blank*] the through [*Blank*] deep, The Shaft is only 6 feet long. The Gudgeons are 22 inches within the shaft, the round hole for the brass 3¼ diameter, this made [*Blank*] & 4¼ in long, the Square for the box 3 inches & 9 inches long.

One o'clock the Masons have continued at their several work as at breakfast. A Warm day. William David, Smith, has been burning horns & hoofs to case harden one of the Clay Mill wheels gudgeons after it was turned true in the lathe by George Ford. The windows for the Clay Mill are sett upon the down wall next the pool to the penstock, the other about a foot from it on the other side of it.

Six o'clock. The Masons are employed as in the morning except Thos. David who left the quarry and worked at the forebay wall. Five Labourers serving Masons. Two raising stones in the quarry, two carrying them to the hurry, one putting them down, one taking them from the foot, Two at Cardiff Mortar, four at common Mortar & two serving Edward Thomas John at great race. David John & his men at the Clay Mill walls upon bargain. Joseph Lucas at the Air furnace stack & Mary David serving him. George Ford in the wood his two men upon the Stamper Wheel frame, William Postlethwaite upon the Clay Mill Wheel shaft. Evan Lewis, William & Morgan William Jenkin sawyer sawing beams & principals for roofs & Lodovick Thomas & Partner, Sawyers, sawing Pannels at 3s 2d p. 100 feet.

William David, Smith has case hardened one of the Clay Mill Wheel Gudgeons very well, it is exceeding hard.

The horse & cattle have brought a piece of Timber 18 feet long & 19 inch girth contents 45 feet.

I have just heard that Isaac Wilkinson is come to the vilage & have sent to desire to see him here, either this evening or of morning. Thomas Clifton & partner have finished the bargain in taking away part of the rock near to the fore hatch which makes room for laying the foundations of the remainder of the forebay.

Mr. Terry & Mr. Guests Brother in Law came here to see the work the former says their metal is now of a black grey, not so good, as some time ago. They have cast three Stamper Cases, the last very good, the two former wanted cutting being lumpy & not usefull until the knots are cut level off, to allow the bottom to lye quite cloase & flatt. He promised to send two men to cutt the lumps off the Anvils, they have sent.

Wednesday June 25th. Half past five o'clock, a fine warm morning the men have been waiting to begin work at Six. Mr. Isaac Wilkinson breakfasted with me here. I showed him the situation we intended for our Blast Furnace, which he much approved of, but advised to take the field on the other side of the road, for a bank to burn Stone & Coke Coal as it will then be down hill to the bridge house across the high road, as the fields are very uneven next to the bank, belonging to us, & will require Levelling at an expense.[1] This is to be further considered. He informed me the intention of the Plymouth Company was to suffer us to lay down our Wear & then prefer a bill against us & obtain an injunction to stop our Work & that Lord Plymouth was prevailed upon to come over and view the premises for that purpose. And if this could be obtained, they would make their own terms with us. That the Dowlais & Plymouth Companys had had a meeting or one of each company had met & agreed. that whatever agreement should be made or entered into with us for make should be for both companys each to have the supplying amenity & at a certain price as it is thought we shall be obliged to come into any measure they may think proper to impose on us.

The Plymouth Furnace I am informed goes at Six charges a turn and 14 Turns in the Week, and 8 cwt of stone at each charge is 6 × 14 = 84 × 8 = 672 cwt as they work fresh Mine, there ought to be allowed for Shale one sixth part, which reduces the real good mine used in one Week to 560 cwt or 28 T. Allow 3 ton of Stone to produce a Ton of metal, They blow then after the rate of about Nine Ton a week and suppose this Blast continues 12 weeks and their raw stone is 8s per dozen, one third of which may be taken off for loss of weight in burning, which will make the Mine when burned at 10/6 per doz. Therefore 2 dozen of Mine at 10/6 p. dozen will be 21s. Their Coal upon the Bank @ 2/6 p. Ton is for 5 Ton, 1s 6d coking, 5s 8d Lime 1s, burning stone 1s, other Wages including Clerk per Week £5, Cut 25s.

2 dozen of Mine for one Ton,				
for 9 T of metal is 18 doz	@ 2/6	£9	9	-
45 Ton of Coal	2/6	5	12	6
Coking 45 Tons of Coal		-	13	6
Lime 9s, burning stone 9s		-	18	-
Wages		6	5	-
9 Ton of pigs @ £2 10s p. Ton £22 18s		22	18	-

12 weeks Blast at 9 T p. week 108 T @ £2 10s p Ton is £270 - .

[1] See above, p. 60, for Wood's own thoughts on the question of creating a coking bank level with or above the charging bridge, not below it.

Therefore that Company will be at the following Expense when they are out of Blast and suppose this metal was cast all into use at £8 15s per Ton the profit be £3 2s per Ton but if in grains @ £4-5s it will be £1 15s p. Ton. The Profit upon 108 Tons at £1 15s p. Ton is £189 for 12 weeks. Blast in one year. This Company and all others, in the like situation must be at the Annual Expense of rent, interest of money advanced, and Workmen's wages etc. which I calculate as under vizt.

Their Capital £4000 @ 5 p. cent for one year	£200	-
Their rent	60	-
Wages for workmen, clerk etc.	300	-
	560	-
The Profit upon metal made in 12 weeks	189	-
Loss	371	-

John Morgan informed me that the Sill horse, that had the rupture, is dead, a loss as he was a good as any for that purpose as any in this Country. Six o'clock. I have been at the Plymouth Furnace with Mr. Wilkinson and examined into their method of working, & if one can give credit to the filler, he says that they put on 3½ cwt of Mine every half charge & 1½ cwt Lime stone, which is 7 cwt of Mine & 3 cwt of Lime stone to the charge & they some time have 6 or 7 Turn in the 12 hours. Mr. Terry tells me that their coal byes them in 2s p. ton getting, & 2s carriage & 4½ per ton coking. Their stone is very badly burned, some of it raw & used as got which is very bad method, as the shale or shell is upon it which produces no Iron and take up the room of better mine that would produce metal & destroy coke. Their bellows are growing bad, their pipes too streight & tuère too small. The wind rebounds back & I am of opinion that the Bellows will not serve another blast, they should not, if I were concerned and could prevent it. Their scrap iron they put into their furnace again which in my opinion is another piece of mismanagement as it would be more profit to sell it for what the metal byes them in which has been offered. Their metal is much altered for the worst from a bright open gray to a dark close grey.

So that upon the whole they are certainly by these short Blasts working at a loss. As far as I can learn, there is not any want of either Mine or Coal, the former may be got and lay them in upon the furnace bank, about 10s p. day & their coal at 4s p. Ton and their Lime stone lyes them in 4s per Ton dd on the furnace bank, then there may be allowed 1s p. Ton for Coal for burning Mine & for workmen. If I have a just account given me their charge will be as underwritten vizt.

22½ dozen of Mine at 10s per dozen	£11	5	-
45 Ton of Coal at 4s p. Ton	9	-	-
Coal for houses & burning Stone	-	9	-
Coking 45 Tons @ 4½d p. Ton	-	16	10½
Lime 24s A man to burn stone 9s	1	13	-
Wages etc	6	5	-
	£29	8	10½
	-	11	1½

9 Ton of metal weekly @ about £3 5s per Ton	30	-	-

Suppose this blast continues 13 weeks @ 9 T per week

£117 first cost		
Int. on the Capital for 1 year	£200	
Their rent £60 and £20	80	
Wages etc for one year at least	300	£580
Their metal £4 5s per ton (will be 20s p. Ton profit)		117
Their loss per annum is		463

Began the further course of the hammer Hutch this day and got the first part of the forebay where the Stampers are finished to the hight. The Masons at it were William Edwards, Harry Williams, Thos. Loyd, Morgan Evan Jenkin, Hopkin David, Thomas David & Joshua Thomas, Thomas Clifton, Richard Harthorn, two of Thos. Clifton Sons & a Labourer were upon the lower part of the rock to clear it for the hammer hatch. Edward Thomas, John & Thomas Samuel upon their bargain the mixing room David John & two Masons were upon their bargain the Clay Mill. Three Labourers raising stones in the quarry, one clearing rubbish, two bearing stones to the hurry, one putting them down, one taking them from the foot, two at Cardiff Mortar, four at Common Mortar, one cleaning the stamper race, one serving Joseph Lucas, two bearing quarry Stone, two bearing Cobbles to Masons & one throwing Stone on the Scaffold. George Ford turning Clay Mill wheel Gudgeons his two men at Stamper wheel frame, William Postlethwaite at the Clay Mill wheel shaft & Lewis Edwards William jointing planks for the Penstocks. Evan Lewis Williams & Morgan William Jenkin, Sawyers sawing footing beams by day wages. Lodowick Thomas & his partner Sawyers sawing spars for roofs by the 100 ft 3s 2d. Edward Farnell & his 3 men framing the roofing and flooring at 4s 6d p. square.

Penree & his 3 partners clearing the great race for another length of Arching @ 4d p. yard for the earth at 8d p. yard for the rock at 2d p. dozen for what Mine they get & there is a vein of iron stone in the rock which is a hard blue sill all the way up in the course of the race & to encourage them to be carefull in saving it they are paid at that rate.

The carriage with four horses & 6 Oxen brought a piece of Timber 36 feet.

Eight o'clock, the wind at South West, rains & looks like a continuous rain.

Thursday June 26th. Half past Six o'clock, a rainy morning & continued all night, as the river is high. Mr. Wilkinson breakfasted with me here at Cyfarthfa. After we cut the form of a furnace and gave Mr. Parry directions to draw a section. Then we went to the Bank where we intend fixing the furnace. George Ford, Joseph Lucas & Edward Parry took the height, near the End and found it 85 feet from the top of the Wear but as this place is too near the road, the Bank for burning the Ironstone & coking the coal would lie below it & the wheeling up hill. But by going lower down, to obtain the high ground above the bridge house for wheeling downhill, there will be 68 feet high for the Stack. Therefore this is the place fixed upon for Erecting it by which is obtained all the advantages for a yard that can be desired and what is in our own possession. Mr. Wilkinson stayed & dined with me & after dinner went to meet Mr. Webb at Doulass Furnace. He says that command of blast and a high furnace will produce as good metal from the Mine or stone as it is capable. He observed there is not any management at the Plymouth furnace, their Blast is weak, their coal too far coked, so much as to destroy the strength of it and the white ash appeared in some of it. The filler struck his rake into the heep as hard as to break them which makes great waste as the small coke (like bray[1] in a charcoal work) are not fitt to put into a furnace, but sound ones only, which bear up the stone until hot & then when it falls to the Tuere is readily fused & allows the Mettalic part to separate & become as pure in quality as the nature of the stone will produce. All ironstone (as well as Iron) requires time to have absorbing heat, too sudden heat does not do so well hence it is evident that low furnaces do not allow it time to acquire the heat & consequently the Iron is not so good but a high furnace must answer this end, as it is longer in sinking down double the hight will give more than double the time in getting to the Tuère.[2] By this form of attack the Iron is made so much purer in the first running as will require less refining in flourishing for what is wanting in the first fusion must be done in the second & often repeated after flourishing. The large coke, with large lump of Mine, keep the furnace hollow and admits

[1] i.e. small pieces of charcoal.

[2] The nozzle through which the blast of air is driven into the blast furnace.

the Air to flow & afford heat to answer the end desired, all small mine should be mixed with slacked Lime & worked up as Mortar & when stiff put into the furnace in Lump, this prevents it falling too soon down, before it can melt, & carry its flux with it, for this small mine, when put on without mixing with Lime, not only fills up the vacancies between the Coke & large lumps of Mine but drops down too soon & mixes with the other metal before a separation of the metal & Scoria is made & becomes a regular they must make the iron bad, of a bad grain & black cases in the middle. Then in my method of working what is wanted in the first refining must be performed in my method by repeated refining before it can be made so fitt as those metals that are better and more thoroughly refined from the ore & mine. But in differing this method of repeated refining cannot be obtained. Hence the necessity of flourishing with some metal & as good Iron from other in one flourishing. The Goodness of Iron depends upon a due proportion of cinders being left in it (as I have observed in some former observations upon the working of iron) too much make it wrotten and redshot, & too little the same.

Near Six o'clock it rains hard has been Showers all day. The Masons Scabbling stone since breakfast vizt. William Edward, Harry William, Walter William, Hopkin David, Morgan Evan Jenkin, Thomas Loyd, Thomas David & Joshua Thomas, David John & his two men Scabbling Stone for Arch over windows, the large one over the Clay Mill Gavel End Wall. Edward Thomas & Thomas Samuel at their bargain the Mixing Room, at intervals of fair weather. Labourers one serving Josh Lucas upon the Stack, three raising stones up in the quarry, two carrying stones to the hurry, one putting them down the hurry, one taking them from the hurry, four carrying stones from the hurry, one serving Masons, two at Cardiff Mortar & four at Common Mortar two getting Sand, George Ford turning Clay Mill Spindle and laying out work, his two men & Lewis Edward Williams upon headstocks for the Wheels & William Postlethwaite upon Clay Mill wheel shaft fixing the Gudgeons and making keys. Edward Farnel & his men framing roof Timbers. Evan Lewis Williams & Morgan William Jenkins Sawyers sawing roofing per day wages. William Rees—it is not Lodewick Thomas as has been set down hitherto—& his men Sawyers Sawing Roof timbers 3s 2d p. 100 feet.

The carriage with horses and Cattle at home the river being too high to fetching Timber, it lying where the water must be forded twice it cannot be brought but in low water. David Lewis was loading fire clay for brick making but the Shade broke & he was obliged to give over. I am much afraid that the weather will not allow us to make sufficient quantity to erect our Air furnace this Season.

Eight o'clock continues raining. Wind at South West, blows hard at times, look very like rain.

Just now received a note from Mr. Thomas Atkinson of Whitehaven desiring to see me at Edward Morgan in the vilage. Waited upon him & found Mr. Robottom, Mr. Glover['s] Clerk of Abergydon furnace[1] with him after enquiring how all friends did and what brought him there he informed me that he had been with Mr. Webb at Doulass Furnace relating some pig iron sold Mr. Dorsett from Cardiff Forge,[2] that Mr. Webb was always looked upon as a Partner there. Mr. Atkinson has procured from Dorsett several of Webbs Letters to him by which it appears very clear that he was a partner, in my opinion I could not prevail upon Mr. Atkinson to wait long enough to take a view of our Work, he said he must be off by five o'clock to meet Mr. Glover at Cardiff. Got to bed about eleven o'clock.

Friday June 27th. Past Six o'clock a rainy morning and as there is a great flood it is very likely that there has been rain all night. Neither Masons nor Labourers can work, only Carpenters & Sawyers as they have Shades to work under.

About eight o'clock Mr. Atkinson came up to Cyfarthfa & stayed with me with Mr. Robottom about an hour showed him what I could of our Plan but seemed so full with the Affair betwixt him & Webb that he could not attend to any other discourse.

Nine o'clock. Workmen at Breakfast. When done the Masons and Labourers sett to work, the former Scabbling stones the Latter carrying stones etc. It is fair. Half past ten the Masons left Scabbling & sett upon the forebay. It is fine weaher the Sun warm, but a cool S.W. Wind. I hear that John Guest came to the Vilage last night.

One o'clock, Showers, but the Masons have continued on the forebay Wall, & farr Hammer hatch next to the rock.

Six o'clock. Mr. Wilkinson & John Guest have been with me & propose selling their shares of Plymouth furnace. The latter asks £100 each share exclusive of the advance which he says is £150 p. share more & he and Mr. Wilkinson will assign over the lease from Lord Plymouth of the premises with the management, & all other advantages, they were to have & was reserved to each in their Articles of Partnership bertween them two, the Original Lease & they declare that neither of them have already alienated any part to any other person whateever. I have offered

[1] Riden, *Gazetteer*, 12 for Abercarn furnace in Ebbw Vale (Mon.).

[2] For the forge near the castle in Cardiff see *Glamorgan County History*, v. 27–8.

him John Guest £350 for his two shares & Isaac Wilkinson 3 shares is agreed for before. They both are to see Thomas Guest this evening, and demand sight of the Books which has been refused them some time ago and to consider of my offer & give me an Answer tomorrow morning, at eight o'clock, & breakfast with me. The procuring these five shares with the Lease & Management, will enable us to make metal soon & before we can be ready, with these works to flourish & shingle & when the other partners find that the two principal persons, have sold, they will be willing to do the same, in Course.

This has been a fine afternoon. The Masons upon the forebay wall were William Edward, Walter William, Harry William, Thomas Loyd, Hopkin David, Morgan Evan Jenkins, Thomas David & Joshua Thomas. David John & two other Masons were upon their Bargain the Clay Mill. Edward Thomas John & Thomas Samuel are upon their Bargain the Mixing room.

Thomas Clifton, his two sons & 3 other Labourers are taking away the rock for the fore hammer hatch. David Penree & three partners clearing the great race for the arching.

Two raising stones in the quarry, four carrying to the hurry, one put them down & one taking them from the foot, four carrying stones to the Masons & one serving them, one clearing the Low quarry, one serving Joseph Lucas, one getting Sand, four at Common Mortar & two at Cardiff Mortar. George Ford turning Clay Mill Spindles, his two men at headstock.

Lewis Edward William preparing a piece of Timber for Shrouds & Wm Postlethwaite making two wheels for a Slade for carrying fire clay to Brick makers—Evan Lewis William & Morgan William Jenkin Sawyers Sawing Principals & William Rees & his men Sawyers Sewing rafters, Panels etc.

The Horses & Cattle ploughing. David Lewis with four horses carrying Tyle from Aberdair.

William Edward showed me a letter that Councellor Kymer agreed to his proposal to direct the Erecting of Bridges for him, which Williams informs me that he is to have 30s p. week & four days every month to go to his family.[1] Which I advised him to accept, upon his promising, that when we were determined to begin the cut for conveying the water to & to erect our New furnace that he would leave the management of

[1] Thomas Kymer of Kidwelly (Carms.); the bridges were for his canal, mentioned earlier (p. 13).

the Bridges to his son, who he said was as capable as himself, and he would undertake the completing them, agreeable to his proposal.

Saturday, June 28. Past Six, a rainy morning but the river is lower than it was yesterday therefore conclude there has not been any rain this last night. The Masons cannot work upon the Wall, therefore are Scabbling stones for the remainder of the forebay.

Eight o'clock. Paid William Edward 5¾ and his son 1 day work & took leave upon his going into Carmarthenshire to undertake the Erecting of two Bridges as mentioned before.

Waited until after Nine o'clock before we breakfasted expecting Mr. Wilkinson & Guest, they promised to be here by eight but have not heard from them. It has continued raining until this time & very like to do so. several workers continue working notwithstanding the rain, & chose to be wet rather than lose any time, it shows care & Industry. David Lewis & Edmund Lewis with 5 horses fetching Tyle from Aberdair one turn the rain prevented his going any more this day, order him to look over & repair the pack saddle against Monday. Twelve o'clock it rains hard the river rises. The Labourers left off the Masons Scabbling stones under the Shade erected for that purpose vizt. Harry Williams, Walter Williams, Morgan Evan Jenkins, Hopkin David, Thomas Loyd, Thomas David, Joshua Thomas, & William Jenkins. William David & his two men scabbling stones, under a shade, they Erected themselves being upon bargain, Edward Thomas John, & Thos. Samuel, not here this day they being upon bargain & no shade to work under, Thomas Clifton his two Sons & two other Labourers, made each of them a quarter of a day untill breakfast.

In looking over this Journal I find there has been 15 fair days from April 11th, to this day, inclusive, four of which were Sundays, therefore the working days 11 only, quite calm, no wind stirring. Three o'clock it has been fair for about two hours, & now rains again; the Wind at S.W.

Five o'clock The Masons & Labourers give over work, as they began at five this morning. Thomas David & Joshua Thomas went home at two, having 14 miles to go, & return on Monday morning. Sometimes showers. George Ford and his men about a Cart for carrying fire clay to Brick makers & William Postlethwaite made a bedstead for George Fords men they do not like being at an Ale house, for Lewenkelly house, Lewis Edward William, upon the Stamper wheel frame. The Sawyers by day wages & by 100 feet the same as yesterday. David Penree and his partners left off work at five. The Wind at S.W. brisk & whistles very cold for the Season, keep good fires.

The horses brought three pieces of Timber this day containing Three Labourers raising stones notwithstanding the rain a day each four carrying stones to hurry, one putting them down & one taking 'em from the foot of the hurry, four carrying stones to the Masons to Scrabble two carrying Sand ½ day each one getting Sand ¼ day, three making up Mortar each ½ day, one serving Joseph Lucas ¼ of a day, One in smithy shop 1 day & one at the Low quarry ½ a day. Thomas William, Smith not here, being sick.

Edward Farnals & his men not having Shade to work under could not do anything this day at the roofing.

Isaac Wilkinson has been with me, & informs me that John Guest & him, dined with Thomas Guest who showed them his Accts. but they are not kept in a regular method for to be examined without a deal of trouble & time. Thomas Guest told Isaac that when we were ready for working they wd begin and get Mine & follow it cross the field adjoining, that we have taken from Lewis John, & by that means they could deprive us of the water. Isaac says that Mr. White allow Terry one hundred pounds p. Annum, that Terry does not understand the management of a furnace and I think that appears pretty evident from what is now doing in the burning of the Ironstone & Coking Coal etc. Isaac says that John Guest informs him that the Colebrook Dale Com'y have obtained a Patent for the making of Pig or cast metal maleable in an Airfurnace without Pots by puting it into an Air furnace upon a Sand bottom & suffering it to remain there untill bro't into Nature then remove it into another Air furnace & further refine it.[1] This method was made use of by one Woodhouse I think a watchmaker 35 years ago & a Patent obtained by him & several Gentlemen supported him in puting this in practice & good Iron was made but the small quantity that could be refined in a Week with great waste of metal obliged them to give it up.[2] I do not mention this to invalidate the method, it may have been improved & a better method, discovered, since that time. The new invention can be supposed to be brought to its utmost perfection at once or by one person others may see an easier or a better, cheaper or more ready method, by only seeing a few operations performed then the inventor, or improver, that have spent many years and a great deal of money to bring it to the state, which the other person see it. If the method of refining the metal

[1] For Thomas and George Cranage's patent of 1766 see R.A. Mott, *Henry Cort: the great finer* (1983), 8–10.

[2] For Roger Woodhouse's patent of 1724 see Flinn, 'William Wood', 57–9; Treadwell, 'William Wood', 104; both discuss the relationship between his patent and the activities of Charles Wood's father in the 1720s.

upon a Sand bottom without pots can produce quantities & little waste, I will then give it the preference to my method with pots, as it will save all that expence and trouble. I do not in the least doubt, but when I come to be in a regular course of working, of improving, both in quantity, quality, nearer & better methods, as I have found in the time I have already been working in this method. And I can see that nearer and cheaper methods are to be found as I hope will appear in time. And I do not in the least doubt but a few years, will show the World that there will not be any need of Wood fuel to make good Iron. When I made use of Sand bottom I could not find any that wo'd stand, longer than two or three days and when the Cinder run, the Iron stuck to the bottom — but perhaps they might have a better method, which I co'd not then think of.

Sunday June 29th. A fair morning. Seven o'clock the Wind at S.E. but cool overcast & no Sun appears.

Twelve o'clock it has been a fine day the Wind at N.E. the sun appears. Mr. Wilkinson has been with me since about 10 o'clock he informs me that John Guest will not take less than one hundred & sixty pounds, for his two shares subject to a further sum for advance of one hundred and fifty upon each share, more, which is the sum that he has advanced, viz. £300 for his two shares the whole sum £460 upon these terms he will join I. Wilkinson in assigning over his Lease with all the privileges of management, disposing of the metal etc. that they have, and as Mr. Parrot who has four shares & Thomas Guest one Share, part of the Ten which the said I. Wilkinson & Guest had reserved to themselves upon their disposal of the other Ten shares subject to the advance of £200 upon each, to Erect the Works & which were to be repaid out of the first profits will, I think join us, if we purchase to carry the work on in the most advantageous manner. And as the whole management of this Work was invested in John Guest that management will be assigned over to the purchaser. But as I have offered no more than one hundred pounds more than the advance of £300 upon Each share the whole £400 Isaac Wilkinson in his Zeal & great desire to have them in our hand, has offered to pay the difference of £60 out of his share, which I have accepted. And in order to get the affair concluded as soon as can be I have sent Mr. Parry with a letter to Mr. Thomas Morgan, Lord Talbot's Steward at Cowbridge to come over tomorrow & bring with him three or four sheets of Stamp Paper in order to draw a proper assignment for the Lease & their shares, with all the priviledges & advantages they were to have, & did reserve to themselves. Isaac informs me that John Guest is very fickle & uncertain to deal with & hard to fix, that he has a great opinion of that Work & the best sort of pig of an open grey grain, has been tryed & found as good for barr iron as any coke metal that is made and that such metal may be made for the most part with management and advise that if we purchase his and Guests shares to Blow out, lay in a good stock of Mine to have burnt to shale (or the shell fall off) and in the mean time be altering the wheel and Bellows, and some other necessary repairs and he will engage to make Sixteen Ton a week, from that furnace. Isaac says there will not be any doubt of one making as good metal in our own furnace when Erected, to save one a flourishing which I verily believe from the command of Blast height of stack & round coke with the Mine in lumps & the small mixed with slacked lime like Mortar, & when hard the mine in lumps in this method carrys conviction, with it to any person of knowledge in the Iron Affair. The purity of the metal depends upon the Scoria being entirely separated from the metalic part & this cannot be obtained without command of the blast etc. The Coal for this purpose must be what they call here, sweet coal, free of Sulphur & I think there is such here, as sweet as in any part I know. Another observation from Isaac is, not to throw on a whole charge at once, only a half one, or less, one or two baskets at one time it does not cool or clog the furnace as a larger quantity nor press down the heated fuel & Mine, so close as a greater weight will do & the lighter & opener the burthen is the better metal is produced as appears evident from what has before, been observed on this head. Although I do not pretend to be a master in knowledge of the managing a Blast furnace yet I know so much as to see & be convinced that what Isaac advances relative hereto, is very judicious in him & very evident to me, and the same observations will hold in all metals whatever. In differing the metal of what kind soever of its earthy part, which is the scoria, depends the purity of it.

Past Six o'clock this has been a fine day, but cool to make a fire necessary to one of my age and I think more sensible of cold than many much older. The weather does not look like settled but has the appearance of more reain. Number of people come to view our work on a Sunday. Therefore I think it may be proper to pay a Man for walking about to see that no mischief is done by any that come. I now have told 18 together, in looking at our cast house.

Nine o'clock it rains hard. Mr. Wilkinson & John Guest have been with me and I believe we shall agree but John Guest wants to keep half a share which I suppose may be with an intent to have the management, but unless he will assign over his right of the Lease with the privileges & advantages he has reserved to himself they should not be purchased. We are to meet tomorrow.

Isaac Wilkinson Estimates of the Weekly Expenses in making 14 tons of pigs at Plymouth Furnace

		£ s d
Coals 70 ton at 4s p. Ton upon the Coking Bank		14 - -
Iron stone raw 49 T allowed for loss of weight in burning @ 4s		9 16 -
Lime stone 16 Ton @ 4s		3 4 -
A founder & keeper £1 2s two bridge Stokers 14s	1 16	
Two fillers 16s, two cokers 15s, Stocktaker 8s	1 19	
A supernumerary man 6s, Clerk £1 5s	1 11	5 6 -
Rent £2, Int. of Stock £4, Wear & Tear £1 5s		7 5 -
		£39 11 -

14 Ton of Metal @ £4 5s p. Ton £59 10s

Monday June 30th. Six o'clock. There has been a deal of rain last night, the river is raised. It is overcast and has the appearance of more rain, but is fair at present.

Eight o'clock begin to rain a wind at S.E.

Nine o'clock Breakfast time it is now fair the Sun appears & it is warm & comfortable. Mr. Wilkinson now with me informs me that Mr. White is expected here tonight & would have me go with him and John Guest to Bristol.

One o'clock Mr. Wilkinson & Guest just now gone, agreed to go with them to Bristol in order to get proper writing drawn for Lease & shares. A fine day.

Two o'clock it rains hard. Six o'clock it has been a fine afternoon since two, Thunder & Showers. The Masons upon the forebay Wall, were Harry Wm, Hopkin David, Morgan Evan Jenkin, Thomas Loyd, William Jenkin, Thomas David, Joshua Thomas, & Walter Williams, David John & three more Masons upon Bargain on Clay Mill, Edward Thomas John, Thomas Samuel & two more Masons that Edward Thomas John has hired, upon the Great Arch.

Thomas Clifton his two Sons & two wheelers at the Rock for the farr Hammer hatch.

David Penree & his three partners clearing for the grand race. Two Labourers bringing up a Level at the low quarry below the Sawyer Shade, to clear it of water, that stone being much nearer the Arching than any other & has been neglected although of as good a quality as any, 3 at the Quarry raising stones, 4 carrying Stones to hurry 1, putting them down, 1 taking 'em from it, 4 carrying to Masons, 4 serving Edw. Thomas, 2 at Cardiff Mortar, 2 at Common mortar, 1 serving Joseph Lucas, George Ford, his two men, William Postlthwaite & Lewis Wm Edward preparing the Wear frame against settled Weather to put it down,

Four Sawyers Sawing Beams, joists & Sparrs etc. for roofing, one pair by the day, the others by piece at 3s 2d p. 100 feet.

David Lewis with four horses brought one tunn of Slate in the Morning. In the afternoon with three horses fetching stone from the farr Quarry, for great Arch. One horse John Morgan took to Brecon with letter to Mr. Bacon, & one enclosed for my wife and one to Doctor Brownrigg & he is to meet me at the Passage[1] or at Bristol with what Letters there may be for me. The horses brought pieces of Timber containing [*Blank*] feet. It rains hard & Thunder Showers. Joseph Lucas upon the Stack.

Mr. Wilkinson thinks that a Stack for Blast furnace may be built cheaper than William Edwards estimates it at and advises when we begin to build the out & inside of good stones, laid in Mortar, & the Inside, between those two walls to be filled with dry stones, placed close & the vacancies filled with smaller stones & over foot or two high, pour Thin Lime & Sand untill all the vacancies are filled continued in the same way to the top leaving a pipe in each corner 18 inches square or round, & other holes or vacancies in an oblique position to come into the large pipe and every night when the Masons have left off work, kindle a fire at the bottom of each hole & let it burn until the Masons come to work again in the Morning. By this method the Stack by the time it is got up, will be partly dry & will not require a great deal of time to compleat it before fire is put in for Blowing.

Mr. Parry returned from Cowbridge with £170 for his bill upon A. Bacon @ 20 days sight as Mr. Morgan would keep 3 weeks or a month before he sent it.

There has been so much rain in the Mountain that it has made a flood in two hours time, the river is very high. Such a sudden raising if part of our Wear had been down, must have carryd it all away which shows the great uncertainty of the weather this year.

Tuesday Morning, July 1st. Set forward with Isaac Wilkinson and John Guest for Bristol to procure proper deeds of conveyance for their five shares in Plymouth work. Left orders with Geo. Lyndon to keep a journal of Weather & Work done etc. in my absence which as underwritten, vizt.

[1] i.e. the New Passage, one of the two landing places on the Welsh side of the Severn used by the ferries to Bristol; see also pp. 82, 85.

GEORGE LYNDON'S JOURNAL
1–14 JULY

July 1st. 20 minutes past five. A Cloudy morning. Wind at West.

9 o'clock Wind at N.W. at 12 Cloudy but fair & very hot, Wind at East. Three o'clock a heavy shower of rain which continued until four attended with Clap of Thunder.

David Lewis with 2 horses carryed 12 Load of clay to the kiln. Edmund Lewis with horse carried Arch stone to Edward Thos. John. The Team with 6 horses & a Yoke of Oxen bro't out 3 pieces of Timber 82 feet, all the Massons at the forebay in the Morning at 9. William Jenkins, Thos. David & Joshua Thomas Scabbling Stone, Harry Wm, Walter Williams, Morgan Evan Jenkins & Hopkin David continued at the Forebay. Labourers two raising Stone, 4 bearing above, 4 bearing below 2 serving Masons 4 at Low Quarry 4 at Common Mortar, 2 at Cardiff Mortar, 4 serving Masons 1 serving Joseph Lucas 1 raising sand.

Lett the cutting the rock under the Arch at 8d per yard in length. Carpenters at several branches of work & Sawyers by 100 feet.

Wedneday July 2nd. A quarter past five a fine morning. Wind at E. Nine o'clock continues fine but cloudy at 12 fair. At four begun to rain and continued until six the Wind at East.

Received from Plymouth Furnace two stamper Boxes weight 2 T 10 cwt 1 qu 14 lb & four bottoms weight 2 T 11 cwt 2 qu 0 lb.

Team with 6 horses & 2 Yokes of Oxen bro't 2 pieces of Timber containing 54 ft. David Lewis with 2 horses carried 12 Load of fire clay to kiln. Edmund Lewis with two horses bro't 8 Loads of Coals to Smiths Shop.

Masons Wm Jenkin scabbling stones forebay. Harry Wm, Walter William, Hopkin David, Morgan Evan Jenkin, Thomas David, & Jos. Thomas, at the forebay.

Labourers 2 raising stones, 1 clearing stones, 1 clearing rubbish, 4 bearing above, 2 bearing below, 2 fetching them to Masons, 3 at the low quarry, 3 at the Common Mortar, 2 at Cardiff Mortar, 3 clearing for Stamper race, 1 serving Joseph Lucas, Carpenters George Ford and his 2 Men, Wm Postlethwaite & Lewis William Edward at the Wear frame.

Nine o'clock at Night fair but cloudy Wind at East.

Thursday July 3rd. A quarter before Six o'Clock, fair but Cloudy, the Wind at East. 9 o'clock fair, at 12 fair, at 6 fair the Wind Westerly.

Received from Plymouth Furnace 2 Stamper boxes 2 T 10 cwt 2 q 14 lb four large plates for mixing upon 1 T 5 cwt 1 q two furnace Mouth plates 3 cwt 3 q.

Team with six horses & 2 Yoke of Oxen brought 2 pieces of Timber 79 feet, David Lewis with two horses carried 13 load of fire clay to kiln. Edmund Lewis with 2 horses brought 13 Load of coal to the Smith shop.

Masons Harry Williams, Walter Williams, Morgan Evan Jenkin, Hopkin David, William Jenkin, Thomas David & Joshua Thomas upon the Forebay.

Labourers 2 raising stones, 4 bearing above, 1 bearing rubbish, 2 bearing stone below, 2 serving Masons, 2 at the Low Quarry, 3 clearing Stamper race, 3 at Common Mortar 2 at Cardiff Mortar & 1 Serving Joseph Lucas.

Carpenter George Ford, his two men, William Postlethwaite & Lewis William Edward at the Wear frame & other odd Jobs.

Wind westerly.

Friday July 4. A quarter before 6 o'clock rains, the Wind westerly. 9 o'clock fair but cloudy 12 fair & very hot.

Horses Team with 6 horses & 4 Oxen bro't 1 piece of Timber 67½ ft. David Lewis with 2 horses carryed 12 Loads of fire clay to kiln. Edmund Lewis with 2 horses brought 10 hurdles.

Masons Harry William, Hopkin David, Walter Williams & Morgan Evan Jenkin Scabbling stones until 9 o'clock. William Jenkin, Thomas Loyd, Thomas David & Joshua Thomas, were all with the first four at the Forebay.

Labourers 2 raising stones, 2 bearing above, 2 bearing below, 3 serving Masons, 2 at the Low quarry, 1 clearing rubbish, 3 at Common Mortar, 2 at Cardiff Mortar, 1 lading water out of hammer race to lay the Sills, 3 clearing Stamper race & 1 serving Joseph Lucas.

9 at night. Fair. The Wind at West.

Saturday July 5th. 5 o'clock A cloudy Morning. Wind at West.

Horses Team with 6 horses brought 1 piece of timber 41 feet. David Lewis with 2 horses carried 12 loads of fire Clay to the kiln. Edmund Lewis with 2 horses leading coals to the familys at Rhyd y Carr.

Masons Walter William, Morgan Evan Jenkins, Thomas David and Joshua Thomas at the forebay.

Joseph Lucas laid the foundation of a Stack for Shingling Furnace.

Labourers. 2 raising stones, 1 clearing rubbish 4 bearing Stones above, 4 bearing stones to the great race, 1 assisting the Smith to shoe oxen, 2 bearing Sand, 3 at Common Mortar, 1 at Carediff Mortar & 1 serving Josh Lucas.

9 at night. Fair Wind Westerely.

Sunday July 6th. A quarter after Six. A fine Morning, Wind westerly continued fair until three, then thundered & rained hard, Wind westerly. 9 at Night fair Wind continues westerly.

Monday July 7th. A quarter before Six o'clock A fair Morning. Wind westerly, continued fair until half past 12. The[n?] Thunder & rain. Three o'clock rain the wind N.W.

Horses 6 horses & 2 Yoke of Oxen brought 2 pieces of Timber 49 feet. David Lewis with 2 horses carryed 12 loads of fire clay to kiln. Edmund Lerwis carryed coals to Llewenkelly & 6 Hurdles to Cyfarthfa.

Masons Henry William, Morgan Evan Jenkin & William Jenkin and Thomas Loyd ½ a day at the Forebay, Hopkin David with Jos. Lucas.

Labourers 2 raising stones at the high quarry, 2 carrying for them 2 bearing below, 3 serving Masons, 1 raising stones at low quarry 4 bearing stones to the Great race, 2 at Common Mortar, 2 at Cardiff Mortar, & 1 Serving Joseph Lucas.

Tuesday 8th July. 5 minutes before six, a rainy Morning, Wind at West, at 9 fair continued all day very hot.

Horses Team 6 horses & 4 Oxen bro't 3 pieces of Timber containing 68 feet. David Lewis with 2 horse carried 12 load of fireclay to kiln and 6 hurdles to Cyfarthfa.

Masons Harry Williams, Morgan Evan Jenkins Scabbling Stone Thomas David, Joshua Thomas ¼ ditto & Hopkin David with Joseph Lucas at the Stack.

Labourers 2 raising stones at the high Quarry, 4 bearing for those, 4 bearing below, 2 raising stone at the lower quarry, 2 carryd to great race 3 at Common mortar, 1 only ¼ at do, 1 cutting the rock below the hutch & 1 with Josh Lucas.

Wednesday July 9th. A quarter before Six a fair morning the Wind easterly, continued fair all day.

Horses The Team with 6 horses bro't 1 piece of Timber 26 feet David & Edmund Lewis bro't with 4 horses 26 Stones from the Wern.

Masons Harry William, Walter William, Morgan Evan Jenkin, William Jenkin, Thomas David & Joshua Thomas at the forebay and Hopkin David with Joseph Lucas at the Stack.

Labourers 2 raising stones in high quarry, 2 bearing from do 3 serving Masons, 2 serving David John 2 raising stone at low quarry, 2 bearing to the great race, 2 at Common Mortar, 2 at Cardiff Mortar, 1 serving Jos. Lucas, 1 lading Water & 2 wheel rock from the hutch.

Thursday, July 10th. Six o'clock a rainy Morning, Wind E. at 9 fair at 11 rain & continued.

Horses Team with 6 horses & 3 Yoke of oxen bro't 4 pieces of Timber 113 feet, David Lewis with 2 horses carryed 12 Load of Clay to kiln. Edmund Lewis with 2 horses brought hurdles.

Masons Harry William, Morgan Evan Jenkin, Tho's David & Joshua Tho's at forebay until rain. Then these with Walter William & William Jenkin Scabbling stones. Hopkin David with Joseph Lucas, untill rain then Scabbled stones.

Labourers 2 raising stones, 4 bearing above, 4 bearing below, 2 raising stone in low quarry each ¾. 2 bearing for ditto at 1 day each, 2 at Common Mortar ¾ each, 2 at Cardiff Mortar 1 day each, 2 wheeling with Clifton ¾ each. 1 serving Joseph Lucas ½ day, 2 bearing Sand ¾ each.

Friday July 11th. A quarter before Six a fair Morning, Wind at S.E. Fair until 11 then began to rain and continued wet until 5.

Horses The Team with 6 horses brought [*Blank*] pieces of Elm Contents [*Blank*] David Lewis & Lewis Traharn with three horses br't 24 stone from the Wern. Edmund Lewis & Wm. Harry with 2 horses carryed Hurdles to Rhyd y Car.

Masons Harry William, Walter William & Morgan Evan Jenkin at the forebay ½ day, these with John Gabriel, Thomas David & Joshua Thomas Scabbling Stones.

Labourers 2 raising at high quarry, 4 bearing above, 4 bearing below, 2 raising in low quarry, 4 bearing to great race, 3 at Common Mortar, 1 at Cardiff Mortar & one serving Joseph Lucas.

Saturday July 12th. 5 minutes before 5 a fair morning. Wind at S.E. Continued fair all day.

Horses Team with 6 horses & 4 Oxen bro't 4 pieces of Timber 100 ft. Edward Lewis with 2 horses bro't hurdles out of the ground to Rhyd y Car.

Masons Harry William, Morgan Evan Jenkin, John Gabriel, Thos. Loyd, William Jenkin & Thomas David at the forebay Hopkin David with Joseph Lucas.

Labourers 2 raising stones in high quarry, 2 bringing stone from thence 2 bearing stones below, 2 digging a Saw pit ½ day, the other ½ day carried stones, 3 at Common Mortar, 1 at Cardiff Mortar, 1 serving Masons, 3 wheeling rubbish & 2 Serving Joseph Lucas.

Sunday July 13th. A quarter after Six, a fair Morning. Wind W. Continued fine until 20 minutes past 2 o'clock then rained at 9 fair the Wind Westerly.

Monday July 14th. A quarter before six a fair morning, Wind Westerly, at 10 begins to rain & continues until one o'clock.

Horses 6 horses & 6 Oxen brought 2 pieces of Timber. David Lewis with 2 horses carried 12 load of fireclay to the kiln. Edmund Lewis with 2 horses brought 32 hurdles for Rhyd y Car.

Masons Harry William, Walter William, Morgan Evan Jenkin, William Jenkin at Forebay, Hopkin David at Stack, John Gabriel & Thomas David, Joshua Thomas Scabbling stone.

Labourers 2 raising stone, 4 bearing stones, 2 at the hurry, 4 bearing Stones below, 2 half a day assisting raising the roofing, 2 more bearing stone, 3 at Common Mortar, 1 at Cardiff Mortar, 1 serving Masons, 3 wheeling rubbish, & 2 Serving Joseph Lucas.

This Ends George Lyndons Journal while I was absent from July 1st to the 14th inclusive when I got to Cyfarthfa.

CHARLES WOOD'S LONDON DIARY
1–14 JULY

July 1st. Set forward at 5 o'clock in the Morning, with John Guest and Isaac Wilkinson towards Bristol. About eight o'clock stoped at Caerphilly & breakfasted, see Mr. Price of Watford.

Set forward about 10 o'clock got to Newport about one, Dined at the sign of the Heath cock at the near end of the Bridge. The landlady who was an obliging carefull woman had been dead a fortnight. Set forward & got to the Rock & Fountain,[1] within 6 Miles of the New Passage where we stayed all that night, had peas & a shoulder of lamb roasted for supper. Set forward about six.

Wednesday July 2 towards the Passage, there breakfasted & posted about 10 & got to Bristol about 2 o'clock, after dinner we talked over the affair in hand vizt. purchasing their shares in Plymouth Works. Then waited upon Mr. Thos. Evans an Attorney below the White hart in the Old Market, and gave him directions to draw up a proper deed of conveyance of their shares with all the rights privileges and advantages they had as Original Lessees & agreeable to an Article of Copartnership masde between them Messrs Wilkinson & Guest.

Thursday July 3rd. Walked about Bristol with Wilkinson until Dinner time, all three dined together. Walked again after Dinner & supped together. Mr. Evans clerk bro't a rough draft of deed read it & agreed to, ordered an Engrossmt.

Fryday, July 4th. Rambled about again with Mr. Wilkinson by the Waterside & happened to be there when the Duke of York[2] went down in a Barge with his Musick in another, returned the Evening to Supper at the White hart in the Old Market.

Saturday July 5th. Waited upon Messrs. Sedgley & Hillhouse & delivered Hillhouse on Fryday the day before Mr. How Letters informing

[1] Still a well-known inn on the main road between Newport and Chepstow and in the eighteenth century often used as a staging-post in the journey to Bristol via the New Passage ferry.

[2] Prince Edward Augustus (1739–67), younger brother of King George III. Created Duke of York 1760; Admiral of the Blue 1766.

them that I was the Standing Partner & was entitled to receive the Balance due to Lowmill Company £148 18s 10d.

Mr. Sedgley not then being at home, Mr. Hillhouse desired I would call again the next day about 11. Accordingly I did & then see Mr. Sedgley, only, after a good deal of talk & he informing me that he had orders from Mr. How to place a parcel of goods sent Younger & Company, amounting to £66 add to said How Debt. I told him I could not agree to that but if he would produce Mr. Hows order for the delivery of those goods to Younger & they would prove that sum, & give me a proper Authority to receive the dividend I would allow it. But I found that he had not any such order but he pretended it was upon the Credit of Mr. How that he trusted Younger. He desired I would call again and asked me to dine with him on Saturday, but as I was for London, the next day, excused myself. The Writing being engrossed & examined, in order to be at a greater certainty & save time, it was thought proper for me to go up in the Fly & carry the Writings for Mr. Bacon to Execute & Accept Bills for the money. Accordingly I took a place & set forward about 10 o'clock on Sunday night and reached London Monday night about 8 o'clock at the Three Cups in Breadstreet, from thence I went to Copthall Court Throgmorten Street, to Mr. Bacons house, but found no one at home but Mrs. Wilkinson, a Servant Maid Mr. Langton & of course being tired I desired a Bed which being ready, I lay untill Seven on Tusday morning, July 8th. Soon I got up & set me down in Mr. Bacons Inner Office when Mr. Bacon & Mr. Richard came from Wanstead. I informed him what I had done & produced the Writing, Breakfasted with him, after he having to go to the Board of Trade, I went with him by Water to Whitehall & then left him appointing to be with him again the next Morning. I went to wait upon Mr. Parritt Plaisterer, in John Street[1] near Hill street Berkley Square, it was after twelve before I got there, sat with Mrs. Parritt near an hour and half about Plymouth affairs, found her a sensible Woman. Mr. Parritt came in gave a deed of Assignment known to be Executed by Wilkinson & Guest to Mr. Evans of Worcester for one share sold by which assignment it appeared that there was a scheme laid to get the work & Stock into the possession of the purchaser of the first Ten Shares, to repay them in the first place for their several sums paid & advanced for the building the work amounting to £2000, whereas they were to be paid out of the Profits only. Mr. Parritt see clearly into their Trap & promised me that

[1] Now Chesterfield Hill, connected to Berkeley Square by Hill Street (B.H. Johnson, *Berkeley Square to Bond Street. The early history of the neighbourhood* (1952), 178–9).

as Mr. Bacon & me were now partners he wd join us to defeat any such purpose & to advance what may be necessary to put the Work in proper condition & a good stock of Mine to be raised, to produce quantities without which no profit could be expected. After Dinner I parted and went to my Brother Cox at the Horseshoe Brew house, found all well staid all night.

Wednesday Morning July 9th. Went to Mr. Bacons at Eight o'clock found Mr. Bacon was come from Wanstead. Breakfasted with him after he read the Ingrossed Deed & we both Executed it & the Bond for performance of Covenant. Drew Two bills for John Guest. One dated this day July 9th on Anthony Bacon payable to John Guest or his order three monthly after date for £440, the other the same date at Six months after date for £444 10s and two bills at Three & Six months to Isaac Wilkinson for £100. Each which four bills Mr. Bacon Accepted. I got a draft upon Charles Argill & Co. for £8 8s. I took my leave of him & called at three Cups in Bread Street in order to take a place in the Fly for that night but they were all taken before for that night and also for Fryday. There was a Mr. Pittman a Plumber in Bristol in the same situation, and we agreed to join in a Post chaise & appointed me to call upon him at Mr. Smith an Ironmanger opposite the White Bear Piccadilly 3 o'clock on Friday morning. Then I went & dined with Brother Cox & one Mr. Asberry, an owner's Son in Bridgenorth was there, upon Turbot and a Green Grass. Staid there all that day & night was called at 2 o'clock. Frank carryed my Bags & Coat and got to Mr. Smith about 3 the time appointed & waited there until near four before the Chaise came & got into it about [*word missing*]. I cannot recollect the several places we called but we got to Bristol about Eleven o'clock on Friday night July 11th. Mr. Pittman sent his servant with me to the White hart in the Old Market found John Guest up. Supped & went to Bed. Lay until seven o'clock informed Mr. Guest & Mr. Wilkinson that I had finished & waited the other part for their Execution. After Breakfast waited upon Sedgley & Hillhouse again after some discourse to the same purport as before they gave up Their claim upon Younger being allowed & told me that they had an order from Mr. How to place the proceeds of the iron the balance amounted to £148 18s 10d to the Credit of Ellison & Gilpin. I desired to see the Letter which they showed me the purport of which was to inform them of his misfortune & desired them to remit that Ballance to Ellison, who had a right to receive it. Their demand upon Ellison & Gilpin was for £107 odd shillings. I told them the Men were good & that I would take their bill upon them for that Sum & the remainder in Cash, which they refused. But placed the proceeds of the Iron to Ellison & Gilpins Credit & wrote a letter to them to draw for the Ballance, but as they refused drawing a bill I appprehended they must be doubtful of their Ballance in Ellison & Gilpin Account, being acknowledged & in such a case my giving them a receipt in full for Lowmill Company would cut us off from any future call upon them, therefore I refused and they refusing to do in any other Shape, I left them & told them that I called last year & had no other business to keep me in Bristol, but there settling that Account. I would make an Affidavit of the debt & endeavour to get it & so we parted. This was after four o'clock in the afternoon. Soon after dinner Mr. Evans Clerk came with the other part & after we had examined it Wilkinson & Guest executed their part & their Bond to perform Covenants & exchanged them paid them the Bills mentioned before as the consideration & so finished. Mr. Guest then gets ready, paid his share of our bill at the Inn & got ready to leave us for Brosley which he did about three o'clock, he paid for their part equally between their 2½ guineas each & me 5 guineas. After I came from Sedgeley & Hillhouse, I waited upon Mr. Evans and informed him the affair in as particular a Manner as I could, he told me they would be obliged to pay & thought they would not stand a Suit and advised me to make an affidavit of the Debt which he said must be in my Name & the Assignees of How & Griffith, Mr. Ellison being a Partner, as Executor his Name sho'd not be in. Which I did, but desired Mr. Evans to inform them before any Writ was Served, which he Mr. Evans proposed himself & then if they would not pay to serve them, for their giving in Bail. After this at night, I sent for Mr. Gundry (Mr. Evans being gone into the Country) & desired he would tell Mr. Evans that I desired every step might be taken in the Gentlest manner & to look over their Acct they offered & if he thought, I was safe in taking them, desired he might do it & told him every particular that passed between Sedgeley & Hillhouse, as near as I could. I borrowed five guineas from Mr. Reeve & gave my Note for it payable to bearer on demand. On Sunday morning I set forward by five o'clock but did not pass before eleven with Mr. Jenkin Post Master in Cardiff, Mr. Thomas William Carpenter, Mr. Howel Boatmen & Mr. Jones of Swansey. We Dined at Newport about four o'clock & got to Cardiff about eight. Went to Mr. Richard & staid with him untill after eleven. Went to the Angel & about Eight on Monday Morning set forward to this place and got here about 2.

See Mr. Thomas Guest in the Vilage & desired to see him, he came here about Six o'clock. I then informed him, that we had purchased Mr. Wilkinsons & his Brothers share & of the conversation I had with Mr.

Parritt. He promised to bring me a list of the deficiencies of the several partners etc.

Tuesday July 15th. Half past Seven, a rainy Morning Little Wind at [*Blank*].

Masons Walter William, Morgan Evan Jenkin, Thomas Loyd and John Gabriel Scabbling stones, likewise Thomas David & Joshua Thomas & Harry William ¼, Hopkin David, with Joseph Lucas at the Stack, David John & his two Masons with a Labourer, Harry William, Edward Thomas John & 2 Masons under him & 1 Labourer are drinking & I suppose are confederating not to work unless such Wages are given as they demand because I refused to give Harry William & Edward Thomas John their demand for Arching.

Labourers 3 raising stones in high Quarry, 4 bearing to Hurry 1 putting them down, 1 taking them from the foot, 4 bearing them from the hurry, 1 clearing rubbish in the quarry, 2 getting Sand, 2 at Common Mortar, 1 riddling Smith dust for mixing with Lime as it is said it binds best with that dust, 1 serving Joseph Lucas. Thomas Clifton & his 2 sons & 3 men at the rock where the Shingling Furnace are to be, these have been omitted by George Lyndon.

Horses brought 2 pieces timber containing 54 feet. David Lewis carryed 12 load of fire clay to kiln.

Carpenters George Ford his two men, William Postlethwaite & Lewis William Edwards at the frame of the Wear. Two pair of Sawyers, Sawing p. 100 feet 3s 2d those & Carpenters were omitted by George Lyndon.

Three Labourers upon Bargain in grand race. One ditto upon bargain on the farr wheel case wall in rock to be blasted. Edward Farnels & his Men upon the roofs of the Squares.

Wednesday July 16th. Seven o'clock a Cloudy Morning but fair the Wind West. Breakfast time 9 o'clock. Fair. Agreed with Henry William for walling & Arching the grand race at 4s p. yard in Length, the former Bargain with Edward Thomas John was 5s 6d p. yard because I would not give him the same price he prevailed upon the several Masons mentioned yesterday to leave their Work and go with him to the Ale house and all were much in Liquor, quarreled and fought, as I am informed for whch I have discharged him, altho' we are in want of Masons, as he is a very dangerous man in a Work & capable of corrupting those who, otherwise, would stick close to their work. And for the building above the forge at 4d p. Perch & for the farr hammer hatch wall, at Common Walling price, he being paid for Scabbling & preparing the stones to lay in Cardiff Lime, next the Water, by the day.

Eleven o'clock a strong West Wind with showers of rain.

Six o'clock some showers the Wind ceased.

Masons Harry William, Morgan Evan Jenkin, at the Arch for a passage through the hutch between the forge & the Stamping house. John Gabriel, Thomas Loyd, Thomas David & Joshua Thomas at the hammer hutch, William Jenkin underpinning the great Arch, where the rock was sunk under it.

David John & one Mason upon the Pine end of flourishing house upon bargain.

Edward Thomas John, & 2 more Masons, walling for Arch in the great race taken at 4s p. yard by Harry William he employ these men.

Hopkin David with Joseph Lucas at the Stack for Shingling Furnace.

Labourers 2 raising stones in the high quarry, 2 raising Stones in the low quarry, 4 bringing stones to the hurry, one puting them down, 1 taking them from the foot, 1 cleaning rubbish, 4 bearing stone, to Masons, 2 carrying stone to David John, 3 at Common Mortar, 3 at Cardiff Mortar, 1 serving mason & 1 serving Joseph Lucas, Thomas Clifton, his 2 sons & 3 more cutting the rock for shingling Furnace, Those clearing the race for great Arch p. bargain.

Horses 6 with 3 yoke of Oxen brought 2 pieces of Timber 48½ ft. David Lewis with 2 horse carrying fire clay to the kiln, with 3 horses carryed Tyle from Aberdare.

Carpenters George Ford his two men bored wood for laying in the hammer hatch to convey water to the hammer & washg house. Wm Postlethwaite & Lewis William Edward at Wear frame. Four sawyers sawing for 3s 2d for 100 feet.

Edward Farnel & his Man upon the roof p. Bargain.

Thursday July 17th. Six o'clock a cloudy Morning. Six at night a fine day. Begun clearing for Wear 16 Labourers at Wear. Harry William & Hopkin David, Masons, each ¼, with the Carpenters George Ford, his two sons, Wm. Postlethwaite and Lewis William Edward.

Masons at the hammer Hutch Henry William ¾, Hopkin David ¾ Morgan Evan Jenkin, John Gabriel, Thomas Loyd, Thomas David, & Joshua Thomas.

Horses 6 brought 2 pieces of Timber containing 50½ feet, David Thos. 2 horses carried 12 L Clay to kiln.

Sawyers 4 sawing by 100 feet at 3s 2d for roofs. Edward Farnel & his Men framing the roof by Bargain.

This day I took from Gervas Powell vicar of this Parish all the great & small Tythes vizt. Wheat, Barley, Oats, Lambs, Wool, Geese, Hide, Pigs, Honey & Easter offering within the Hamlet of Gellideg, at the yearly rent of £29 & four fat Geese, payable in May & November, the first payment to be made in Nov. 1767. This Hamlet takes in all our farms as also the whole district of Lord Talbot & Mr Richard Liberty, therefore I thought it right to take it to prevent any dispute or trouble from any other person that might Lease it. The term is 11 years.

Friday July 18th. Six o'clock rainy morning.

Eight o'clock it took up & is fair. All hands in general upon the Wear vizt.

Masons Joseph Lucas, Harry William, Walter William, Morgan Evan Jenkin, Hopkin David, Thomas Loyd, John Gabriel, Thomas David, Jos. Thomas, William Jenkin, Edward Thomas John, David John, John Jones, David Humphry, John Richard, Morgan William, 16 in Number.

Labourers Thomas Clifton, Jack Clifton, Robert David, Howel Rhys, Howel Powel, William John William, Thomas John William, John William, Evan William, Evan Harris, Llewellin John, David Lewis, John David, David John, John Jones, Thomas John, Edwd William, Thomas Price, John Watkin, Wm. Edw. Rhys, Henry Richard, Luellin Edwards, Watkin Rhys, William Richard Rhys, Christmas David, James Thomas, John David Williams, William Robert, William Clifton, Thomas William Luellen & his son & Aaron Wedgwood, 32 in number.

Carpenters George Ford, his two men, William Postlethwaite, & Lewis William Edward 5 in Number.

Horses 7 brought 2 pieces of Timber containing 45 feet David Lewis with 2 horses carryed 12 L of clay to kiln. with 3 horses bro't Slate or Tyle.

Sawyers 4 sawing roofing @ 3s 2d p. 100 feet. Edward Farnell has been framing roofs upon Bargain. This has been a fine day & warm.

Saturday July 19th. Six o'clock a fine warm Morning.

All hands at the Wear vizt.

Masons Joseph Lucas, Harry William, John Gabriel, David John, Edward Thomas, Hopkin David, Thomas Loyd, Tho's David ¾, Joshua Thomas ¾, John Richard, John Jones, David Humphry and Morgan William, 13 in number, 3 Masons went to Caerphilly Fair.

Labourers Howel Rhys, Thomas Clifton, Howel Powel, Thos. John William, William Robert, John David William, Evan Williams, Luellen John, David Lewis, John David, Edward William, Tho. Price, John Jones, Thomas John, William Edward Rhys, William Richd. Rhys, Christmas David, Llewellyn Brod his Son, Mary David, William Black, Moses Abraham Evan, William Abraham Evans, Evan Abraham, Aaron Wedgewood & Thomas William Smith 25 in Number.

Carpenters George Ford, Joseph Gibson, David Milligan, William Postlethwaite & Lewis William Edward 5 in Number.

Horses 7 brought 2 pieces of Timber containing 61½ feet

Sawyers 4 Sawing roofs @ 3s 2d p. 100 feet.

David Lewis 2 horses carrying 12 L of clay to kiln. Edward Farnel framing roof p. Bargain.

Sunday July 20th. Eight o'clock a fine Warm Morning Nine o'clock Breakfast at the Rock, with George Ford, Joseph Lucas & George Lyndon. Stayed within untill past 10, Then we all went to Lewenkelly. All well there, at near Eleven went to Rhyd y Carr all well there, but James Mason who was poorly, he shaked on Saturday. But they all thought that he looked better than he had done.

After 12 o'clock we all went down to the Vilage & dined before one. This being a yearly meeting of Mr. Samuel Davies a Dissenting Minister[1] in Chapel, Numbers of that Sect, come from all parts, which occasioned every Publick House full of these people therefore we left Edward Morgan soon after we had dined. I went alone to Thomas Guest but as he had not dined I left him & returned to the rock. He and his brother in Law (who is a farmer & understands the Management of Land from Shropshire) came to speak to me, to talk about the case of both Plymouth Company Land and our three farms, Rhyd y Carr, Lewenkelly & Cwm Glo. He proposed to view the Land, which John Morgan shew him, by going with him through the whole.

We all took a walk about the work, untill near Seven. David John daughter brought a few Bilberry & Rhys David Son some Wood strawberrys & milk which my Brother in Law, Mr. Parry, George Lyndon & myself partook of. After Eight George Ford & Joseph Lucas came in. My Brother & Edward Parry went to their Lodging at the Vilage. At Nine went to bed.

Monday July 21st. Past Six o'clock a rainy Morning. Calm a great Fogg therefore hope that it may take up about Nine o'clock.

About Nine, it took up & has been a fine day. We have gone on with the Wear briskly having let part of it to David John & his three Men. Henry William & four others at 6d p. Square yard the setting, And then supplying them with Setting stones by eight Labourers at 3d p. squ. yard.

[1] Samuel Davies (d. 1781), minister of Ynysgau chapel, Merthyr Tydfil, 1750–81. Son of James Davies, minister of Cwm-y-glo and Ynysgau, 1724–60: *Dictionary of Welsh Biography*, sn. James Davies; see also below, p. 127, for the chapel.

Hopkin David, Walter William ½ a day, Thomas Loyd & John Gabriel, were not willing to take any part by the yard therefore they work upon it by the day & they do well there being an Emolation[1] which shall do most.

Labourers upon day wages vizt. Thomas Clifton, Rhys Howel Rhys, Thomas John William, William Robert, Evan Harris, David Lewis, John David, Thomas Price, Thomas John, ½ day, James Thomas, William Richd Rhys, Christmas David, Henry Richard, Thomas William Smith, ½ day, Wm Black, Aaron Wegwood, Llewellin Edward his son, John Clifton, Wm Clifton, Mary David, William Harry, Moses Abraham, William Abraham, & Evan Abraham. In Number 24.

Carpenters George Ford, his two men, Wm Postlethwaite and Lewis William Edward.

Horses brought 1 piece of Timber containing 29½ feet forward. David Lewis with 2 horses carried 12 Load of Clay to the kiln.

Sawyers 4 sawing roof timber at 3s 2d p. 100 feet. Edward Farnels & his men framing roofs p. bargain.

I was this morning with Thomas Guest viewing the Plymouth Furnace. I observe, that their Dam to convey the water to the Wheel is too Narrow, and low. The bridge too low to take all the water in a flood, which occasion the high road to be overflowed, & if not remedied will occasion an Indictment. The Mine comes in much faster than I expected but is very foul and dirty by which there is paid a higher carriage as well as for raising, & if weighed before burnt, must defraud the furnace of the quantity and as it is newly raised, the Shale or Shell is put in with it, which occupy the space that good Mine should & consequently the furnace cannot produce so much metal, but will consume the same quantity of Coke, as it would, if it was all clean Mine. Where coal is near, I think the Mine should be burnt upon the spot it is raised this would save in the Carriage, as the Mine would be lighter & the Shale left behind. I walked to see the New pit Sinking about 700 yards from the furnace. when finished the coal will be raised at 18d p. Ton or 21 cwt & if a rail or waggon way is laid (as Terry proposes to do it for £130) the carriage will be small. Thomas Guest says that two horses will supply the furnace. The Bellows loose a deal of wind & the keepers do not take the proper care of the furnace. The tuère was black, upon the whole I do not think that this furnace will produce any profit under the present Management. If the nose of the pipes of the Bellows were wider, & to blow into one it would be better.

[1] Wood appears to mean that there was competition between the masons.

Tuesday July 22. A quarter before Six, a cloudy, but fair Morning. One o'clock a fair Warm day. The Wear goes on briskly.

After Six o'clock this has been a fine day and the Wear has gone on well.

Masons by days wages vizt. Walter William, Hopkin David, John Gabriel, Thomas Loyd & Joshua Thomas, David Thomas & 3 men Sttg stone by yard @ 6d. Edwd. Thos., Henry William & 3 more Setting by the Yard 6d.

Labourers as mentioned yesterday Serving Masons at 3d p. Yard.

Labourers p. days wages Thomas Clifton, Howel Rhys, Wm Robert, Jo'n David William, Evan Harris, David Lewis, John David, Tho's Price, John Jones, Thomas John, Wm Edwd Rhys, James Thomas, Wm Rbt Rhys, Christmas David, Thos Wm Smith, Wm Black, Aaron Wedgwood, Evan Abraham, Wm Abraham, Moses Abraham, John Clifton, Wm. Clifton, Edwd Lewellin, Thomas William, & Mary David. In No 25.

Horses brought 2 pieces of Timber containing 51¾ feet. David Lewis with 3 horses carried 5 turn of Clay & 15 load of Coal to the kiln.

Carpenters, as yesterday.

Sawyers as yesterday & Edwd Farnel & his men upon framing the roofs.

Mr. Anthony Richardson sent me John Harris's Letter found among his paper contained Spedding Hicks & Co.[1] note so long wanted.

Wednesday July 23. A quarter past five o'clock a fine warm morning, quite calm.

About one o'clock began to rain, continued Showery. The river raised a little which I am afraid will give us trouble in turning the water to lay the remainder of the frame for the Wear, three parts is fixed. Ordered John Morgan to go with the Wagon tomorrow to Cardiff to fetch Clay Mill rolls, & sundry things bought at Bristol & to take in the Waggon 30 cwt of pig iron from Plymouth Furnace, they carry it up on the top of the Hill where the Waggon receive it.

Masons p. day wages Walter William, Hopkin David, Jon. Gabriel, Thomas Loyd & Joshua Thomas.

David John & his 3 men setting stones in the Wear at 6d yard. Harry William Edward, Thos. John & 3 men setting ditto, at 6d p. yard.

Labourers who serve the Masons with stones @ 3d p. yard they fetch them from the Quarry vizt. Wm John, Wm Wm, Richard William, Thos.

[1] Of Seaton furnace, near Workington (Cumb.): Riden, *Gazetteer*, 120–1.

Jon, Wm Wm, Richard William, John Wm Evan & Wm Howel Powel, Lewelin John, Edward William & John Watkin, 8 in Number.

Labourers p. day Rhys David, Howel Rhys, Thomas Clifton, Wm Robert, in the Quarry John David Wm, Evan Harris, David Lewis, John David, Thomas Price, John Jones, David John, James Thomas, William Richard Rhys, Christmas David, Harry Richard, Aaron Wedgwood, Moses Abraham, Evan Abraham ¾, William Abraham, John Clifton, William Clifton, Edward Lewelyn, Thos Wm, Mary David, Thomas Wm Smith & William Black. In Number 26.

Horses brought 1 piece of Timber containing 22 feet. David Lewis with 3 horses carryd Clay & Coal to kiln.

Carpenters George Ford, his 2 Men, Wm Postlethwaite & Labourer William Edward at Wear.

Sawyers 4 Sawing Roof Timber p. 3s 2d for 100 ft. Edward Farnels & his Men framing the roofs & floorings.

Thursday July 24th. Half past five o'clock. The Morning is overcast & looks very like rain. About Seven it began to rain & has rained all day. The river higher but I hope the Wear is secure. Six o'clock the rain has continued to this time & very like to do so. Wrote to Mr. Gale junior, my daughter Betty & Doctor Brownrigg, enclosed Messrs. Spedding Hicks & Company Note to the Doctor & a Letter for William Nicholson. As the water was high & it run strong thro' the Sluice in the near end of the Wear, I employed several Labourers to thro the rubbish into the stream which carryed it clean off, the most ready method to get rid of it out of the high pool next the flood gates. All the panes in the Wear being sett & finished, that were ready, the Masons upon days wages were employed this afternoon in Scabbling stones for the Stacks vizt. Thomas Loyd, Hopkin David, John Gabriel & Jos. Thomas Labourers Rhys David, Howel Rhys, William Robert, David Lewis, John David, John Jones, Thomas John, William Edward Rhys, Wm Richd Rhys, David John, William Black, Aaron Wedgwood, Moses Abraham, William Abraham, Evan Abraham, Henry Richard, Thos. William Smith, 17 in Number all of them a day each.

Labourers combined Thomas Clifton ½ day, Wm John Williams ¼, Thomas John William ¼, Howel Powel ¼, Evan William ¼, Evan Harris ½, Edward William ¼, James Thomas ½, John Clifton ½, & William Clifton, Edward Lewelin ½, William Harry ½.

Carpenters George Ford, his two men, William Postlethwaite and Lewis William Edward worked very hard in the rain to secure the Wear as did Joseph Lucas. The Masons & Labourers, work daily in the water, therefore to encourage them I give drink to some & advanced wages to others who do not chose drink.

Sawyers 4 Sawing roofing @ 3s 2d for 100 feet.

Horses & Waggon at Cardiff. David Lewis leading clay in the morning, but the rain drove him off.

Edward Farnels & his men at the Low furnace putting in hub in furnace wheel, which ought to have been done before, but Terry neglected it.

Gave William David 5 Letters for his son to take to the Post Office in Brecon, tomorrow morning, & bring back what Letters there may be for me etc.

A strong gale at South Wind, in the morning, abated before Noon.

Fryday July 25th. A quarter before Six o'clock. This morning is overcast, there has been a deal more rain, the river high, little wind at S.W.

Six o'clock, this has been a day for work, but showery. The river fell, and rose again, by a deal of rain, in the Mountain, as I suppose.

Masons Hopkin David, John Gabriel & Thomas Loyd, Scabbling Stones for the Stacks.

Labourers four saving a Ladder that was carryed away by the flood & bearing stones to the great race, 6 bearing Stones in the high quarry, one at the hurry, one at the foot of it, Thomas Clifton ¾ with 3 more & 2 Labourers wheeling rock. 5 Men with Mary David & Cornelius Thomas wheeling & carrying rubbish against the inside of the Wear & 2 in placing it.

George Ford, his 2 men, Wm Postlethwaite & Lewis Wm Edward at the clay Mill wheel.

Sawyers 2 Sawing joists & rafters, the other two sawyers not here, Edward Thomas John & his two men upon the mixing room by Bargain Henry Williams & his Man upon the great race Arch @ 4s p. yard squ. length.

Three labourers, the Abrahams, upon their bargain in clearing the Walling & Arching the great race.

Edward Farnel & & his Men raised the Mixing Room Garret floor, and roof. The Horse at Cardiff with Waggon which I ordered to stay there a day to draw all the Bellows plank together & put in a store until wanted.

Saturday July 26th. Six o'Clock a fine clear calm Morning Wind but only a little at South West.

The river is faln but not so much in the time as usual, which I impute the Springs & small brooks being quite filled with the great quantity of rain that has falled these last three days.

Masons John Gabriel only upon days wages, Scabbling stone for Stack.

Labourers at Wear 8 filling & wheeling to the inside of the Wear & making a dam to drain the water for laying the remainder of the frame. 6 in the quarry, 2 bearing Sand, 2 raising stones at Low quarry, 4 Serving Masons at great race. Thomas Clifton, his 2 sons & 3 Men at the Rock. The three Abrahams clearing at the great race p. Bargain, & 1 sinking in the rock for hammer race. Total in Number 32.

David John, Mason & his 3 Men upon Clay mill p. bargain. Edward Thomas John & his 2 men, Masons, upon Mixing Room p. bargain, Harry William & his Man Arching great race at 4s p. yard in length.

Horse & Waggon at Cardiff to fetch Clay Mill rolls etc. David Lewis with 2 horses carrying 15 turns of Clay to kiln. Edward John Morgan with 3 horses fetching Tyle from Aberdare.

Carpenters George Ford his man David & Wm Postlethwaite at the Clay mill wheel. Lewis Wm Edward & Joseph Gibson at the Wear, nailing listings on the top next the pool.

Sawyers 2 Sawing boards for the Clay mill wheel p. days wages.

This has been a fine day.

Wrote a Letter to Mr. Tho. Morgan by Edward Parry, for money for a bill drawn by Edward Parry, as it is not known what sum he can spare.

Sunday July 27th. Half past Seven o'clock. A rainy morning, but the river is much lower, therefore conclude it has been a fair night. The Wind westerly.

Eight o'clock there has been rain all day, a large flood the Wind at W. it looks like a continueance of rain. Staid within all day, with George Lyndon, Ford & Joseph Lucas our Landlady sent Dinner for one only, expecting all would have gone to vilage to dine, except me. I dined upon Bread & cheese, and drank water & the Meat & Beer, the Men & Geo. Lyndon got. I wrote my wife, that if Affairs in Cumberland would allow me to remain here all Winter, to come here by way of London, but if I was to return home, in September, as Mr. Ellison wrote me than it would be too fatiguing, but I would bring her at my return. I wrote to the Doctor, to the same purpose.

Sam & Edward Parry came, about three & staid with me untill near eight.

George Ford & Joseph Lucas went to Rhyd y Carr, but are not yet returned, returned between 8 & 9 o'clock. James Mason is much better, but Aaron Wedgwood is ill with the Rheumatism. I put goose grease to warm & [*word illegible*] to dissolve to be ready for Jos. Lucas & those who are troubled with that disorder.

Monday July 28th. Half past Six o'Clock a rainy Morning. The Wind westerly. Very cool weather for the Season. Seven o'clock. Evening has been a fine day since Nine o'Clock in Morning.

Masons John Gabriel only, Scabbling stones for Stack p. day. Edward Thomas John & one Man upon Mixing room. Harry William & one man upon the Great Race Arch. David John & 2 Men upon the Clay Mill.

Labourers 2 in the quarry, 2 serving stones to David John Mason 2 raising stones in Low quarry, 2 carrying stones to great race, 2 carrying Sand. Clifton ¾ his 2 sons ½ & 1 man 1 day wheel rock from Forge.

Wear 9 Labourers backing the wear, 1 beginning the dam to run the water for laying the remainder of the frame the third time. It has been washed down by floods twice.

Carpenters Geo. Ford his two men, William Postlethwaite and Lewis William Edward at the Stamper wheel it being upon the frame, it was thought best to finish it & then put up the Clay Mill Wheel.

Sawyers 2 Sawing at 3s 2d p. 100 feet the other two have not been at work of several days past.

Joseph Lucas Scabbling stones for foundation of Stack. A cold whistling wind at West denote more rain.

Gave Thomas Guest a copy of letter to be sent to each proprietor at Plymouth Furnace and some particulars for him to prepare state of the Work etc. to lay before the Company at their meeting, he came here and informed me that Terry had discharged several of the Colliers and counteracts him in all the directions he gives, this method of proceeding must be greatly prejudicial to the proprietors. There ought to be no more than one Manager & him to be answerable for any neglect, or wrong proceedings.

Sir   Merthyr July 28, 1766.

You are Ernestly desired to meet the rest of the proprietors of the Plymouth Furnace [*Blank*] on the [*Blank*] of August next when and where a full & clear state of the Company Affairs, will be laid before you; When also it will be proper, to consult what method will be expedient to pursue, in order to carry on the same for the future more profitably for all concerned; And what further advances will be necessary for that purpose. I am Sir

Yours obedient Servant
T. Guest
Agent at the Plymouth Furnace.

In order to form a clear state of the Plymouth Work, to lay before the Company at their next meeting It will be necessary to take an Inventory of the Stock in hand; the debts due, to & from the Company. The Books settled, in a regular method, & Ballanced. The Quantity of Mine, Coal etc. with the several rates they have costed at, & prepared for the furnace. An Estimate of a railway and of other necessary Alterations & repairs. The quantity of Mine that ought to be raised & brought upon the furnace bank, for a long Blast, & all other materials for that purpose in order to send metal to Market on such a footing, as to answer the End proposed by the proprietors vzt. Dividing a profit. Without this it will be in vain to Expect that the work can be continued long, as the proprietors must be weary in advancing when there is not any probability of a return. Gave the letter & this to Thomas Guest this day.

There is a writ served upon 2 of the Workmen for a Trespass in getting Mine & as T. Guest informs me there is an agreement signed by the Tennant for leave at certain which Mr. White has in his possession and as the Writ is returnable next Tuesday night he was obliged to go to Mr. White at Bridgnorth for that Agreement. Therefore he set forward this afternoon.

The underwritten from Mr. Terry

Plymouth Works July 28th 1766
Sundry Articles requisite for Establishing the said Works
so as to continue in blast vizt.

		£	s	d
1.	A railway as p. Estimate	130	13	11
2.	Three kilns to burn the Mine	36	-	-
3.	An Air Furnace to Melt a Ton of Lime	22	10	-
4.	A stable with Store rooms & 2 dwellings over	75	-	-
5.	To Coal Work with 2 pitts	12	15	-
6.	A stock of Pitwood	10	-	-
7.	Level head to drain the Mine 14 yards	70	-	-
8.	Six Months Stock of Mine on the Bank or 1248 Ton at 5s 4d p. Ton	270	11	-
9.	Deal planks 100 for boxes & patterns	18	-	-
10.	Drs & cr equal	-	-	-
11.	Stock in Trade for 6 Months Cr.	1152	-	-
		1797	9	11

If all the iron be sold to Mr. Wood & Co. in grains & pigs, as proposed to draw for the Cash in 3 Months the bills payable one Month after date, then 4 Months Stock in Bank is only required

	£		
	576	-	-
Convenient for Shelling	10	-	-
Brought down above the Stock	655	9	11
	1241	9	11

Observations. I do not see any charge for Lime Stone, Wages Sand and several Incidents Charges that must unavoidable happen. There cannot be too large a stock of Mine, as the Air and time will meliorate it, clear it of the Shale or Shell by which the metal will be so much better, as to pay more than double the Interest of the money it will take to lay in a large Stock.

There are several other alternatives that are necessary to be made before this Furnace can be in a proper state for profit not mentioned in Mr. Terry's Estimate vizt. The Bellows altered for a better Blast. The nose of the pipes widened, & blow into one pipe. The Wheel raised or a back race drove to free it of Back water. The Dam to be raised & the Water in a flood, to be prevented going into the high road. To prevent an Indictment from the Parish. The Stack to be raised higher & to make it still more Compleat in order to turn out a larger quantity of metal, & of a better quality, lay aside the Leather Bellows & fix in their room Cylinders.

Robert Wilson & John Edge have burnt a kiln of firebrick, but they are so Tender from the wett weather & their want of skill in setting them in the kiln that they will not bear carriage upon a horse back. Therefore I sent Aaron Wedgewood our Potter to instruct them in setting them better and draw the flame through them the want of which, I apprehend to be the chief cause of their miscarriage. Aaron Wedgwood informed me this night that he had been with them all day, & he believed they would do better, but that the bricks were so coted with the wet weather, they cold not be expected to turn out so good as in dry weather.

Tuesday July 29th. Past Six o'clock a rainy Morning. The largest flood we have had this year by which I conclude that it has rained all night. The Water runs over the Wear, the vacancy, where the frame is not fixed, of 5 panes & the double Sluice, not being sufficient to receive the whole quantity of water.

One o'clock. Showers untill now. The Masons could not lay stones in Mortar. The river continued high, no damage done to the Wear, or backing.

Lett the remainder of the great race, to the junction of the two hammer race & those two; to Evan Abraham & his partner; at the same rate as the other cut, that he has finished, he to take the chance of the hardness of the rock but we finding gunpowder to blast where necessary. The rate is 4d for the Earth & 8d p. yard for the Rock. This is the same that was given to David Penry & his partners. 4 of these Labourers.

Masons John Gabriel, Hopkin David, & Thomas Loyd ½ day each scabbling stones it being rain, and the other ½ day laying stone in the Stack.

Harry William, Edwd Thos John & 2 Men upon their Bargain the mixing room this afternoon, the morning, the rain prevented 'em. David John & his three men upon their Bargain the Clay Mill ½ day.

Labourers 4 bearing stones out of the quarry upon the bank for carts to fetch them to the race Arch, 3 bearing stands, 2 clearing the mixing room & carrying the rubbish to fill up the Clay Mill, Thomas Clifton his 2 sons & 2 Men cutting the rock for Air furnace and carrying into the river, 2 carrying stands to Daniel John, & clearing the Pool of Cobble stones & one throwing them over the river. 19 in No.

Carpenters George Ford, his 2 men, William Postlethwaite, Lewis William John at the Stamper wheel, & preparing Wood for the inside of the Clay Mill rolls.

Sawyers 2 Sawing shrouds for wheels @ 3s 2d p. 100 feet.

Past seven o'clock this has been a fine afternoon & the river is lowered. The Wind at S. West.

Wednesday July 30th. Six o'clock a rainy morning. The Wind but little, at S.E.

Nine o'clock continues rain. No Masons can lay Mortar, but some Labourers work in throwing stone out the Pool & clearing the Mixing room & filling the Claymill floor level with the door. The Labourers who have taken the digging for the great race upon bargain are likewise at work upon it.

Near Eight o'clock. Wind at S.W. There has been rain all this day, little work done.

Masons Hopkin David, John Gabriel & Thomas Loyd preparing stones under the shade for the Stack, per day.

None of the Masons by bargain would work.

Labourers 2 raising stones ¼ day, 4 bearing ¼, 6 clearing in the pool ¼, 2 clearing the Mixing room 1 day, do ¼, 4 bearing stone ready for Masons in Bargain ¼, 2 bearing sand, 1 at Mortar ½ & 1 do ¼.

Carpenters George Ford, his 2 men, Wm Postlethwaite & Lewis Wm making Bucket boards under the shade

Sawyers 2 sawing odd piece for sundry uses @ 3s 2d p. 100 feet.

Lett unto John William & Edward William the filling up the great race upon the Arch about 40 yards in Length for 18s & if I see that is a hard bargain, to give them 3s more.

Lett unto Hopkin David, John Gabriel & Thomas Loyd, Masons, the building of a necessary house 6 feet by 5 at 10d p. Perch which is 18 feet in lenght one foot high, & 2 feet thick. To have the stone & Mortar delivered them upon the spot & the foundation dug ready for them.

Agreed with Reece David & his partner to serve the Masons with stone from the great Quarry, for the great race Arch @ 8d p. yard in length for one length of Arching as a tryal & if they cannot get wages then they have liberty to quit the Bargain. But in order to enable them to make wages I have made them a way behind the Office to carry them to the nearest road to the race.

Horses Team at home since the floods as the Timber must be brought through the river. David Lewis with 2 horses carryed 18 Load of coal from Penwane, the level not being brought up to that coal, near the Brick kiln. The other horses at grass to recruit,[1] being worn down by Work & the bad weather.

Thursday July 31st. Past Six o'clock a fair Morning but overcast & very like rain. Wind at W. a little to the Southward. Nine o'clock rain and after cleared up & proved a fine day until near One o'clock but cloudy & very like showers. Past six o'clock this has been a fine warm day & I am in great hope the weather will take up & settle.

Brother and I have been to Plymouth Furnace, they go on much at the same rate, very uncertain, both in quantity & quality. Mr. Terry gave me the underwritten Estimate to look over vizt.

[1] To rest and recuperate.

An Estimate of the yearly Expenses of Plymouth Furnace supposing the Iron to be sold to the Cyfarthfa Company, as per proposals delivered.

	Ton		£	s	d	£	s	d
Mine from David Thomas's Land	1446	@ 1s	£72	6	-			
Do raising		@ 3/9	270	18	6			
Do carriage		@ 1/4	96	8	-	439	12	6
Mine from Company side 1446 T raising		@ 3s	216	18	-			
Do carriage		@ 1/4	96	8	-	313	6	-
Coals 2469 Waggons each 36 cwt 3/9 p.			383	15	-			
Do Tickets & Workmen			20	-	-	403	15	-
Lime stone 728 Tons Labour delivered on bank		@ 3/9				136	10	-
Ground rents & damages						100	-	-
General repairs if continued in blast						80	-	-
Clerks salarys & Incidents						70	-	-
Riding charges						20	-	-
General Incidents & small sundries						20	-	-
Weighing Lime Stone & Mine 3610 T		@ 1½d				22	11	3
Workmen, 2 keepers @ £1 7s						70	4	-
						1675	18	9
Workmen for 20 Ton of Castings		@ 5s				5	-	-
2 Fillers @ 21s Stocker of bridge 10s, & Mine burners 8s						101	8	-
Lime stone breaker		@ 8	20	16	-			
Cynder wheeler		@ 7	17	14	-			
Unloader of the Coals		@ 7	17	14	-	56	4	-
Coaking 3800 Ton at 4½d p. Ton						70	18	10
Carpenters @ 12s, Smiths		@ 18s						
& Labourers		@ 7s				95	14	-
Total charge for one year						£2005	3	7

Produces p. year	£	s	d		£	s	d	£	s	d
650 T of grain Iron	@ 4	2	6	p. Ton	£2681	5	-			
20 of Castings	5	12	6	do	112	10	-			
20 of Pig Iron	4	-	-	do	80	-	-			
10 of Scull & Scraps	@ 2	10	-	do	25	-	-			
					2898	15	-			
Profit p. Annum								893	11	5
								2898	15	-

Totals vizt.	£	s	d
Mine @ 2892 T @ 5s 2½d p. Ton	752	18	6
Coals 4493 @ 2s 1d	383	15	-
Limestone 728 T @ 3s 9d p. Ton	136	10	-
Coking @ 4½d	70	18	10
Wages	371	1	3
Ground rent & damages	100	-	-
General repairs	80	-	-
Clerk, Incidents & charges	90	-	-
General Incidents & small Sundries	20	-	-
	2005	3	7

All 4 ton of Stone, & 6 ton of coal to the Ton of metal & nearly ¼ of Lime to the stone, the metal at first cost about £8 p. Ton & about 25s p. Ton profit upon [*blank*] of metal.

Masons Hopkins David, John Gabriel & Thomas Loyd Scabbling ½ day work. Harry Williams & Edward Thomas, with 2 Men upon the great race Arch at 4s yard in length 8 feet wide in clear, David John & his Men upon the Clay Mill p. bargain

Carpenters five upon Sundry work, Wheel, Bucket boards & Door Cases.

Sawyers 2 sawing General work.

Labourers 2 raising stones, 1 clearing rubbish in the quarry, 3 at Common Mortar, 4 carrying sand to the Lime, 2 bearing stones to David John, 7 cleaning the Pool of Stones, 2 half a day clearing a foundation for a necessary house, 1 carrying Stone, Six serving Arch stones at the great race at 8d p. yard in Length, Clifton, his 2 sons & 3 more cutting the rock for an Air furnace for Shingling.

Horses Team brought 2 pieces of Beech containing 44 feet David Lewis with 2 horses carryed 18 load of coal to the Brick kiln and 3 load for the use of the Office & 2 horses brought 2 turns of Tyles from Aberdare. Total 200 in Number.

Evan Abraham & his Men 4 more at the great race p. bargain.

Fryday August 1st. A quarter past six a fine Warm Morning but overcast. The Wind at W. a little to the N.

This has been a fine warm day. We begun the dam again to turn the river, in order to lay the remainder of the frame for the Wear. The horses were ordered to draw Timber this day into the Road, to be ready at any time when wanted, bro't 2 pieces of timber 60½ feet. David Lewis with 5 horses at the Hay.

Masons Hopkin David, John Gabriel & Thomas Loyd, with Joshua Thomas, at Necessary House.

David John & 3 more at his Bargain upon Clay Mill. Harry William, & 3 more upon the Walling & Arching great race.

Carpenters George Ford, his 2 men, William Poastlethwaite & Lewis William John Squaring Stamper shafts & forge helves.

Sawyers Two sawing joists for the floor over the Buildings for dweling of Workmen.

Agreed with David John, to allow him 6d p. Perch, to serve him self with stone for the building that he has undertaken p. Bargain, he breaking, & making use of the stones now in the Pool.

Labourers at the Wear making the Dam to return the river 12 for ½ day & 8 the other ½ day. Thomas Clifton, his two sons & 3 men taking up the rock for Air Furnace, 4 loading Stones to the great Arch, 3 making Mortar, 2 bearing Sand & 2 bearing Stones to David John.

Saturday, August 2nd. A quarter past six, a rainy morning. Calm.

Eleven o'clock continues rain, the river rises, and I am afraid the Dam for turning it, to lay the remainder of the Wear frame, will be washed down a third time?

Six o'clock, Continued rain, a big flood, the Water runs over the part of the Wear that is finished, notwithstanding the Sluice & about 40 feet of the old channel of the river open. Very little done this day.

Masons Hopkin David, John Gabriel, Thomas Loyd & Josh Thomas, Scabbling Air furnace Stack stones. No other mason at Work either by day or bargain.

Labourers 4 with Joseph Lucas, ¼ each at the Wear, serving the dam cross the river from the end of the Wear that is finished, 1 cleaning for the Tyler ¾ & ¼ clearing the Mixing room & the other 3 bearing stone to the Arch & Sand upon Cardiff Lime 5 in number only this day.

Carpenters George Ford, his 2 men, William Postlethwaite, and Lewis William John making Hubs for Wheels.

Sawyers 2 Sawing Beech for Stamper Shafts, & Joists of Oak. Wind continues South West.

Half past seven, a fine evening, very little Wind at S.W.

Received from Plymouth Furnace, 2 stamper boxes, 4 plates for washing & 34 small plates for furnace Stoke hole & Cynder holes weight 4 T. Mr. Terry informed me that they had made but a poor number, workers have made only 32 Ton of Metal, Pigs & castings, and that not more than 6 Ton of the pigs were fit to go to Market.

Horses bro't 1 piece of Timber 27 feet & David Lewis with 6 horses bro't 12 Load of coal to Smith's shop.

Sunday August 3rd. Half past seven o'clock, a fine clear morning, the Wind a little to the S.

The river is not lowered so much as it usualy is in the same time, without rain, therefore I conclude there has been some in the night. George Ford & Joseph Lucas with their Spouses to John Edge child this Day.

Breakfasted at home, about Nine. Brother Sam came, we two stayed untill after Eleven then took a Walk upon the hill untill after Twelve, and walked down to the Vilage, a little before Dinner came Mr. Jenkins of Morlas,[1] he dined with us. After Dinner came Captain Samuel Hughes. I desired my Brother Sam to tell Mr. Jenkins, that as we were concerned in the Plymouth furnace we should be glad to compromise all disputes relative thereto, he said he was willing but as he had not any time to stay. No more was said. Captain Hughes, my Brother, George Lyndon & Mr. Parry walked up to Cyfarthfa viewed the Wear & found the water in the river much lowered & if it continue fair I think tomorrow will give us an opportunity to put the remainder of the Wear frame down. We all walked up the hill, to the Quarry, and drank Sugar & Water at Spring there. Then returned to the Office and Capt Hughes took leave, his horse being brot from the Vilage. Bro. Sam & Mr Parry left George & me about ½ past Six. This has been a very fine day & I am in hopes the weather may be up to have some settled, fit for getting in the Hay & fixing our Wear, as well as forwarding our Buildings.

Monday August 4th. Six o'clock. A fair Morning but overcast Little Wind at West.

Past eight o'clock at Night. This has been a fine day, the river much lowered, & by the Dam being made, we have fixed the remaining part of the Wear frame very near ready for setting the Stones.

The Carpenters & several of the Labourers have been in the Water all day and have worked very hard and deserved the 5s for drink given to them, besides drams. They all worked untill Eight o'clock. The Wear frame, within, is boarded from the Sills upward, Moss placed close at the bottom, & a Clay that lay upon the Quarry, put upon the moss & then filled up with small stone, thrown into the river from the Quarry, The outside well paved with flatt stones, sett Edgeways, whch bind one upon another, like into an Arch, & so long as the foundation continues, which

[1] Possibly Richard Jenkins of Marlas, Pyle, and Corrwg Fechan, Glyncorrwg (1719–83), high sheriff of Glamorgan in 1750. He owned land in Aberdare and Merthyr. R.L. Brown, *Two papers on the history of Glyncorrwg* (Tongwynlais, 1982), 31–2. See also below, p. 140.

is a rock there cannot be any fear of its failing. The persons employed at this day are, vizt.

Labourers 4 at 1/6 p. day, 1 at 2s, & 14 at 1s p. day, and all of these worked 2 hours over, to be paid for, 19 in Number.

Carpenters, at it George Ford, his 2 men. Wm Postlethwaite & Lewis William, Joseph Lucas Mason at the Wear, David John & his Men at the Clay Mill upon Bargain Edwd Farnel & his Men Carpenters raised the Beam & floor upon the Clay Mill. Henry William & his Men upon the great race Arch.

Sawyers 4 sawing Boards, at days wages.

Horses bro't 2 pieces of Timber containing 64 feet.

Tusday August 5th. A fair but close Morning, ½ past Six o'clock. Wind at West, but very little of it.

All the Masons are setting stones in the Wear, & the Labourers filling the panes, with stone & gravel. Except 2 raising Stone & 6 carrying setters, the latter @ 3d p. Square yard, the former by the day.

Past seven o'clock. This has been an exceeding fine day, & this Eveng as pleasant a one as we have had this year & the Moon changing at six this evening, I am in great hope of having a fitt of fine fair weather, quite calm, not the least Wind.

We have finished 3 paines of the Wear. One of them p. Henry Wm and his Men, one by David John & his Men, at 6d p. Square Yard, the other by Walther William, Hopkin David, John Gabriel, Thos Loyd and Joshua Thomas p. days wages. The other two panes I hope will be finished tomorrow, by Harry William & Co. & David John etc. Joseph Lucas repaired the pane that was damaged by the floods. The inside of the Wear is filled & rammed with clay & small stones near as farr as is sett.

Labourers 6 serving Setting stones at 3d p. square yard, 2 getting stones for the Wear & 12 wheeling clay & rubbish to fill the inside of the Wear & 2 Serving Gravel & fill under the Stones

Carpenters finishing their part of the Wear.

Sawyers 4 sawing

Horses. David Lewis John brt the Smith shop 12 load of Coal from the small Vein.

James Mason began this day to work at one of the Air furnaces.

Wednesday August 6th. A quarter past 6 o'clock. A fine morning, no wind stirring.

Nine o'clock. Warm & very like settled weather. Harry Williams & his Men, & David John, & his Men, are upon the last two panes of the Wear.

Edward Thomas John is gone as an Evidence, in a Cause to come on this Assize at Cardiff, between Lewis Jenkins, & some of Plymouth Furnace Men, upon a Trespass, in getting of Wood & other damages.[1]

Past Six in the Evening. The Wear is secured within, & near finished by the setting of the panes, & when a Wall is Erected at the End, upon the Sill stones, it will, I think be compleat and a very good one & Erected in as short a time as any in England from our first beginning to this day inclusive is 9½ days & reckon tomorrow for the dry Wall at the End will be 10½ days. Not any Masons working at the Wear by day wages but these men worked alone by Bargain.

Labourers About the Wear 2 raising stones for it & 1 more ½ day, 2 clearing the rubbish, & 10 wheeling, filling & ramming the inside, 2 serving the Setters with gravel, 17 at the Wear. 2 serving Masons at necessary house, 1 at Common Mortar, 1 Tampering clay & 1 Serving Joseph Lucas at the Stack, 6 upon Job at carrying stone & 4 upon Job in great race.

Masons Walter William, Hopkin David, John Gabriel, Tho. Loyd, Thomas David & Joshua Thos. with Josh Lucas & James Mason.

Horses brought 1 piece of Timber containing 18 feet. David Lewis with 3 horses br't 18 Load of Clay to sett fire brick, with 3 do fetched Slate.

The charges in setting the Wear in 10½ days vizt.

	£	s	d	£	s	d
George Ford 10½ day @ 3s 4d a day	1	15	-			
ditto 2 Men each 10½ days	2	5	6			
William Postlethwaite 10½ days @ 1/8	0	17	6			
Lewis William 10½ days @1/8	0	17	6			
Carpenters				5	15	6
Masons Josh Lucas 10½ @ 2/6	1	6	3			
47½ days work @ 1/6	4	1	3	5	7	6
Labourers 200 days work @ 1s				10	-	-
Masons Setting by the yard 191 yards @ 6d	4	15	-			
Labourers Serving @ the yard 231 yards @ 3d	2	17	-	7	12	-

[1] i.e. an action at the Court of Great Sessions held at Cardiff.

Building the Wall at the Ends	1 17 6
Ale & drams to those working in water	3 10 4
The whole Expenses in fixing the Wear	£34 2 10

Thursday August 7th. A quarter past five o'clock. A fine warm fair morning. Wind is so little one cannot know where.

Past Six at Night, this has been a very warm, fine day.

Masons Hopkin David, John Gabriel, Thomas Loyd, Thos. David, & Joshua Thomas No 5 at the Wall at the farr End of the Wear. David John & his 2 Men, at their Bargain the Clay Mill. Harry William and his two Men at their Bargain, the Arch in great race. Joseph Lucas & James Mason at the Stack, lining the pipe with Fire brick.

Labourers Three in the quarry raising stones for the Wear Wall, two leading them to the Masons in hand Barows, 1 Serving them and 4 carrying Clay & Stone to fill up the End of the Wear. 2 making up Mortar 1 man at Quarry, Thomas Clifton, his 2 Sons & 2 Wheelers at the rock for Shingling Furnace, 6 serving Josh. Lucas & James Mason, & 2 at the quarry ¼.

Carpenters Geo. Ford, his 2 men, Wm Postlethwaite & Lewis Wm making Gate for the Sluice in the Wear.

Sawyers 4 Sawing Boards etc.

Four Labourers upon their Bargain in the great race

Horses 7 in Team Trailing Timber into the road with the Plymouth Company horse the same, the former bro't 1 piece 20 feet the latter bro't 1 piece 18 feet. The Small horse turning Hay.

Captain Hughes & his Brother (a Parson) paid me a visit this Evening. Wrote to Mr. Bacon as p. copy.

Friday, August 8th. Half past five o'clock, a Warm calm morning. No Wind.

Nine o'clock very warm Mr Terry sent two Men to cut an Anvil etc. he began cutting himself but a piece of Iron struck his Eye and obliged him to leave off. He gave me the under written Monthly Account of the charge & the metal made at the Plymouth Furnace.

Plymouth Works Anno 1766

Pig iron received from July 5th to August 2nd

		T	cwt	q		£
To Watkin Watkins for raising		2	15	-		
of Mine @ 2/8						- 7 4
To John Williams	do	1	4	-	do	- 3 9½
To Widow Lewllin	do	4	3	-	do	- 11 -½
To Thomas Harry John	do	-	6	-	do	- - 9½
To Thomas John	do	9	3	-	do	1 4 4½
To William Evan	do	2	13	-	do	- 7 -½
To David Evan	do	5	12	-	do	- 14 11
To David William	do	7	8	-	do	- 19 9½
To Thomas Watkin	do	9	1	2	do	1 4 1½
To Henry Lawrence	do	117	14	2	do	15 1310¾
To William William (by day work)		3	18	2		
		163	18	2		20 14 7¼

		T	cwt	q		£	s	d
To Edward John for carrying		11	18	-				
of Mine @ 18d						-	17	11
To Widow Lewellin	do	4	3	-	do	-	5	6½
To Watkin John	do	30	13	-		2	5	11
To Thomas Rees	do	19	6	-	@ 16d	1	5	8½
To Thomas Lewis		29	14	-	@ 16d	1	19	7½

	T	cwt	q	lb		£	s	d
	95	14	-	-		6	14	8½
William David	1	14	-	-	@ 2s	-	3	4
Morgan Thomas	8	7	-	-	@ 18d	-	12	6
Howell Evan	4	2	-	-	@ 2s	-	6	1½
Watkin Richard	-	13	2	-	@ 2s	-	1	3
David Williams	-	16	2	-	@ 2s	-	1	7
Richard Thomas	-	14	2	-	@ 2s	-	1	5½
To Company	51	19	-	-	@ 16d	3	5	11
	164	-	2	-		11	6.10.½	

	T	cwt	q	lb		£	s	d
John & Donald Wm								
for raising coal	122	8	-	-	@ 18d	9	3	8
Do David William	102	1	2	-	@ 2s	10	4	2
Do raising by Wm Bill	29	5	3	-	@ 2s	2	18	7
Raising @ Tickets						-	7	-
Raising by river side	11	16	2	-	@ 1s	-	11	9½
	265	11	3	-		23	5	2½

	T	cwt	q			£	s	d
John Evan for Carriage of Coal	86	20	-	-	@ 2s	8	13	10½
Watkin Richard	40	17	-	-	@ do	4	1	9
Watkin John	20	-	-	-	@ do	2	-	-
Morgan Robert	29	16	1	-	@ do	2	19	7½
Rees Griffith	29	6	1	-	@ do	2	18	7½
Widow Lewellin	1	7	3	-	@ do	-	2	9
Howel Evan	20	8	2	-	@ do	2	-	10½
William David	8	13	-	-	@ do	-	17	4½
Llewellin John	9	10	-	-	@ do	-	19	-
Company	7	-	2	-	@ do	-	14	-¾
Watkin John								
for riverside Brick kiln	5	3	2	-	@ do	-	5	3
Company for do	6	4	-	-	@ 1s		6	2½
Tickets etc	-	9	-	-				
Carried forward	265	11	3	-		25	19	4¾

		T	cwt	q		£	s	d
Limestone vizt.								
Edward William								
raising & Carriage of		14	11	-	@	£ 2	14	6¾
John Richard	do	10	1	1	@ 3/9	1	17	8¾
Richard Thomas	do	8	2	-	@ 2s	1	10	4½
John Richard for raising	4	3	2		@ 3d	1	-	-½
Company		4	3	2	@ 3/6		14	6
		36	17	3		6	18	2½

	T	cwt	q		£	s	d
To Evan Jones for weighing							
Coal	245	10	3				
Mine	163	14	2				
Limestone	26	17	3				
Coal to burn the brick	56	10	-				
	436	1	-	@ 1½	2	14	6
John Roberts for coking	209	-	-	@ 4½	3	18	4½

William Bill Sinking 2 pits in Jenkins Wood for coal
15 yards @ 7/6 & 7 yards at 10s — 9 2 6
William Bell for sinking a pit at Pentrebach — 2 2 -

	Days		£	s	d	£	s	d
Thimothy Davis Carpenter	8	@ 20d a day	-	13	4			
Thomas Cox do	14	@ 17	-	19	10	1	13	2
John Rees Sawyer	10	@ 18	-	15	-			
Evan Richard do	5	@ 14	-	6	8	1	1	8
Anthony Lewis Blacksmith	2½	@ 18	1	12	3			
Thomas Williams do	24	@ 17	1	14	8½	3	6	11½
Thomas Watkin Labourer	11½	@ 1s	-	11	6			

Thomas Henry do	3½	@ 1s	- 3 6	
Edmund Lewis do	2	@ 1s	- 2 -	- 17 -
William William Miner	10	@ 20	- 16 8	
John Roberts do	10	@ 20	- 16 8	1 13 4
				26 9 6

To William Cope for 1 Month	3 - -	
Ditto for 6 Tons 5 cwt of Castings 25/-	1 11 3	4 11 3
To William Lewis for 1 Month		2 8 -
To Richard Hammonds filler for 1 Month		4 4 -
Thomas Lewis Stocker at the Bridge for 1 Month		1 16 -
Edmund John Limestone Breaker for 1 Month		1 8 -
William David Calciner for 1 Month		1 12 -
		15 19 3
Thomas Rees Cynder Wheeler 1 Month	1 8 -	1 8 -
		17 7 3

To Morgan Robert for carrying 6 plates to Penhole	- - 6
John Evan do 10 do	- - 10
Lewellin John Carriage of 10 cwt of pig to Mountain	- 1 -
Company do 20	- 2 -
Mr. Wood for do 30 cwt of pigs to Cardiff	1 1 -
Edward John f. Carriage 8 Ton 10 cwt of Iron to Neath	4 5 -
Richard Thomas do Machen Forge	4 10 -
Edward John	1 4 -
William George	- 6 0
Thomas David 2 to Cardiff	1 12 -
Watkin John Carriage of pit wood	- 4 8
Company	- 13 4
ditto 2 Load of Castings to Cyfarthfa	- 10 -
ditto for Load of Sand back	- 2 6
ditto for drawing 106 feet of Timber	3 19 6
	14 12 4

	T cwt q	T cwt q
Pig Yard Dr To Blast		
To Pig iron for	26 - -	
To Sundry Casting	6 6 -	32 6 -

Sundry Dr To Pig Yard	T cwt q		
Mr Wood to Sundry Castings-	4 6 2	@ 5/15	£24 17 4½
Mr. Mayberry To Pig Iron	2 10 -	@	
Mr. Dorset To Pig Iron white	6 - -	@ 3/15	22 10 -
Ditto To Pig Iron motley	4 - -	@	
Mr. Mound To Back Plate	- - 3	@	
Mr. Parrot To Pig Iron	20 - -	@	
Farm To Back Plate	- 1 -		
So farr Mr. Terry	36 18 1		

Furnace Dr.

To Mine raised 163 T 18 cwt 2q @ 8½ p T @ a medium	£20 14 7½	
To carriage of do at 1/4	11 6 10½	
To Coal raised 265.11.3 @ abt 1/9	23 5 2½	
To carriage do about 2s	25 19 4½	
To Limestone 36.17.30	6 18 2½	
To Coking	£3 18 4½	
To Weighing	2 14 6	
To Wages founder etc.	17 7 3	
To Extra	19 16 7½	
To Expense	14 12 6	
	58 9 3	
		146 13 6½
Rent to Lord Plymouth for 1 month	5 - -	
ditto To David Thomas	1 12 -	
Clerk Wages	8 - -	
Interest of Capital	16 - -	30 12 -
Other Expenses in side charges, damages etc.		2 14 5½
		180 - -

Pigs 26 T @ £4 p. Ton	£104	
Castings 6 T 6 cwt	36 4 6	
Loss	39 15 6	£180 - -

Eight o'clock. I have had the pleasure of seeing this Evening water run over the Wear.

Masons p. day Walter Harry William, Hopkin David, Thomas Loyd, Josh Gabriel, Thos. David & Joshua Thomas in No 6 at Wear Wall. David John & his 2 Men at their Bargain the Clay Mill. Harry William & his Men at the Great Race Arch p. Bargain.

Labourers Serving Masons at the Wear Wall, 4 carrying Stones to it, 2 Getting Stones, 3 in Number 9 for Wear, 4 at great race p. bargain, 4 at the Rock where a Shingling Furnace is to be.

Carpenters. George Ford, his 2 men, Wm Postlethwaite and Lewis William at the Stamper Wheel.

Sawyers sawing Shrouds & house Timber.

Horses 2 of our own, & 4 of Plymouth Co. bro't 1 piece 22½ ft four of our own brought 1 piece 10 ft.

David Lewis with 2 horses leading Stones from Quarry to great race. The horses bring but little Timber, orders given to do better.

	£	s	d
Mine to make 32 T 6 cwt of metal			
@ 4 cwt to the Ton is 129 T 4 cwt			
@ 3/10 p Ton	28	4	11
Coal for ditto @ 6 Ton to the Ton including burning Stone @ 3/9	36	-	-
Lime stone 1/3 to the stone 33 Ton @ 3/9	6	3	9
Coking & weighing	7	6	6
Total of Wagess Sundry kind with Expenses	58	9	3
Rents etc.	33	6	6
One month real Expenses	169	10	11

	£	s	d	
Pigs & Castings	140	4	6	
Loss Monthly	29	6	5	169 10 11 Look over this leaf

Saturday August 9th. Near Six o'clock a fine Morning. The Wind due North.

Near Eleven o'clock Excessive hot weather, the hay makes as fast as it can. We are very busie in cutting & getting it in.

The charge for a Month supposing the furnace called at Plymouth is well stoked, & the alterations & repairs Intended were made & to make 16 Ton of metal Weekly drawn from the last month Acct but deducting the sinking of pits for coal & several extra charges that will not come into the yearly general Acct for the future vizt.

	£	s	d
Mine for one Month @ 16 T of metal p. week 258 @ 3s 10d p. Ton	£49	9	-
Coal for do @ 6 Ton for 1 T of metal 384	72	-	-
Lime for do 66 Ton @ 3/9 p. Ton	12	7	6
Coking & weighing @ 6d p. Ton	14	13	-
Wages for founders etc. for furnace	17	7	3
Extra Wages £5 5s 7d	5	5	7
Rents as per monthly Acct	30	12	-
for one month	201	14	4
Multiply by 12 for one year	2420	12	-
64 T of metal for 1 Month is 768 Ton for one year @ £4 2s 6d @ ton is £3081 12s			
Profit	661	-	-
	3081	12	-

By this there does not appear to be so much profit as Mr. Terry make in his estimate by £232 11s 3d which should be examined into as by that Estimate there appears to be full enough charged for every article.

This has been a fine warm day & the several branches of work have gone briskly.

Masons at the Hammer Hatch Walter William, Hopkin David, Thomas Loyd, Thomas David & Joshua Thomas. John Gabriel asked leave to be absent a day or two. p days wages.

Labourers 2 raising stones in the Quarry, 4 bearing stones out of the quarry for carts to lead to the races. Thomas Clifton with 3 men & his 2 Sons at the Rock for Air furnaces 2 clearing about necessary house, 1 Serving Common Mortar, 1 Cardiff Lime, In No 16. & 2 men serving Masons with stones, which makes the No 18. 2 more with Josh Lucas at Dam Wall in Total 20. 4 at the great race per bargain, 2 with Masons at the great race p. bargain.

Masons p. Bargain Harry William & his Men at great race Arch. David John & his Men at Clay Mill.

Carpenters George Ford, his 2 men & Wm Postlethwaite & Lewis William at Stamper Wheel.

Sawyers 4 Sawing shrouds & several odd pieces into Spares.

Horses Loading Hay with the Waggon horses. David Lewis with a Man & 2 horses & Carts loading Arch stones from the Quarry. Horse loading 36 Loads of Coal to Brick kiln and 4 load to each of the familys vizt. Wm Postlethwaite, Aaron Wedgwood & James Mason.

Joseph Lucas & James Mason at the flourishing Stack, lining the pipes. This day gave the Men a Barrel of Ale, agreeable to promises, at the completing the Wear, & when the water run over it.

Sunday August 10th. Half past Six o'clock, a fine Morning. Wind continues due North.

About 10 o'clock I went down the Vilage, to wait upon Mr. White & Mr. Thomas Guest, but he was gone to the Plymouth furnace & I went there & saw him & his Brother, then we entered into discourse, about that furnace. Upon enquiring we found, that under present management, and condition of that furnace, it worked to Loss therefore I proposed, that it shall Blow out, and order all the accounts to be settled & Ballanced, an Inventory taken. An Estimate made, of all the Alterations & Additions that may be necessary to procure a long and profitable Blast. This Mr. White seemed to think could not be done, untill affairs, & the dispute with John Guest are settled. I told him that I did not see, that that affair could be any hindrance to the Company Acct and Affairs being settled, and brought to a head which I thought absolutely necessary, that each Partner might know the state thereof which in the present one could not be expected. I told them that for our parts, we were willing to come into any Measures for the benefit of the whole. After this conversation we walked up the Vilage, to Mr. Guests House, staid there some time & Mr White showed me a paper of the several

Advances & decrease (a Copy of which I had from Mr. Guest, some time before). And then I repeated my desire & the necessity of the affairs of the Company being settled & brought to a head, but could not find Mr. White inclined to come to any resolution herein, altho he & his Brother agreed to the Utility of it

About 11 o'clock Mr. White proposed taking a walk to Cyfarthfa and I agreed & we viewed every part with the Wear & Walked back. He invited me to Dine at Mr. Guest. I left him and promised to return at One. Went to Edward Morgan where I met my Brother Sam, Mr. Parry, Mr. Jones the Officer of Excise, & our Men Geo. Ford, & Jos. Lucas with George Lyndon. About one I went to Mr. Guest to Dined & stayed with Mr. White talking of indiferent Affairs untill Evening. When I told Mr. White I desired him to consider what I had said and I would wait upon him to Morrow he said he should leave the Vilage at One, go up to their farm in the Morning, & view the damage done Lewis Jenkins for which an Action was sought it was agreed to refer it. and would be glad to talk further for half an hour before he went, and so we parted.

The Charge for clearing, Walling & erecting the great race vizt.

David Parry & Partners for 1400¾ yards of Earth at 4d p. yard		£23	6	11
for 790 yards of Rock at 8d		26	6	8
Arching & Walling 65 yards by John Ford, including Stones Lime @ 4s & 2s 6d				
Total 6s 6d p. yard 4s for Labour & 2/6 Stones, Lime		21	2	6
William Edwards 56 yards @ 8/6 p. yard he being by day & prided himself upon excelling other work which made it dearer		23	16	-
Edward Thomas John 37 yards @ 5/6 & 2/6 8 ft wide				
the others were but 6 ft wide		14	16	-
Evan Abraham & partners for clearing				
Earth 286 yards @ 4d	4 15 4			
Rock 31 @ 8d	1 0 8	5	16	-
For covering what is mentioned above 158 yards in Length		5	18	-
The workmen inform me that Wm Edwards back Wall was from the Extra Scabbling work, at least 4d p. Yard more than charges		11	4	-
Abraham Evans & Partners for				
162 yards of Earth at 4d	2 14 -			
26.¾ of rock 8d	- 18 6	3	12	6
Labour & Costs to fetch stones for the Arches		5	12	-
Paid Harry Wiliams & Edward Thomas for Aug. 29 Arching		17	5	6
Clearing for Arching for Rock & Earth		7	12	3
Carried to August 12th		166	8	4

Monday August 11th. Near Six o'clock a fine Warm Morning. The Wind N. West.

Thomas Guest was with me this morning and informed me that Mr. White asked him if I wanted possession of the Works he answered him Not that he knew of. That he supposed I was not against their having, their first advance paid out of the first profit, he said he supposed not, but if the Works did not make any, they could not have it. Mr. White said he tho't The Works & Stock shod be liable.

This conversation T.G. said he tho't proper to inform me before I met them again.

About Seven o'Clock I waited upon Mr. White & his Brother. The Workmen came to him so often to demand the money due that I had but little time to say anything to him but his brother mentioned that if some proposal could be thought of to rent the Work & free them of that trouble they had, he should like it. I told him I had had thoughts of offering to give or take 10 p. Cent for what money had been advanced after Accounts were Settled and all Arrears paid to put every partner upon Equality. This seemed to be agreeable but Mr. White he said he did not care if the works stood 2 or 3 years. After this I said no more but as the Men will not work, the Furnace must be Blow out and I think they will be glad to agree upon reasonable terms.

Masons p. day wages Walter William, Hopkin David, Thos. Loyd, Thomas David & Joshua Thomas upon the Hammer Hatch.

Labourers 2 raising Stones in Quarry, 6 carrying stones out, for the carts, 2 Carrying stones to Masons, 1 @ Cardiff & 1 at Common Mortar, 4 at the Mouth of the great race, Tamping Clay, 2 Serving at the Stack, Joseph Lucas & James Mason & 1 leading Stones.

Carpenters George Ford his Men & Josh Gibson & Wm Postlethwaite at the Stamper Wheel. David Millingin & Lewis Williams in the Mountain to cut wood for a Brick Shade.

Sawyers 4 sawing Bends by the day.

Horses Six brought a piece of Timber 17 feet, after they had been dragging Timber out of the Wood. & Gills into the road 2 pieces of timber 40 feet. David Lewis with 2 horses & Carts leading Arch Stones from Quarry. Joseph Lucas & James Mason at Stack & furnaces. Four Labourers at the Great Race clearing it for Walling & Arching by Abraham Evan, Moses Evans, Lewis Edward & Philip Thomas. Upon Bargain 4d p. yard for the Earth & 8d for the Rock, as was given for the former they are able Workmen.

David John & 2 More Masons upon the Bargain the Clay Mill Harry Williams & one Mason upon the Great race Arch p. Bargain Edward

Thomas & one Mason upon the Mixing room p. ditto Two Labourers upon Bargain in clearing for the Stamper Wheel Cases.

Wrote to Dr. Brownrigg & enclosed one to my wife. Wrote to Mr. Bacon & John Guest sent p. the Postman. Locked up in Case.

If the Plymouth furnace falls into our hands, it must be upon the condition as under, 10 p. Cent upon their advances as rent, the Lords rent & others to be paid by the partners, as also all damages that may arise & railway to be made by them to allow the charges thereof out of the Rent otherwise we shall lose that Sum at the end of 10 years the time it is proposed to take the furnace also all the repairs and additions that may be necessary.

Tuesday August 12th. Five o'clock a fine warm Morng the Wind at NE.

Suppose the whole Capital of Plymouth Co. be at present

		£5000	-
A railway to cost, as p. Terry Estimate		131	-
Three kilns	36		
A Stable with store room	75		
An Air furnace	22		
Level head to drain the Mine	70	203	-
		5334	-

Call it £5400 @ 10 p. Cent is £540 p. Annum this rent should not commence untill we begin Blowing (but Cyfarthfa to pay the Lord & other Rents until that time) & when the blast begins the Interest or Rent to begin & the Lords & other rents & charges to be paid, by the Lessees and deducted out of the Rent. The Plymouth Co. to Secure to the Cyfarthfa Co. free egress & regress for the Coal, Mine & other loads necessary or to be at the Expense of any Litigation upon such Trespasses. The Works & Utensils to be viewed & the Cyfarthfa Company to deliver them in as good Condition as they received them. If the Cyfarthfa Co. should make any improvement in the Blast, or in any other Shape that may appear to be advantageous to the Plymouth Co. at the Expiration of this Lease, they should pay for the same, or the Cyfarthfa Company have the Liberty alter such & leave the Work in the same Condition they received them.

Half past 4 o'clock. This has been a fine Warm day untill this time, but now it rained hard, Wind at S.E. Past Seven, the rain over but very like to be more.

Masons Hopkin David, John Gabriel, Thomas Loyd, Thomas David & Joshua Thomas at the Hammer Hatch, upon days wages. Joseph Lucas

& James Mason at the Stack and furnace. David John & his Men upon Clay Mill p. bargain. Edward Thomas John upon the Mixing room upon bargain. Harry William & his Man upon Great race Arch p. diem.

Labourers 2 raising Stones in the quarry 4 bearing them out, for Carts, 2 Carrying stones to the Masons, 1 at Cardiff Mortar, 1 at the Common Mortar, 1 Tempering Clay and weighing Sand, 2 Serving Josh Lucas & James Mason at the furnace, 4 at the rock where the Air furnaces for Shingling is to be. 1 wheeling rubbish out of Mixing room & 1 leading Arch stones from Quarry Number 19.

Carpenters George Ford, his Men, Josh Gibson & Wm Postlethwaite at the Stamper Wheel & turning a Pattern for a Gudgeon box. Lewis William & David Millinkin upon the Mountain cutting wood for a Brick shade.

Horses The Carriage & 6 horses bro't 3 pieces of Timber, containing 52 feet. 3 horses carrying hay to the Barns & Stacks. David Lewis with 2 horses & Carts carrying Arch Stones to Great races.

Sawyers 4 Sawing bends p. the day.

There was the 4 Labourers clearing the great race for Walling & Arching.

One of the Labourers left his work, at 12 in order to go to Brecon, as an Evidence against a Woman for poisoning her husband he being a Lodger was being desired by her to buy some yellow Arsnick to kill ratts, which she put into some Broth & gave to her husband. An Acct came this day that as soon as she heard the Trumpet sound upon the Judge going into Brecon she expired in Goal. However the Man went to Brecon.[1]

N.B. This being fine weather for the hay, several of our Labourers are cutting grass & leading hay & several Masons & Labourers stay at home for that purpose.

As the Plymouth furnace will soon blow out, & we shall want Stamper heads & having but 2 Shanks, I ordered the Smith to take two of the Cams, made for the furnacee Bellows, & wield two of them together to make other Shanks which was done & I have ordered them to be taken to the furnace to have 4 cast, for one sett of Stamps which may Serve untill they or we Blow again. I likewise ordered the box pattern to be sent to have three of them cast.

[1] William Thomas (*Diary*, 169) gives a very similar account.

Charge of clearing, Walling Arching etc. of the races from the river to wheels vizt.

Brought from August 10th	£166 8 4
Quarrying & leadg stones out, for carrying,	
The grand race with the several branches 300 yards	
8d p. yard at the medium	10 - -
Sept 13th Harry Wm 5½ of Arching @ 3s 14 yard	
2 ft 6 in @ 2/6 p. yard	2 13 7

Wednesday August 13th. Six o'clock a Cloudy Morning has the appearance of rain. Wind at East.

Being informed that Lewis William John, has sunk a New pit, to get Coal upon Penwane Common, & he being confined to a pit he was then driving Level of his Lease to A. B. & Co. I sent for him this Morning in order to talk to him & protest against such proceedings.[1]

Nine o'clock Went to Plymouth furnace with patterns for Stamp head and box for Claymill Gudgeons and gave direction for them & one frame. Order should be completed before they Blow out which they promised to do. On my return, Lewis William John came, upon my reading the Agreement between & Mr. Bacon & Co. I could convince him that he was wrong in working in any other place than the pit, he had liberty to do by said Agreement. I must go up with him upon the spot, & see what can be done there.

Masons John Gabriel, Thomas Loyd, Joshua Thomas & Thos. David each one day & Walter William ¾.

Joseph Lucas & James Mason at the flourishing furnace. David John & 2 more upon his Bargain the Clay Mill. Edward Thomas & 1 more upon his Bargain the Mixing room. Harry William & 2 more upon the Great race Arch p. bargain.

Labourers 2 raising Stone in the Quarry, 1 clearing rubbish 4 carrying Stones out for Carts, 2 carrying to Masons, 2 clearing the Mixing room, 1 Sinking a Sawpit lower, 1 at Common & 1 at Cardiff Mortar, 5 at rock & wheeling it off & 1 Serving Josh Lucas, 1 loading Cart, Number 21.

Carpenters George Ford, his 2 Men & William Postlethwaite at Stamper Wheel & Lewis William puting up a shade of Brick.

Sawyers 4 Sawing joists & Spares

[1] See also 14 and 23 Aug., 23 Sept.

Horses 6 brought one piece of Timber 35 feet. Three in Carrying hay to Stacks & Barn. Two leading Arch Stones from the Quarry. Two at Grass to rest they being worn down.

Four Labourers clearing the great race for Walling & Arching.

Husbandry An Account of Mowing etc. is bro't in every fortnight by John Morgan.

Thursday August 14th. Half past five o'clock a fine Warm Morning, no Wind that one can see from whence it comes. About Eleven, I took a Walk with Sam & Thomas Clifton to Penwane, to view the place where Lewis William John is getting Coal and if the agreement can be understood to confine him to the Pit he was driving, or pretended that he was driving a Level to, he is certainly getting coal now contrary to the Express words of that Agreement. His plea is that the meaning of the Word pit is any part of the same vein of Coal.

About three o'clock it rained about one hour only but not so hard as to put the Men of their work.

Six o'clock, rain again. The Wind at West.

Masons Walter William, Thomas Loyd, John Gabriel, Thos David and Joshua Thomas p. day. David John & 2 more at the Clay Mill & Clay Mill race Arch p. bargain. Edward Thomas John & Harry William with 3 more at the great race Arch. Joseph Lucas & James Mason at the flourishing furnaces.

Labourers 2 raising Stones in the Quarry, 1 clearing away the rubbish, 4 bearing stones out for Carts, 2 bearing Mine & filling in the Temporary Claymill race & filling in over the great race Arch, 2 Serving Masons with Stone, 2 bearing in fire brick, one serving Joseph Lucas, 1 Striking for Smiths, 1 leading Stones from Quarry with horse & Cart. Thos. Clifton making a Conduit in the rock under Air furnace & his two sons carrying Mine out of the Pool whch was got there.

Carpenters George Ford his 2 Men & William Postlethwaite about the Stamper wheel, & Lewis William fixing a shade for Brick makers.

Sawyers 4 Sawing roof Timbers by the day.

Horses The 6 horses have not bro't any Timber. David Lewis with 2 horses leading Stones with Carts from Quarry to Arch. Abraham Evans & his 4 partners at the great races, clearing for the Arching p. Bargain.

Edward Farnell & his men putting up the Clay Mill roof ready for Slate. Evan John the Tyler begins to Scaffold in order for Laying on Laths for the Tyles, or stone slate by the yard he gets the Tyle, in the Quarry dresses & prepares them, & lays them on for 8d p. Square Yard.

Friday August 15th. Half past five o'Clock, A Fair but Cloudy Morning with a cold strong N.W. Wind very like rain.

Past eleven o'clock, it has been Showery since Nine, but not so hard as to prevent the Masons, & other hands, working. But the work does not go on so well as in dry weather.

Horses Six in the Carriage bro't one piece of Timber 52½ feet. Daniel Lewis with 2 horses & Carts leading Arch stones from Quarry. 3 horses at the farm to carry hay in the Morning before the rain, & 2 at grass to turn it.

Masons Walter William, John Gabriel, Thomas Loyd, Thos David and Joshua Thomas at the hammer Hatch. David John & his two men, at the remainder of the Clay Mill & Stamper race Arch. (the Clay Mill being finished & the Slater, is now covering it). Harry William & Edward Thomas John & their three Men upon the great race Arch (the Mixing room Gavel, or pine End as called here, is postponed untill the Arching is finished) the whole Number of Masons is 13 viz. 5 upon days wages & 8 upon Bargain.

Carpenters George Ford, his 2 Men & William Postlethwaite upon the Stamper wheel. And Lewis William, at the Brick Shade on Penywain Mountain.

Sawyers 4 Sawing joists & beams for the floor over the Stamping house & forge. The Clay Mill mixing room & flourishing house having the roofs, & floor laid, only want boarding & doors. Abraham Evan & 4 more upon clearing the great race p. bargain.

Labourers p. day 2 raising Stones in the Quarry, 4 bearing Stones, out for race Arch, 2 at the hurry, 2 Serving Masons, 1 at Cardiff & 1 at Common Mortar. 3 at the rock for furnaces 1 serving Jos. Lucas & Tempering Clay, & 2 serving at races.

Saturday August 16th. Half past five o'clock a fine clear morning but cool the Wind at N. West.

This day sett out, the other Shingling furnace stack, two of them which makes three of them for Six furnaces four only will be built at the first to see whether those will keep two constantly at Work & if it should be found that a Sixth is necessary, the Stack will be ready for another.

Masons p. day. Walter Williams, John Gabriel, Hopkin David, & Thomas Loyd. Thomas David & Joshua Thomas, I discharged yesterday as they were not Extra Workmen & there was not so great a want of them. David John, Harry Williams & 6 more Masons were all this day upon the race Arch.

Joseph Lucas & James Mason were upon the Shingling Furnace Stacks, laying the foundation of 2 Stacks.

Labourers 2 raising Stones in the Quarry, 4 bearing them out for Carts, 2 serving Masons, 2 Serving Joseph Lucas & James Mason at the Stack, 1 at the Cardiff, 1 at the Common Mortar, 3 cutting the rock for flourishing furnaces, 2 Wheeling rubbish from the Hammer race; 3 filling upon the Arch. Number 20 p. day. Abraham Evan & 4 more upon Bargains in clearing the race for Walling & Arching. No 5.

Carpenters George Ford & 1 of his Men laying the fall in Clay Mill, the other of his Men David Milleken & William Postlethwaite & Lewis William upon the Stamper wheel all upon Wages.

Tyler or Slater Evan John covering the Clay Mill p. bargain.

Sawyers 4 sawing roof Timber for the dwellings above the Stampers & Forge.

Horses Six bro't 2 pieces of Timber containing 42½ feet. 2 in Carts leading Arch Stones fm field nr the Quarry. 3 Carrying in hay to stacks and 2 at Grass recruiting. the whole 13.

My Brother, Joseph Lucas, & George Lyndon went with me to show 3 Masons, vizt. Harry William, Edward Thomas John & David John the place where we have pitched upon to erect our furnace and I gave them untill Monday to consider & let me know how much p. Perch they would build it their finding every particular, but Lime the Company laying that down at the most convenient place they might chose near the work; and they to build it agreeable to mine or to our agents direction.

Wrote to Mr. Bacon & my wife at Mr Brownrigg, Keswick, put them into the Case, locked up, & sent by John Morgan who goes with them to carry Mr. Parrys cloaths to Brecon on his way for London; Mr. Bacon having sent for him.

Sunday August 17th. Past Seven o'clock a fine clear Morning the Wind due North.

Mr. Parry came up to Breakfast here at Cyfarthfa about eight & then went forward, with John Morgan, to Brecon on his way to London, John to bring the horse back.

This has been a fine day but cool. I dined at Edward Morgan, the Anchor & Crown, & returned to Cyfarthfa with my Brother, George Lyndon & George Ford. Stayed at home all the afternoon looks like a change of weather.

Monday August 18th. within a quarter of Six o'Clock & Cloudy Morning with the appearance of rain. The Wind but little at N.E.

One o'clock a fine Warm Day. Sent three more hands, to the farms to assist getting in hay. We think Rhyd y Car & Lewinkelly will produce 160 Tons. Borrowed a Net of William David & another of Rees the

Cobbler, with the Tyler at Tamour, put together we fished & took about 5 dozen Trout. Sent a dish to Thomas Guest and to Mr. Jones the Attorney, and kept as many as dined 4 of us, at Cyfartrhfa.

This day I agreed with Harry Williams, Edward Thomas John & David John, Masons, To Build a Stack for a Blast Furnace upon Terms following, vizt. me to find them with Lime near the place & they to have 3s p. Perch, they themselves to provide & bring to the place Stone, Sand & Water and all other necessary having the use of the Quarry for that purpose. The Company to provide them with Crows & Sledge Hammer & to repair their hammer when needed, the same to be returned or paid for if lost. The whole building to be carried on & completed without delay or loss of time, in a strong solid workmanlike Manner. This is to be begun as soon as they have finished the Bargain they have now undertaken. The Company to Erect a shade, near the place alloted for the furnace, for them to Scabble stones under in rainy weather. Agreed likewise with the said three Masons, to digg the foundation for the furnace, at 4d per Square Yard for the Earth & 8d p. yard for the rock and to supply them with powder for Blasting the rock if found necessary. Signed by them & witnessed by Samuel Wood.

Masons upon day wages Walter William, Hopkin David, John Gabriel, & Thomas Loyd at the hammer hatches. David John & 2 more upon the last length of Stamper Arch. Harry William, & 4 more upon the great races Arch.

Labourers 5 carrying gravel to Wear to fill the joints, 2 serving the Masons, 1 at the rock for flourishing furnaces, 4 wheeling rubbish from the races to cover the Arch, 1 filling upon the Arch, 1 serving James Mason at the Stack, 1 at Cardiff & 1 at Common Mortar. Joseph Lucas at the Mountain building a small kiln for burning fire brick. James Mason at the shingling stacks.

Carpenters George Ford & one of his Men David Millikin up on the Clay Mill wheel fall. William Postlethwaite, Jos. Gibson & Lewis William, upon Bucket boards for wheel.

Horses Six brought 2 pieces of Timber containing [*Blank*]. Six carrying hay to Stacks. 1 at grass to recruit.

Sawyers 4 sawing for floors over the Stamp house p. day.

Wrote to Mr. Bacon, Mr. How & Mr. Kendall, locked them into the case & sent to Brecon p. Postman. My Brother took them to the Postman. This has been a close day, little sun, but warm. The Clay Mill and Stamper Arches, are quite closed, and joined to the great race. One side of the Clay Mill roof is covered and the Scaffold fixed for the other side.

Tuesday August 19th. Half past five o'clock, a close warm Morning. Little Wind at N.W. Past six o'clock, this has been a fine warm day but now there is a whistling wind at [*Blank*].

Masons p. day wages Walter William, Hopkin David, Thomas Loyd & John Gabriel upon the hammer Hatch. David John & two more upon the Stamp house upon Bargain. Harry William & 4 more upon the great race Arch. Joseph Lucas on the Mountain, erecting a small kiln for fire bricks this makes two days. James Mason at the Shingling Furnace Stacks.

Labourers 2 Raising Stones in the Quarry, 2 bearing stones out for Carts, 2 bearing for Hurry, 2 Serving Masons, 1 Serving James Mason at Stacks, 4 covering the Arch on great race, 1 at Cardiff 1 at Common Mortar, 5 filling and wheeling rubbish from the race, in Number 20.

Carpenters Geo. Ford & David Millikin at Clay Mill wheel fall Wm Postlethwaite & Josh Gibson making Buckets for Stamper wheel and Lewis Williams making a door for my Brothers Room over the Office.

Abraham Evan & his 4 Partners sinking the rock for the hammer races, p. Bargain.

Sawyers 4 Sawing for floors & roofs, over the Stamp house & the high end of the forge p. day 1/6 each. Evan John, the Tyler has lathed the other side of the Clay Mill ready for puting on the Stone Tile.

Thomas Rees called upon me & told me that he had been at Hensol & Mr. Morgan desired him to inform me that he intended being here next pay day that Mr. Rice & his Lady had been there & prevented his being here sooner.

Horses Six brought a piece of Timber containing 32 feet. Six carrying in hay to Stacks. One at grass recruiting. 13 our whole number.

Dug the foundation for the stamping House side Wall, from the Stamping House to the Stamper Hatch p. David John the Mason, he is to have the use of the Cobble stones that now lye contiguous thereto upon condition that he take out, at his charge, all the Stones that shall remain in the Pool, after the vacancy is filled that was left for a passage. I agreed to allow 6d p. perch his supplying himself with Stones.

Wednesday August 20th. Near five o'clock a fine warm Morning. Little Wind, not to discern from which part it comes.

This Morning David John began to lay stones in the foundation for the Stamping house side Wall for flourishing house to the Hammer Hatch.

This has been a very warm fine day & the work has gone on well.

Masons upon days wages. Walter William, Hopkins David, Thos Lloyd & John Gabriel upon the Hammer Hatch. Harry William & 3 more upon Great Race Arch upon Bargain. David John & 4 more upon Stamper cross wall upon do.

Labourers 2 getting stones in the Quarry, 1 clearing rubbish, 6 bearing Stones out for Carts, 2 Serving Masons, 3 serving Josh Lucas & Jas Mason at Stacks. 2 filling barrows, 2 wheeling rubbish, 1 Spreading, 1 filling up in Arches, 1 Leading a Cart with Arch stone, 1 at Common Mortar, & 1 wheeling Lime to heap. In No 23. Jos. Lucas & Jas. Mason at Shingling furnace body next the rock.

Abraham Evan & 4 more Labourers clearing the great & hammer races for Arching upon Bargain.

Sawyers 4 sawing for floor & roof for rooms above the Stampg house & forge p. day.

Horses 6 drawing Timber into the road out of Gulleys and other bad places. 4 Turning hay. 2 Carrying Stones to Arches. 1 at Grass recruiting. on whole No 13

Carpenter George Ford & 1 of his Men p. Clay Mill Wheel fall. Wm Postlethwaite, Josh Gibson upon Buckets & Lewis Wm upon Jobs.

Thursday August 21st. A quarter before Six o'clock a close Foggy Morning quite calm.

Yesterday Conor our farmer or Husbandman Sold to Tho. Rhys 2 of our Oxen which cost £13 10s for £16, we had worked them untill they were lame then put them to grass.

Past Six, this has been a warm fine day the work has gone on well. The great race is Arched within one length of the end to the joining the two hammer & Chafery races. Joseph Lucas & James Mason are upon one of the Shingling Furnaces.

Masons upon day wages Walter Williams, Hopkin David, John Gabriel & Thomas Loyd at the Hammer Hatch.

Labourers 2 raising stones in the Quarry, 1 cleaning rubbish, 4 bearing Arch stones for the Carts, 3 attending Jos. Lucas at Stack 2 serving Masons with stones at hammer hatch, one at Common Mortar, 5 filling & wheeling rubbish that is thrown out of race 2 filling in upon Arches.

Carpenters George Ford went into the Wood this morning to see some timber and this afternoon he and one of his Men were upon the Clay Mill wheel fall. William Postlethwaite, Joseph Gibson and Lewis William were making buckets for Stamper wheel.

Sawyers 4 sawing roof & flooring for Stamp House p. day.

Horses 6 dragging out Timber into the road to be ready for fetching and bro't 1 piece home containing 21½ feet. 2 Leading Stone from Quarry to races. 4 leading Coals to the workmen.

David John & 4 more Masons at the Stamp house Side Wall p. bargain. Harry William & 4 more Masons at the great race Arch p. bargain. Abraham Evans & 4 more Labourers upon clearing the great race for Arching and the two hammer races in the rock, a hard Coal Sill upon Bargain. All the shingling furnace & Stack are built upon the hard blue Coal sill. Wrote to my wife.

Friday August 22. Half past five a fine warm clear Morning very little Wind at West.

This has been a fine Warm day & the work has gone on well. The wall for Arching, is made at the junction of the 2 hammer & chafery races to begin Arching tomorrow.

Masons upon day wages, Walter Williams, Hopkin David, Thos. Loyd & John Gabriel upon hammer hatch. Joseph Lucas & James Mason upon one of the Shingling furnaces. David John & 4 men upon the Stamper side Wall upon Bargain. Harry William & 1 more, upon the Arch Wall p. Bargain. Edward Thomas, & one more upon the Gavel End of mixing room.

Labourers 2 raising Stones in Quarry 6 bearing stones out for Carts to lead to race, 2 Serving Masons with stones, 1 at the Stack, 2 filling upon Arches, 4 filling & wheeling to the hammer races.

Carpenters George Ford his two men & Wm Postlethwaite upon the wheel Buckets, Lewis William on the Mountain puting the brick shade that fell down.

Abraham Evan & 4 more clearing the hammer race in the rock for Arching p. bargain.

Sawyers 4 sawing Timber for floor & roof over Stamper house etc.

Horses Six brought 2 pieces of Timber containing 42½ feet. 2 in Carts Leading stones for Quarry to races. 4 Leading Hay. 1 @ grass recruiting. whole No 13

Saturday August 23rd. Six o'clock a fair Morning but a deal of rain fell last night or Early this Morning. Wind at South West.

Mr. Thomas Morgan, Lord Talbots Stewart, came to the Vilage last night. I expect him here this morning with money being out. About 8 Mr. Morgan came & paid my Brother £100 for his bill upon Mr. Bacon, about Eleven Thomas Rhys came to settle his part of the Wheat that he owed upon part of Lewinkelly Land, before we took possession but after the Death of the Tenant, and it being referred to Mr. Morgan he awarded £12 for ploughing & Harrowing & Sowing seed which was paid him & a receipt taken in full of all demands relating that Estate. Lewis William was sent for & came to settle the disputes about his raising Coal to sell upon Pen Wain he being confined to one pit by his Lease to Anthony Bacon & Co. but he had worked in several pits & was then working in another vein on open cast, after several arguments Mr. Morgan, Richard Philips, Lewis Wm & myself walked up to Pen Wain to view it & it appeared that he Lewis William had encroached & had no right to raise Coal in any other pit than one that he had left off as he had not possessed Level he ought to have drove up to clear it of water to enable him to work that pit he was confined to. After many disputes he at last agreed that if Mr. Bacon was of opinion that he ought not to get Coal at any other place than the pit he worked in, where & at the time he granted lease he would leave off & return to the first pit as aforesaid.

Masons upon days wages Walter William, Hopkin David, Thomas Loyd & John Gabriel upon the hammer hatch. Joseph Lucas & James Mason upon one of the Shingling furnaces. David John & 3 More upon the Stamper side Wall upon Bargain. Henry William & 4 more upon the race Arch upon Bargain.

Labourers 2 raising Stone in the Quarry bearing them out for Carts to carry for race Arch, 2 Serving Masons with Stone, 8 filling in upon Arch & filling & Wheeling the gravel & stones that is thrown out of the race in clearing for the Arch, 1 serving Josh Lucas & James Mason 1 at Common Mortar & 1 with Cart fetching Stone for Arch. Abraham Evan & 4 more clearing in the rock for two hammer races upon bargain.

Carpenters George Ford & one of his Men free the fall in the Clay Mill, William Postlethwaite & Josh Gibson making buckets for Stamper wheel & Lewis William fix a Shade for brick, that fell down.

Sawyers 4 sawing for room & roof above the Stamp house & forge p. day.

Horses Six brought one piece of Timber containing 55 feet. 4 fetching Stack Stone from the Wern Land. 2 in Cart fetchg Arch stone from Quarry. 1 at grass recruiting. 13. This day has been showery.

Sunday August 24th. Seven o'clock a fair Morning but overcast & like rain, Wind at South East. This has been a very rainy day, which has occasioned a flood.

Mr. Morgan with me all day. The water ran over the Wear very smooth about 9 inches deep but as the stone & gravel lay higher than the Apron it prevented the Water flowing off smooth but occasioned a boiling which I think may raise some of the sett stones, therefore they should be taken away and given a fare passage for the water to race off, & then I think there will not be any fear of its failing. In the Evening Mr. Morgan went down the Vilage & brought up Mr. Davies of Landaff it being then more moderate but yet rained a little to see the work. There has been strong wind all day.

Monday August 25th. Five minutes past Six o'clock a fair but cool morning overcast & like for more rain the Wind at N.W.

This has been a fine day and the Arching stone gone on briskly. Mr. Morgan & Zachary Philips with my Brother & myself went to the Wern, to view the damage complained of by Philip David, the Tenant by our washing & laying the mine but he was gone to Abergenny, therfore could not be ascertained. Went from there to view the Farm called Cwm y Glo which Land is very poor, but as there is Coal & Mine it is in the Companys Interest to have it, there is a 6 feet vein of Coal near the house very good which has supplied the Tenant with fuel. The house was formerly built by Mr. Davis for Presbyterian meeting. Father to the present Samuel Davis, the Minister of the Meeting near the Bridge.[1]

Mr. Morgan & Zachary agreed to take off 30 Ton from our Account of Timber for Shakes, damaged Trees which were felled by Isaac Bates, our former Carpenter in who we confided to see the trees felled such as were sound & usefull but he acted very treacherously & felled such as were not sound nor fit for our purpose & this allowance not equal to our Loss.

This day Mr. Morgan discharged Lewis William John, from being Bailey to Lord Talbot & Mr. Richards, in very mild, genteel manner and declared to him, that it was not, for any ill usage he had shown to us, but from his not having the Lords Interest in view in discharge that office & the small pittance he was allowed was not worth his action. Mr. Morgan desired that I would send our Carpenter George Ford, to take an Account of all Trees left upon the Estate & those particularly they were sound after leaving sufficient for the use of the Tenements, we should have the remainder. He informed me that Mr. Glover of Abergwiddon Furnace[2] had applied for Contract for all the coal wood in the joint Estate but that we should have the first offer & as we are to have, by our Lease, all Winterwood, for a rail or Waggon way at the rate of

[1] Merthyr Tydfil was an early centre of Dissent. After 1660 a group met secretly at Cwmglo farm; sometime after 1689 a meeting-house was built there and this remained in use until 1749 when Ynysgau chapel in Merthyr village was built. Glanmor Williams, 'Earliest Nonconformists in Merthyr Tydfil', *Merthyr Historian*, i (1976), 84–95. In 1763 the rector of Merthyr described Ynysgau as 'a pompous meeting house': J.R. Guy (ed.), *The Diocese of Llandaff in 1763* (South Wales Record Society, 1991), 66. James Davies was a preacher at Merthyr between 1724 and 1760, his son Samuel between 1750 and 1781: Wilkins, *Merthyr Tydfil*, 169ff. See also above, p. 90.

[2] For which see Riden, *Gazetteer*, 11–12.

Cordwood we should have the whole, & whatever was not useful for us we might sell to Mr. Glover.

Mr. Morgan & Zachary left us about 5 o'clock.

Masons upon days wages Hopkin David only. Harry William & 4 more upon the Arches upon Bargain. David John & 4 more upon the Stamp House ditto.

Labourers 2 raising stones & clearing rubbish in Quarry. 6 serving for Carts, 2 bearing stones to Joseph Lucas at the Stack & Hopkin David. 1 serving Joseph Lucas, 1 at Cardiff & 1 at Common Mortar, 1 wheeling Lime to Arches, 4 Covering the Arches, 1 wheeling Saw dust from the Sawpit, & 2 ridding before the Clay Mill. Total 22.

Abraham Evan & 4 more Sinking the hammer race in the rock for Arching p. Bargain.

Carpenters George Ford, at Aberdair to look for Timber fit for hammerbeams & his two men, William Postlethwaite & Lewis William making Bucket boards for Stamper wheels & Centres for Arching.

Sawyers 4 by day Sawing Boards for Stamper Wheel.

Horses Six brought a piece of Timber containing 38 feet. 4 Issuing hay. 2 leading Stone from Quarry to the Arches. 1 at Grass recruiting. in whole 13

Agreed with William Lewis, the Mine burner at Plymouth furnace to burn all our Mine upon Penwain @ 2d p. Ton to be weighed at the bank were the furnace is to be & 18d p. Ton Carriage this method saves the Carriage of coal it being within about 60 yards from the Mine Stack & of Mine, as it loses 1/3 of its weight in Carrying.

I ordered John William Walter to cut coal where Lewis Wm John is getting for the use of Brick kiln, one Ton of Coal will burn about 3 ton of Mine. The Coal that John William Walter cuts in Lewis Wm John work is too weak for burning brick therefore I ordered more to be cut in another vein more under cover.

Tuessday August 26th. Half past five a a fair fine Morning, Wind at South East.

This Morning after breakfast, I rode up to Penwain, to view the brick & Coal, the last rains have spoilt a Number of fire bricks that were ready & fit for the kiln. They have set a small kiln with fire brick with only 300 of Stack brick and the large kiln with the same & make soft any that were not burnt enough.

Ordered our own horses to fetch Coal from where John William Walter is cutting there for the Brick kiln.

Called at the burning of Mine they were drawing of ashheap, that was burnt, & carrying to the rock as p. agreement before mentioned.

Brought Aaron Wedgwood down to the rock in order to set out the kiln & drying house for Pots.

George Ford & Joseph Lucas are gone to Level the Water in the river for the Blast Furnace. I walked up the river to meet them, we find that there is 30 feet of fall to the Top of our Wear.

	Feet
From the taking in of the water to the rock, Earth is	248
Then there must be a Trough to where the rock is to be cut	150
A rock to be cut 11 feet deep & 5 feet wide in length	178
Earth to be cut 3 feet deep & 4 feet wide	726
A rock to be cut 16 feet deep & 6 feet wide	760
Earth & Rock as supposed	440
A trough across a dingle	180
Earth & rock to the wheel	300
	2982
Yards	994

William Edwards makes	rock	560.yards
	Earth	400
		960

We make rock that is visible 938 feet or 312 yards 2 ft & 681 yards 1 foot of Earth & Trough but it is expected that there will be a great more rock under the present surface of Earth when opened.

Masons upon days wages. Walter William & Hopkin David, Harry William & 2 more at the Arch in hammer race & two more at the Gavel End, on what they call here the pine End, of mixing room p. bargain. David John & 4 more at the race Arches next the Stamper wheel Cases.

Labourers 2 raising stones in the Quarry, 1 clearing off rubbish, 5 repairing a road for Cart to fetch stones for the Stack from the Wern Land, 2 Leveling the floor before the mix room & Clay mill, 3 filling upon the race Arch, 1, Robert Thomas directing of mending the road to the Wern, 2 fetching stone from the Wern upon horses backs, 2 bearing Stone out of the Quarry, 2 Serving Masons, 1 serving James Mason at the Stack & 2 at Common Mortar.

Carpenters George Ford Leveling the water for a cut to bring it to the furnace wheel, his 2 Men, William Postlethwaite & Lewis William at the Bucket boards for Stamper Wheels.

Sawyers 4 Sawing Boards and Roofs for Stamper Wheels & rooms.

Horses 6 brought home 2 pieces of Timber containing 56½ feet, 3 carrying stone from Wern to Stacks, 3 Carrying Coal to Brick kiln 24 load, 1 CW had to ride to the Mountain, whole No 13.

The whole length of Earth & rock as it appears at present is 994 yards of which there is 178 feet of rock in length to be cut 11 feet deep & 5 feet wide, 760 ft of rock to be cut 16 feet deep & 6 feet wide. The deeper the rock is to be cut from the Top the wider it ought to be made to carry the water, as the face of these kinds of rock being softener by the Sun & Air so much as to be open & retain the Water & we suppose the whole charge in bringing it upon the wheel will be vizt.

178 feet of rock in Length & 5 wide will be	11 feet to be taken off	feet 9790 solid		
760 (feet of rock in Length) & 6 (wide will be)	16 (feet to be taken off)	72960 do		
		82750		
÷ 27 = 3065 Solid Yards @ 8d p. yard the same we give as in our race		£102	3	4
1746 feet or 582 yards in Length of Earth at 1/6 p. yard		43	13	-
Trough 450 feet in Length 1 foot deep & 2 feet wide; I reckon that 360 feet of Timber will make the whole length 2s @ ft including sawing & Carriage		36	-	-
Standards to Support the Trough at every 10 feet		5	-	-
Nails 1 cwt		3	-	8
Workmanship for the woodwork		10	-	-
		199	17	-

Since dinner & this Estimate being made I went up the river & waded the shortest way to view every part with George Ford, Jsh Lucas, my Brother (& Abraham Evan and with their Labourer who propose undertaking the Cut) And I find that by going up the river 378 yards higher there will be obtained an additional fall of 20 feet which will make the whole fall to the wheel 50 feet and although we do not require more than 30 feet, yet the advantage in taking the water at the highest place will save a great deal in cutting the rock & Timber for Trough as we may carry the water nearer the Top of rock and have very little cutting & that but in a few places and on the whole I am of opinion it will be the best and cheapest and will be performed in near half the time; and I am further of the opinion will be performed in as little time as the Stack will be in building, these several advantages must give the greatest distance the preference. We wanting Line would not measure how much further the higher place is than the first place. the convenience of taking in the water at both places I think near equal as each has the rock to guide it into the intended cut by nature much securer & better than any Art could make it & turn it on the side of the river that is in our Lease, belonging to Lord Talbot & Michael Richard Esq. many of these Natural Wears are in the river, one above another as convenient for such

Aquaeducts as one could wish the rock is limestone & the opposite side belongs to Mr. Gwin and Penrice Watkins, an Attorney in Brecon, his stewart for him who faithfully promised to procure one Lease of part of the Limestone for our work at 2 guineas a year. I have sent & wrote often to him since that promise but have not received any answer which I impute to the neglect of a gratuity & my not receiving him in person for that purpose, which ought to be done before we begin to blow as we shall be at a loss for the want of that flux.

Wednesday August 27th. Six o'clock a close overcast Morning with small rain, Wind at S.E. Rain until eleven when it cleared up and appears to be a fine day.

The Question of bringing the water higher up the river, on the other side of this leaf, should have come in here as it was transacted this day.

Masons upon day wages Walter William, Hopkin David & John Gabriel.

Joseph Lucas & James Mason upon the Shingling Furnace Stack, Harry William & two more upon hammer race Arches & 2 more of his Men upon Pine End of the Mixing room p. bargain.

David John & 4 more of his men upon the latter end of the Stamper races next to the wheel cases p. bargain.

Labourers 3 in the Quarry raising stone for the Arches, 2 Leading stones out of the Quarry, 4 bearing Arch stones to David John, 4 covering the Arch, after finishing, 4 wheeling the rock raised in both the races for hammer & chafery, 2 serving Masons p. day work with stones, 1 at Common Mortar, 2 serving upon the flourishing stacks. In Number 22.

Abraham Evan & 4 more cutting the rock for hammer & Chafery races p. bargain.

Carpenters George Ford, his 2 men, Wm Postlethwaite & Lewis William upon Stamper Bucket for wheel. George for day up the river as before.

Sawyers 4 sawing hammer wheel arms p. day.

Horses 6 brought a piece of Timber containing 42 feet, 3 horse carryed 18 load of Coal to brick kiln, 3 horse brought 4 large stones from the Wern & bearing them ready for the Low Furnace, 1 Galloway at Grass, [*Total*] 13.

This day there has been Showery but not to prevent the work going forward. Wrote to the Doctor[1] & my wife.

[1] i.e. Brownrigg.

Thursday August 28th. Half past five o'clock a fine Morning. Wind at South West.

Eight o'clock it is overcast & rains & very like to continue.

Part of the burnt Mine is brought down & laid upon the Bank near where the furnace is intended and is well done & looks like such as makes good metal.

As it is the opinion of several colliers that there is coal occurring a few yards of the surface of the rock, now cutting for the hammer races I borrowed the Low furnace boring rods, & this day set 2 Men to bore for them & got 9 foot through into the Sill this day.

Near Seven o'clock Wind continues S.W. it has been a fair afternoon.

Masons upon day wages Walter William, Hopkin David, John Gabriel, & Thomas Loyd upon the hammer hatches. Morgan Evan Jenkins has been absent some time, came this day, and is upon his bargain, the flourishing furnace Ashpit. David John & 4 more Masons upon his bargain the Stamping House p. bargain. Harry William & 4 more Masons upon hammer race Arch p. bargain.

Joseph Lucas & James Mason Scabbling stone for Shingling Furnace Stack.

Labourers 2 raising stones in the Quarry, 1 removing rubbish 4 carrying stones out for Cart, 2 serving Masons with stones upon the hammer hatch, 2 clearing the Stamp house 2 serving the Masons with stones, for Arch walls, 2 boring in the Sill rock, 6 wheeling the rock from the races, 1 at Common Mortar, 1 serving Joseph Lucas & 1 Leading Arch stones in a Cart from the Quarry Number 23.

Carpenters George Ford & his 2 Men, William Postlethwaite & Lewis William upon the Stamping Wheel, fixing the buckets and odd jobs.

Sawyers 4 Sawing Arms for hammer wheel per day.

Horses 4 with 2 Men ploughing at Plymouth Co. Estate, 3 in Cart fetching Stone from Wern for Stack, 1 Leading Arch stone from the Quarry, 4 Leading Coal to the Brick kiln, 1 Galloway that I rode to the Wern Land, Whole No 13.

Abraham Evan & 4 more Labourers cutting rock for hammer & chafery race p. bargain.

Agreed with the burning of Mine to allow them 6d for every Ton of the Mine they burn for their cutting the coal in the vein & carrying it to the Mine. The bargain as it now stands is 6d p. Ton or 21 cwt for getting & carrying the coal and burning the Mine at 1s 6d p. Ton carriage to the furnace bank the whole charge upon the bank 2s per 21 cwt.

Philip David of the Wern having stoped up the road that we made to fetch the stones in his Land, pretending that we had no right to come through, althou I sent him word that I would pay him all reasonable damages, this would not satisfy him, therefore I rode to the place & pulled down brushwood that was made up with & gave liberty for our Cart to go through, we having free Liberty by our Lease from the Lords as also under his own hand to cut any water course we might have occasion to make for the use of our Works.

Edward Farnel & his men putting up the Sparrs upon the mixing room roof p. bargain.

Friday August 29th. Six o'clock a cloudy Morning. Wind South West.

This morning sett out the drying house & pot kilns & set 2 Labourers to level for the foundation.

Near one o'clock Showery weather. George Ford & Joseph Lucas with my Brother went up the river to mark out & measure the distance of the Cut from the higher place to gain 50 feet fall by which the Water will be brought to high upon the rock, as to save the cutting of rock, which would have cost at least £100 which will give us liberty to raise our wheel as high above the back water to free us from any fear from flood etc. The distances are as under vizt

	Yards	
From the higher place to the first intended one is	378	-
To the rock which would be cut 11 ft deep & 5 ft wide, if the water had been taken at the first place	132	-
To a Dingle where a Trough must be about 4 yards long	77	-
To the rock what would have been cut 16 ft deep & 6 feet wide had the water been taken at the first place	80	-
To this rock in Length will be cut 6 feet deep	364	-
To a Dingle	188	2
The Dingle, a Wall & Trough	60	-
To the delivery of the water	66	2
	1346	1

This we imagine may be performed for 2s p. yard in length which will amount to £134 12s.

		£		
The remainder of the great Arch clearing	85 yards @ 4d	1	8	4
Part of do	59¾ 4d	1	19	11
Rock in hammer & Chafery race	109½ 8d	3	13	-
Abraham Evan & 4 partners for a fortnight work		6	1	3

Harry William & David Thomas f. building mixing room 109 perch				
		£5	12	2
Arching grand arch 61½ yards	@ 4s 8ft wide	12	6	-
do 4ft wide 20 yards 2 ft	@ 3s	3	2	-
do 3 ft wide 15 yards	@ 2/6	1	17	6
		22	17	8
37 yards of great Arch	@ 5/6 p. yard	10	3	6
for setting part of the Wear		2	7	6
5 Arches @ 1/6 p. Arch		0	7	6
		35	16	2
rock in chafery race	44 yards at 8d			
	2½ yards at 8d	1	9	-

Masons upon day wages Thomas Loyd ¼ of a day only, Morgan Jenkins & John Gabriel are finishing their bargain, the flourishing furnace Ashpit. Walter William & Hopkin David were Scabbling stones for finishing their bargain the side of the Pool wall.

David John & 4 more Masons upon their bargain the Stamp house. Harry William & 4 more Masons upon the hammer race Arch as per bargain.

Labourers 2 raising stones in the Quarry, 4 bearing stones and 4 serving Masons upon bargain, 4 levelling floor for kiln, 2 boring for coal, 5 wheeling rock for race, 1 @ common Mortar, 3 placing brick 2 clearing in Stamper Mill No 24.

Sawyers 4 sawing beams for Stamp house

Horses 4 ploughing at Plymouth furnace, 3 fetching stone from the Wern in Cart, 4 do on their back, 2 at grass.

Saturday August 30th. Near Six o'Clock. A Warm Morning there has been a deal of rain this last night the river is raised and the water goes smoothly over the Wear. Wind at S.W.

Mr. Terry called this morning and gave me underwritten Estimate of a railway 1800 yards with 8 Waggons each Waggon to carry 36 cwt vizt.

3800 yards of rails & Strikers @ 6½d p. yard		£97	10	10
3600 sleepers if cut of cordwood @ 4d		60	-	-
Laying them at 3s 6d per score or 20 yards		15	15	-
Making the ground at 2s p. Score		9	-	-
Filling & packing up at 1s per Score		4	10	-
Incidents		5	-	-
	Railway	191	15	10
8 waggons @ £6 14s 6d p. waggon		53	16	-
		245	11	10

If the sleepers were of Timber of Oak they would be 9d p. piece therefore by having the Liberty, by our Lease of such at the price of cord wood a saving of £75.

Expenses of a Waggon vizt.

Timber & boards	£2	4	-	
Iron work 1 cwt 2 q @ 3d p. lb	2	2	-	
Brasses 16 lb @ 1s	-	16	-	
Nails	-	2	6	
Cast wheels 3 cwt @ 8s @ cwt	1	4	-	
Making	-	6	-	£6 14 6

Expence of 100 yards of rails if of oak Bought at present price

36 feet of Timber @ 35s p. Ton	1	11	6	
Carriage	-	15	-	
Sawing 220 feet	-	7	-	2 13 6
1 Yard is about 8½d				

This day agreed with Abraham Evan & his partner to make the Cut mentioned the 29th Instant.[1] In length 1346 yards, the width & depth as they shall be directed at 6d p. solid yard rock or Earth, as it may happen, we finding them Gunpowder if necessary, sharpening their tools & lending them chisels or Crow & what picks already made that we can spare, they paying for them if not returned and they are obliged to finish it by the 11th day of February 1767.

We allow the breadth at the bottom 3 feet, to slope at the top to 5 feet and the depth at the medium suppose at 6 feet.

1346 × 3 = 4038 × 4 = 16152 × 6 = 96912 : 27 = 3589 solid yards at 6d p. yard is £89 14s 6d, allow 2 cwt one barrell of powder at £5, Walls upon the rock £2 & £3 5s 6d for mending tools, the whole £100.

[1] See above, p. 134.

This sum I expect will complete it. The distance is 378 yards more than William Edward proposed to bring it to gain 27 feet fall & asked £300 for doing it and I thought then should not dear, before I waded the river (there being no other way to examine it) & went higher I found by going 378 yards higher up I gained 23 feet more fall which carryed me above several rocks that must have been cut from 11 to 16 feet deep as before mentioned and although the length was more the charge of sinking it would be reduced two thirds and much sooner.

Abraham Evan & his 4 partners have finished the Cutting the rock for the hammer & Chafery races & the Arches are being brought up within a length which may be finished in 2 days. One hammer hatch is finished & the other has about a week work. When that is done the most difficult & tedious work will be over which I rejoice at.

Masons p. day not any having done in that method. David Johns 3 Men at the Stamphouse side Wall p. bargain. David John, Harry William, Edward Thomas John & three more all at the ale house & I hear that they are very Drunk.

Labourers 2 raising stones in the Quarry. Clearing it of the rubbish, 4 shifting heaps of Mine that was gathered in diging foundations races etc. 5 covering arches, 2 with Josh. Lucas & James Mason at the flourishing Stack, 1 Tampering Clay to lay the fire brick in the inside of the Stack, 3 boring for Coal, 3 at Common Mortar, 2 making a floor for pots.

Carpenters George Ford, his 2 Men, William Postlethwaite & Lewis William taking a Stamper wheel to pieces that is finished & odd jobs.

Sawyers 4 Sawing Beams for dwellings above the Stamphouse and forge.

Evan John is covering the Mixing Room.

There has been showers but moderates all this day not to prevent those hands that were at work continuing on it. There is bored 9½ yard in the rock or blue Sill, without any alterationin 3 days & as much above it so that this rock from the surface of the hill will be near 20 yards & how much is there time must show.

Some very fine Common & fire brick are burnt down, made in the last fine weather & now they have a shade to put them under when dry I hope we shall not loose any more by wet weather. We have had great loss in the Brick, as also the makers by the wet season.

In considering the carriage of Coal & Mine to the furnace and Coal to the flourishing & shingling furnace. The upgrading of a rail or Waggonway will appear by the underwritten Observations. The Blast Furnace I expect will make 18 Ton of metal weekly which with the coal for that quantity & Workmen will be 100 Ton weekly. The flourishing furnaces, suppose but 4 kept constantly at work, will take 80 Ton p. week. Two shingling furnaces @ 20 Ton Each is 40 Ton a week, Workmen, Pot kiln, & Drying house 20 ton a week. The whole Carriage will be as under vizt.

				£	s	d
Coal	for Blast Furnace	100. T				
do	for flourishing do	80				
do	for Shingling	40				
do	for Pots etc.	20	240.T @ 1/6 p. Ton p. Week			
				£18	-	-
Mine	3½ Ton to a Ton of Metal		63.T @ 1/6	4	14	6
Clay & Brick			50.T @ 3s Ton	7	10	-
	The Weekly carriage			30	4	6
	For one year will be			1571	14	-

The charge for a railway	£ 200		
8 Waggons	60		260
Interest of the Sum for one year	13		
to keep the railway in repair p.	47		
8 horses at £10 p. annum	80		
8 Men @ 7s p. week Each	145	12	285 12

By this it appears that there will be a saving, in the Carriage by having railway £1286 2s p. annum.

Sunday August 31st. At quarter past Six o'clock. A fine morning. Wind at West but very little of it.

About Ten o'clock Mr. Thomas Guest came to the rock & gave my brother & me an invitation to Dine with him; we accepted it and about One went to the vilage & waited upon Mr. Guest. After Dinner we set talking over affairs, & he was of my opinion that it would be long before the Plymouth furnace would Blow again as there would be necessity of a call of £100 p. share to prepare the furnace, lay in a stock of Mine, make a railway, & several additions for a long profitable Blast, which he said several of the Partners were not able to do.

Mr. Powel, Rector, came in & drank Tea with us, after he walked up to see the Wear & Work with us & then parted to return with Mr. Guest back to the Vilage.

This has been a fine day and not any rain. Mr. Powel says they have had, for a fortnight past very fine weather at Brecon & that most of their wheat is got in but a short Crop from Number of deaf Ears which is the same with us in this Valey.

This is the last day I dine with our Landlady as boarder. Tomorrow we begin to keep house ourselves and we have hired Ann Owen our

Landladys servant with her leave & Consent. Bought a quarter of Mutton yesterday to begin with cost 1s 9d. Our Meat Markets are Saturday & Tuesday.

Monday September 1st. A quarter past six o'clock, a dark cloudy morning with small rain; the Wind at West.

Wrote to Mr. Bacon and sent him the underwritten estimate.

Mr. Terry Estimate of a railway 1800 yards in Length, with 8 Waggons each Waggon to carry 36 cwt vizt.

3800 yards of rails & Strikers @ 6d p. yard	97	10	10
3600 sleepers (if out of Cordwood at 4d)	60	-	-
Laying at 3/6 p. Score or 20 yards	15	15	-
Making the ground at 2s per Score	9	-	-
Filling & packing up at 1s p. Score	4	10	-
Incidents	5	-	-
	191	15	10
C. Wood adds	8	4	2
	200	-	-

	£					
8 Waggons £6 14s 6d p. Waggon	53	16	-			
CW adds to make p. Waggon hold 2 T	10	4	-	64	-	-

N.B. If the sleepers were of Oak & purchased at the Customary price they would be 9d each.

This charge of £200 is for one way only. But as we have different veins of Coal, and different qualities will be used, the Mine got in various places. Throughout to be branches from the direct rail way. But the distances of each branch cannot be ascertained until we have experience of the Quality of the several vains. But I will call the whole charge

	£400	-	-
8 Waggons at £8 to carry a Ton	64	-	-
10 horses with gear for such work @ £15	150	-	-
	614	-	-
10 Men to drive and attend them at 7s p. week	182	-	-
Interest of £614 for one year	30	14	-
10 Horses keeping at £10 each per annum	100	-	-
To keep the railways in repair for one year	50	-	-
yearly charge	362	14	-

100 Ton of Coals	carried weekly for Blast Furnace	
80 do	for flourishing furnaces	
50 do	for Shingling furnaces	
30 do	do for Pots, brick & workmen	£
260 of Coal a week the Carriage at 1/6 p. Ton for 1 year		1014 - -
63 of Mine weekly	at do do	245 14 -
Clay for pots & brick at 3s p. Ton for one year		390 - -
		1649 14 -

This is the Total of the Annual Carriage if there is not a railway and if it was to be let off. But what the charge of keeping a Number of horses & men, to perform this ourselves, These I have not considered This sum is exclusive of the charge of making a road & repairing. But in the present situation everything must be brought down upon Horse-backs.

The Annual Expense upon the railway will be	362 14 -
The Annual saving by having a railway	1287 - -

N.B. In that sent to Mr. Bacon I have made a mistake in the Annual Expense upon rail way charing £692 14d instead of £362 14d, the difference as much as £330. Wrote this day to my wife.

Showery weather.

Masons p. day Morgan Evan Jenkins as he is a good Workman and willing to work in own way by direction. I employ him in Scabbling stone for Air furnace Stack the only one by day. David John & his Men, it being a rainy day, scabbled stone in the Pool for their bargain, the Stamper House. Harry William, Edward Thomas & three more Masons were drinking Saturday, Sunday & this day. These are not to be depended upon, must be kept short of money, the only method to keep them from the Alehouse. Joseph Lucas & James Mason upon altering the flourishing furnace for a Casting furnace in order to cast the Cylinders etc. for Bellows. And if I can agree with the Plymouth Company stock for all their pigs and metal, after the Cylinders are cast etc. the remainder of the metal may be granulated in the furnace & when they are altered into flourishing this metal will be ready for that operation.

Labourers 4 Boring. 2 filling upon the Arches, four making a Saw pit, to cast the Cylinder, 6 clearing the Stamp house & the back to fix the wheel frame & sill for Stamping, 1 making up Common Mortar.

Carpenters The same as Saturday, but Lewis William absent.

Sawyers 4 sawing Principals for roof over the Stamp House & forge.

Horses Six brought two pieces of Timber containing 45½ feet. Seven bringing stones from the Wern for Stack. The whole No 13.

This day the Labourers began upon cutting the water course for the Blast Furnace at 6d p. solid yard.

Tuesday September 2nd. Six o'clock a cloudy morning a strong West Wind with rain.

One o'clock there has been rain all this day, the river is raised & by appearance it is very like a continuance of rain. After two my Brother went with me to meet Mr. Jenkins of Morlas at Edward Morgan in the Vilage. I proposed agreeing with him for the Liberty of procuring the Iron out of the Cinderheap near the Plymouth Furnace to give him 10s p. Ton for what Iron I could get by washing or any other method. He told me that I was welcome to begin & do as I pleased, & that he would not differ with me, that after I had begun & we could not then agree I could leave off. This was the purport of our discourse relating this affair.

Mr. Terry brought me Account of the Castings we have had & desired that I would let him have money to carry him home. I let him have 2 guineas all I had spare & gave him leave to draw upon me, for his board, which he said would amount to 3 or 4 pound more. He said he was calculating the value of their metal in Stock vizt. 95 Ton of Pig of different quality and the Scrap metal about 9 or 10 cwt, that the pigs he thought should be at 3/10 and the Scrap at £2 10s p. Ton delivered at their furnace present money. I told him that I would give that price delivered here And as he will see Mr. White & the other partners he would inform them of it, & he thought they could not do better.

Masons Morgan Evan Jenkins Scabbling stones for the Air furnace Stacks p. day.

Harry William & three more upon the hammer race Arch p. bargain. David John & 3 more upon the Stamp house upon Bargain.

Joseph Lucas & James Mason upon two casting furnaces for casting the cylinders.

Carpenters George Ford & his Men & William Postlethwaite upon the Clay Mill wheel. Lewis William absent.

Sawyers Sawing roof timbers for Forge & Stamper house.

Horses Six brought 2 pieces of Timber containing 69 feet. 2 in Carts leading Arch stones from Quarry. 2 leading fireclay to the Brick kilns. 2 at the Wain fair[1] to fetch Oatmeal etc. and taking two Bullocks to sell. 1 at grass. 13 our whole Number.

No Oatmeal to be bought at the fair, & cattle the dearest that was ever known, a quarter of Mutton cost 2s, did not sell the Bullocks.

[1] For which see above, p. 4, and below, p. 165.

Wednesday Sept 3. Half past six o'clock, fine calm Morning. The Wind at West.

Past Six Evening. This has been a fine day, untill about four o'clock when it overcast and rained small rain.

Masons Morgan Evan Jenkins Scabbling Stones for Stock upon days wages. Walter William Amos & Hopkin David upon the pool wall that was left open to carry Earth & Stones out upon bargain.

David John & 4 more upon the Bargain the Stamp house. Harry William & 3 more upon the last length of the Arching the hammer hatch Arch upon Bargain. Joseph Lucas & James Mason upon the flourishing furnace Stack.

Carpenters George Ford his 2 Men & William Postlethwaite upon Clay Mill Wheel. The Stamper being finished.

Labourers 4 Boring (they have got near 16 yards in the blue sill) Called in Shropshire Clunch (must wait until we get more rods made to go thro' it when we expect Coal) 4 serving Clay & Brick on the Stack, 3 clearing the Stamp house for laying p. wheel case & Stamper frame Sills & 2 filling the Sandpit with sand for casting, 1 serving Walter William & Hopkin David, 6 p. Cardiff Lime, 1 at Common Mortar, 3 in the Quarry raising Stone & 7 went to House hay & wheat, No 26.

Sawyers 4 raising roof timber for Stamping House and the dwelling over the Forge.

Horses Six brought 2 pieces of Timber in the morning 54½ feet. After carried in hay & wheat. Too wet for timber. 3 leading clay to kilns. 4 leading coals to do. Our whole No 13

My Brother and I walked to the head of the cut for bringing the water to the furnace wheel the Men go on well about 4 feet deep is a clay, then hard rock which requires blasting.

Thursday September 4th. A quarter past six o'Clock a close thick Morning with small rain Wind in West. After Six this has been a fine day we got in all our hay & one field of wheat & it has the appearance of fine weather.

Masons Morgan Evan Jenkins Scabbling stones p. day wages. Walter William Amos & Hopkin David at the Pool wall p. bargain. David John & 2 more upon the Stamp house p bargain. Harry William & 3 more upon the Forge race Arch p. bargain. Joseph Lucas & James Mason upon the flourishing furnace stack p wages.

Labourers. 2 raising stones in the Quarry, 1 clearing rubbish, 2 Carrying stones out for Cart, 1 leading with horse & cart to Rock, 4 wheeling the earth that came out of the race upon the Arches, 9 shoring the foundations in the Stamp House for wheel case & stamper frame sleepers 4 serving with brick, mortar & clay upon the Stack, 1 serving Walter Hopkin at Cardiff Mortar & 1 at Common Mortar. No 26.

Carpenters. George Ford & his 2 Men, William Postlethwaite and Lewis William upon the Stamper wheel case fixing one of them to Stamper frame cheeks, preparing them to fix.

Sawyers 4 Sawing beams & principals for the Stamperhouse and forge roofs.

Horses 6 brought a piece of Timber in the Morning. Leading hay & Corn all day. 2 fetching Clay for the Mountain to lay in firebrick kiln. 3 loading Coal for the kiln to burn Brick. 2 Lead stone for Arches & 1 at grass. Our whole No 13.

Friday Sept. 5th. Six o'clock. A fine Morning but cool the Wind at West.

Six o'clock This day has been a fine day but cool, the air is much changed. Rered the floor over the Stamp house for dwelings.

Masons Morgan Evan Jenkins scabbling stones for Air furnace Stack, David John & 2 Men upon the Stamp house upon bargain. Walter William Amos & Hopkin David upon the Pool Wall bargain. Harry William & 3 more upon the hammer race Rock do. Joseph Lucas, James Mason & Wm Benj'in upon the furnace stack.

Labourers 2 raising stones in the Quarry, 1 clearing away rubbish, 4 serving brick, clay & Mortar upon Stack, 4 wheeling away rock that came out of the race, upon the arches 2 filling the sand pit in casting house, 1 with Walter William & Hopkin David, 1 at Cardiff & 1 at Common Mortar, 2 at the Stamp house & cleaning the foundation for wheel cases & Stamper sleepers, 5 assisting Edwd Farnels to rear the floor above the Stamp House & 2 went to house wheat, No 25.

Carpenters George Ford, his two men, William Postlethwaite and Lewis William at the Clay mill wheel & Stamper frames.

Sawyers 4 sawing roof timber & Bends for forge wheels

Horses Six bro't 2 pieces of Timber containing 71 feet. Two leading Clay to the Brick kiln. One leading Arch stones. four at farm. The whole 13.

The rooms above the Stamp house, will be very convenient for Workmen the whole house is 42 by 33 feet, in the clear, divided into 4 dwellings and the same over the hatches & forge.

Saturday Sept. 6th. A quarter after Six o'clock. A fine Morning, little Wind at West.

Near Eleven a fine day so far, I am just now returned from viewing & letting the back race from the river to the furnace Wheel there to

Rosser Thomas, his brother, William Rhys & William Lewis, to be made 10 feet wide & drive up 18 inches, below the river as it now is, about three inches above the Wear, at 3d p. Earth, Sand etc. and for the rock 8d p. Cubic Yard.

Finished the flourishing Stack & took the Scaffolding down, the pipe 22 inches diameter & 32 ft high from the joining Flue to the Stack.

The Stack is 8 ft 6 in. by 5 ft 9 in. Common brick 18 inches to the pipe Brick about 1 ft thick, then one offcut 2 inches which makes further inch & about 10 foot higher another offsett & then 9 inches to the pipe brick. The making of such a substantial Stack is very necessary, which reduces the fear workmen have in our lining then when the fire brick is burnt thin, when the case is thin & the lining is taken out there is great danger of it falling as we have at Lowmill is of this sort, & must be taken down before it can be made use of as no workmen would venture to go in to take out & put in a new lining. But when strong, workmen go upon it with pleasure the thinner clay & Mortar & when building the difference in the Expence is no great affair, to obtain that pleasure they in the end will always be found the cheapest method.

Showers since 3 o'clock. Put down Chafery wheel case & Edward Thomas John is preparing the Arch up to it.

Masons Joseph Lucas, James Mason, William Benjamin upon one of the Shingling Air furnace Stacks upon wages. Morgan Jenkin was not here this day, could not work as he had a large boil upon his arm. David John & one more finished the Arch in one of the hammer races, up to the Wheel & preparing to do the same to the Chafery wheel p. Bargain. Harry William & one more Scabbling Stone in the Quarry, for the far hammer hatch p. Bargain.

Labourers 2 raising stones in the Quarry, 1 clearing rubbish out of it, 2 bearing stones out for the Cart, 1 Leading stones for the Arches over the Case, 5 fitting & wheeling the rock that came out of the races, to fill up vacancy in the road, 2 bearing Scabbled stones to the hammer hatch, 2 bearing Sand to the Lime 1 at the Common Mortar, 7 clearing the forward end of the Stamphouse & rock for the wheel cases & Stamper Sills, & 1 with Joseph Lucas & 1 striking for Smith. No 24.

Carpenters George Ford, his 2 men fixing the Chafery Wheel case, William Postlethwaite & Lewis Williams upon the Clay Mill Wheel.

Sawyers 4 sawing for Stamp house & forge roof & shrouds for Clay Mill wheel.

Horses 6 brought 3 pieces of Timber containing 49½ feet. 1 leading stones for race Arches. 2 leading clay for bricks. 4 at grass being poor & requiring rest. Whole Number 13.

Evan John Tylor has covered the mixing house, all but the rigging & is preparing for flourishing house.

Edward Fernals & his men are preparing the roofs for Stamping house & forge per bargain.

Walter William Amos & Hopkin David worked at the pool wall this month and no more this day, upon bargain.

The farms are under the care of John Morgan, he brings me Account of what is done there about twice every week, all our wheat is got in.

Sunday Sept. 7th. Seven o'clock, a rainy Morning & there has been rain most of the night as there is now a flood. The Wind at West.

It rained until eleven then cleared up & was fine fair weather the remainder of the day. After dinner took walk with my Bro'r, George Ford, Joseph Lucas & George Lyndon to Lewenkelly and drank tea with William Postlethwaite & his wife where we met our Landlady Jane Morgan. Viewed that house to see if it could be made convenient for my wife. But it is the opinion of Geo. Ford & Josh Lucas that it would cost too much money & that it would be more prudent to build three or four rooms & to make the present house into offices which will be the best & cheapest method.

Monday Sept. 8th. Half past six small rain there has been a deal last night or this morning the river is high Wind at NW.

About eight my Brother went to Cowbridge to Mr. Morgan for money being out of Cash & obliged to borrow to pay some small sums.

This has been a rainy day, no Walling could be done the river has been higher than I have seen it since I came here this year.

Masons Joseph Lucas, James Mason & William Benjamin Scabbling Stack stones p. wages. David John & his brother Scabbling do p. foot at 9d. Henry William & 3 more absent this day. Walter William Amos, Hopkin David & Morgan Evan Jenkins absent.

Labourers. Two in the Quarry, raising stones, 1 clearing rubbish out, 1 bringing stones out for Cart, 1 Leading flags for mixing room, 2 wheeling rock upon Arches & 2 filling, 2 Leveling the bank before the Stamping house, 7 clearing the foundation in Stamp House for wheel cases & Stamper frame sills, 1 beating & sanding the pavement in the Clay Mill & 1 at Common Mortar. No 20.

Carpenters George Ford his two men & William Postlethwaite at the Stamper frames. Lewis Williams absent.

Sawyers 4 sawing Shrouds for Clay Mill wheel.

Horses 6 brought 4 pieces of timber containing 58½ feet. 1 Leading flags to Mixing room. 2 with my brother to Cowbridge to fetch money. 4 at grass being run down. Our whole No 13.

Wrote to my wife.

Tuesday September 9th. Six o'clock a fine Morning, the Wind at N.W.

This morning Rosser Thomas & his partner begun the cut, from the river for the back race for the Blast furnace wheel as p. agreement mentioned Saturday the 6th instant.

Agreed with Rhys David to make a road join the Quarry, under the rock, next the river, for a Cart to carry stones to the Blast furnace Stack for two guineas.

Leveled the bank against which the furnace is proposed to be built it is 47 ft high to the flat part of the field & from thence, to the surface of water (about 6 inch rising over the Wear) 19 feet more, in the whole 66 ft. The stack may be 50 ft high, the foundation 6 feet & then there will remain 10 ft for the cistern & cut or back race for a flat bottom boat to convey the metal to the flourishing furnace etc. It may be contrived for the metal to be put into the Boat, out of the Cistern, which will save the room for Binns, & Labour in taking it out of the bins. This may be considered of.

Masons Joseph Lucas, James Mason & Benjamin John at the Stacks upon day wages.

David John & 3 more up the Stamp house upon bargain. Harry William & 2 more up the Chafery race Arch next the wheel do.

Labourers 2 raising stones in the Quarry, 1 clearing rubbish 4 bearing stones each ¼ and 2 more a whole day to the hammer hatch, 5 filling & wheeling rock from the races, 1 half day do, 1 Leveling before the Stamp house, 1 Lading water out of the hammer wheel race, 1 Serving Joseph Lucas & 1 at Common Mortar, No 19.

Carpenters George Ford, his 2 men, William Postlethwaite and Lewis William upon fixing another Stamper wheel case Clay Mill wheel & Stamper cheek & sills.

Sawyers 4 sawing shrouds for wheels & joists & spars for Stamp house.

Horses 6 brought a piece of Timber containing 64½ ft. 2 carrying clay to Brick kiln. 2 housing corn. 2 with my brother to Cowbridge. 1 Lent workman wife, to Brecon fair. In whole 13.

This has been a fine day and a deal of corn got in. Wind at N.

Agreed with sundrys to raise in Penwain Common 200 dozen of Mine at 2/6 p. dozen reckoning a Solid yard @ dozen, or 12 bushel in measure to be taken either way at the option of the Company & they agree to leave 6d p. dozen in Sam'l Wood hands, untill the whole quantity is raised by them.

Peter Jones was agreed with the 12th of August last to raise 500 dozen of Mine @ 2/6 p. dozen or a solid yard & 2 inches higher than 3ft.

Wednesday September 10th. Seven o'clock a rainy Morning Wind South West.

This has been a very rainy day in Walling, another week could be done but under cover.

Masons Joseph Lucas & James Mason paving Clay Mill floor & Benjamin John Scabbling stones for Stacks. David John & 4 more Scabbling by the foot in length under cover. Harry William & 2 more preparing flags for mixing room floor.

Labourers 4 making a road next the river under the rock for Cart p. bargain, 1 attending the paviour in Clay Mill, 5 Cutting & wheeling rock, 2 leveling the bank, 4 bearing sand to Cardiff Lime, 2 carrying flags into Mixing room & 1 at Common Mortar, mixing Lime & Sand in the rain.

Carpenters. George Ford, his 2 Men, William Postlethwaite & Lewis William upon the Stamper Cheeks & Sills in the house.

Sawyers 4 Sawing shrouds for Stamper Wheel & Spars for Stamper roof.

Horses 6 brought 2 pieces of Timber containing 45½ feet. 2 Carrying Clay to Brick kilns. 2 Carrying Coal to Workmen & our room. 3 at Grass they are quite poor & require rest. Our whole 13.

5 Labourers cutting the Blast furnace back race p. bargain. 6 ditto, cutting the water course to the furnace p. bargain

Thursday Sept 11. Half past Six a rainy Morning, the Wind N.W.

Nine o'clock Breakfast, it continues raining, no work to be done by either Masons or Labourers therefore the former Scabble stones, under cover p. foot in length and the latter have not any work to do, in the house. Exceeding bad weather the Corn must suffer greatly. The river is high and like to increase. Wind strong North Western.

Five in the Evening it has rained all day & occasioned a large flood, the highest we have had since I came into this County.

Masons Joseph Lucas, James Mason & Benjamin John at the casting furnace.

Labourers 6 Cutting rock for chafery Stamper & wheeling it away ¼ day. Leveling the Bank ¼, 1 at Common Mortar ¼ & 1 serving Josh Lucas at the Casting furnace, No 16.

Carpenters George Ford, his 2 men, William Postlethwaite & Lewis Williams upon stamper frame, putting Gudgeons in Clay Mill rolls and making helves for hatches.

Sawyers 4 Sawing Stamper cheeks & joists for floor.

Horses all at rest this very rainy day.

Robert Wilson came down and informed me, that they had put all the Brick under the shade and preserved them from this wet day, that they had the small kiln filled with Stack brick, except a few flat ones at Top, that the large kiln was filled with fire brick ready for burning, when it was fair & the Wind abated.

This day studded the mixing room floor for binns for metal, and Harry Williams, Edward Thomas, & their two men were flaging where the Binns are to be.

David John & 3 more Masons were scabbling stones for the Shingling furnace Stack bottoms p. the foot in length vizt. 3d p. foot. The river was within 22 inches of the top of the Wall next the grate at the flood gate. But my Brother & several others say there has been floods near three foot higher, therefore it will be prudent to raise the Wall at the Ends of the Wear, three feet higher than they are at present, which will certainly save them from any future flood. The danger being the Water getting behind the Wall and washing the Earth from it, undermine it & the Wall to lett down which may prove of bad consquence to the Wear.

Friday Sept. 12th. Six o'clock A fair fine Morning. The river much lowered. Wind N.W.

About Eleven o'clock a smart shower of rain for about 10 minutes, then fair & Sun warm & clear. Wind continues N.W. Staked out the Cut for the Canal, & back race, from furnace wheel.

George Ford took the Clay Mill wheel of the frame & is fixing it on to place in Clay Mill.

Two of the Clay Mill roll spindles broke in driving into the Center of the rolls in the round, where they were case hardened therefore that method must be laid aside. The Iron of a good grain & sound in every other part.

Evan John Tyler is covering the flourishing house.

Five o'clock it rains again & looks like continuing.

Masons Joseph Lucas, James Mason & Benjamin Jones at the stacks p. days wages. Hopkin David upon the Pool Walls per bargain. David

John & 4 more upon the Stamping House p. Bargain. Harry William & 3 more upon the Chafery race Arch & hammer Hatch p. Bargain.

Labourers 6 cutting rock for Stamper Sills & wheeling it off. 6 Leveling the Bank, 2 bearing stones to hammer hatch, 2 serving at the Stack, 1 bearing stones to the pool walls, 1 at Cardiff Lime & 1 housing fire brick. Number 19. This being pay day we have discharged 5, as we shall continue to do, as work is drawing to a conclusion & not so much wanted. 4 making a road under the rock next the river p. Bargain. 5 Cutting the back race for Furnace wheel p. bargain 6 Cutting the race to carry the water to ditto p. bargain.

Carpenters George Ford & his 2 Men, William Postlethwaite & Lewis William removing & fixing the Clay Mill Wheel & preparing the Stamper frames.

Sawyers 4 Sawing for Stamping House roof. Evan John covering the flourishing house with Stone Tyles.

Edward Farnel & his 3 Men framing the Stamp house roof.

Saturday September 13th. A quarter past six o'clock & a fine Morning Wind in West.

About eight a large shower of rain, cold & a strong Wind at West.

Six o'clock this has been a Cold showery day the Wind continuing W.

Masons Joseph Lucas, James Mason & Benjamin Jones at the Shingling furnace stacks.

Harry William & 2 more have finished the Arching all the races, up to the wheel cases and made up the hatch at the farr hammer ready for the Sill & frame for the Sluice this has taken 7 Load of Cardiff Lime, which must make it quite firm & waterproof & as it is all upon the rock can never fail. David John & 4 more were upon the Stamphouse Gavel or Pine end p. bargain.

Labourers. 4 cutting the rock for the Chafery Stamper sill 2 bearing stones for the hammer hatch, 4 Leveling the Bank 1 Serving Joseph Lucas at the Stack, 1 making up Mortar, 4 Making a road under the rock next the river p. bargain. 5 cutting the back race for Furnace Wheel p. bargain 6 Cutting the Water Course for conveying the water to Stack Wheel p. Bargain.

Carpenters. George Ford his two men, William Postlethwaite & Lewis William fixing the Clay Mill wheel, rabitting the shrouds & odd jobs.

Sawyers 4, 2 sawing planks for the side of the wheel cases & 2 sawing planks & sparrs for the stamper house roof. Evan John, Tyler, covering the flourishing house. Edward Farnels & his 2 men preparing the stamping house roof.

Two Smiths & a striker have been employed in shoeing horses, oxen & making & sharpening Tools for Masons, Boring Chisel and sundry other work. The Cobble & the Quarry Stones are so exceeding hard, the hammer & picks require often sharpening & steeling & it being the Custom to sharp & aneal the Tool for Masons & any bargain lett for cutting the race in the rock etc. which is a great addition to the Expence.

Horses for yesterday & this day 1 piece yesterday 40 ft & brought 1 piece this day 45 ft. The other five were at grass to recruit.

A very rainy night with strong wind.

Sunday. September 14th. Seven o'clock a fine Morning but little Wind at North West.

About Ten o'clock Mr. Bedford[1] has been with me, he is building a Slitting Mill near Newport & proposes to slitt iron rods for us when we are ready. He says that the road from Caerphilly to Newport is near his Mill and by much the best & that Newport is a cheaper Port for sending to Bristol or any part up the Severn & that there are several vessels from that port in the London Trade. The freight from Newport to Bristol is 2s p. Ton & from Cardiff to Bristol 3s or 3/6 p. Ton. Therefore, when we draw Iron for slitting ourselves his Mill will be the most convenient and cheapest of any we can send it to. All this I think right & it will be our Experience if we cannot agree with the Ironmasters for half blooms. A double hammer forge will draw 20 tons of Mill Iron per week from the bloom. Newport I am of opinion will be a more convenient Port for us to get Scraps from London to & ground may be obtained there much cheaper and more convenient than at Cardiff. I am informed that vessels can go out of Newport oftener & more certain than from Cardiff. This may be enquired into.

This has been a fine day & there is an appearance of some fair days. It is cold weather more so than it usual has been of some grey at this time of the year.

[1] For John Bedford and his project to build a forge at Bassaleg, near Newport, see P. Riden, *John Bedford and the Ironworks at Cefn Cribwr* (1992). It is not clear whether the forge ever came fully into use, and in general Bedford was a theoriser rather than a successful practical ironmaster.

A state of the Plymouth Companys shares with the
First the 10 shares purchased from Wilkinson & Guest

Dr	shares		£		
John White & Co. for	7	@ 200 p. Share	1400	-	-
Francis Evans for	1		200	-	-
Blakeway for	2		400	-	-
	10		2000	-	-

Dr The Several Proprietors To six several calls agreed to

John White & Co. for	7	@ 205 p. share	1435	-	-
Francis Evans for	1	@ do	205	-	-
Edward Blakeway for	2	@ do	410	-	-
Willm Parritt for	4	@ do	820	-	-
Sarah Guest for	1	@ do	205	-	-
Isaac Wilkinson for (Now A.B. & Co.)[1]	3	@ do	615	-	-
John Guest for (do)	2	@ do	410	-	-
To John White which may be reckoned as part of his purchase of £50 charged by him for Writings			19	3	8½
			4119	3	8½

To Plymouth Company for debts owing & Debts due

To Sundry debts now due as p. List dd[2] by Tho. Guest	£555	11	2
To Lewis Jenkins for Trespass a suit commenced but agreed to be deferred			
To John Evans do not yet settled			
To Rees Griffiths do do			
to Mr Edwards Lawyer his bill not dd			

Several advances & payments until September 1766 vizt

The original Leases £200 for each share to be repaid out of the first profits

CR			Paid		
John White etc. for	7	£50 - -	£1350	-	-
Francis Evans	1		200		
Blakeway for Wilkinson & Guest	2 Bond	200 - -	200	-	-
			250	-	-
	10		£2000	-	-

[1] i.e. Anthony Bacon & Co.
[2] i.e. delivered.

		Not paid but due			paid Cr		
to be advanced amounting to £205 p. share							
John White has paid for	7				1454	3	8.½
Francis Evans	1	72	8	7	132	11	5
Blakeway	2	410	-	-			
Parritt	4	80	-	-	740	-	-
Sarah Guest	1	50	-	-	155	-	-
Isaac Wilkinson (now A.B. & Co.)	3	395	3	6	219	16	6
John Guest (do)	2	142	1	11	267	18	1
Already paid					2969	9	8½
To Pay					1149	14	-
					4119	3	8½

				Cr		
With their Stock in hand September 1766						
By Wm Parritt 20 T of Pigs sent him @ £5	100	-	-			
John White 5 do	25	-	-			
Jon Phillips 1 do	5	-	-			
A. Bacon & Co. their Bill for castings	117	12	2			
Francis Dorset his Bill for pigs	70	6	6			
By Pigs in stock in Cardiff 24 T 10 cwt	122	10	-			
By do Scrap metal at for 107 charged by T.G.[1]	401	5	-			
By Farm Stock there valued at	242	-	-			
				£1083	13	8

Monday September 15th. A quarter after Six o'clock a fair Morng the Wind at N.W. but little of it.

This being appeal day for the Militia, most of our Workmen are gone to Llantrissant to appeal as they have three children each, or more.[2] As the Millers in the Country are very exorbitant in their Tolls which occassions meal much dearer than it otherwise would be, George Ford informs me, that he can at small expense fix a pair of stones to be twined to the chafery wheel, which will grind all the Corn the workmen may use, without the least detriment to the other work, And as we have stone

[1] i.e. Thomas Guest.

[2] The Militia Act of 1757 provided for the re-establishment of the militia after it had been dormant for some time. A form of conscription was introduced under which petty constables made lists of adult males aged 18–50 and ballots were held to choose some of them to serve: J. Gibson and M. Medlycott, *Military Lists and Musters 1757–1876*. Two meetings of the justices to hear appeals from those chosen are mentioned here, one at Llantrisant for the hundred of Miskin, the other at an unidentified Penyrheol Isaf, probably for the hundred of Caerphilly, in which Merthyr Tydfil was situated. William Thomas (*Diary*, 171) mentions another such meeting for the justices of the hundred of Dinas Powys on the same day.

in our own Land fitt for grinding any grain I have ordered George Ford to provide for such a Mill, to put up when occasion calls. It will be prudent to use all the means in the Companys power to free their Workmen from the imposition of this Country which is very great und unless this can be done there will not be any possibility of preventing the Workmen getting into the Company Debt or advancing their wages or loosing them as they cannot maintain their families with the wage agreed for, unless they can be supplied with their provisions at the Market price which they have not been hitherto.

Nine o'clock. It now rains, is overcast & I am afraid no one will be got in this day.

About one I went with Thomas Guest & Evan Jones to view some Mine in the Parish of Aberdaire belonging to Lord Plymouth & included in the Lease granted to Wilkinson & Guest by the said Lord, which Mr. Mabery agreed with carrier to carry it to his Furnace at Hirwain,[1] Mr Thos. Guest went to Ludovick Nathaniel a Sawyer & desired him to inform his Brother in Law (who is the carrier) not to carry any more, if he did he would be sued by the Plymouth Company.

Horses 8 brought 4 pieces of Timber containing 93½ feet, 3 Carrying coal to Bank below office, 1 C. Wood rode to Aberdaire, 1 at grass, Our whole No 13.

Masons Josh Lucas & Benjamin Jones Scabbling Stones for Air furnace Stack. James Mason went to the Justices in Pen rule Isa to get clear serving in the Militia having 3 Children, as did Harry William & David John.[2] Edward Thomas & 3 More upon part of the forge, p. bargain.

Four Masons (of David Johns) upon the Stamper Gavel End p. bargain. Walter Williams & Hopkin David, upon the Pool Wall p. bargain.

Labourers 4 Boring, 2 bearing stones to Edward Thomas at the forge, 1 Serving at Pool Wall & 1 at Common Mortar & 1 serving Jos. Lucas

Carpenters George Ford in the Wood to choose some Timber to be brought home, his 2 Men at the Clay Mill wheel, Lewis William at the Stamper frame. William Postlethwaite to get clear of the Militia.

Sawyers 2 Sawing 1 roofing for Stamper, 2 went to get clear of the Militia.

[1] For John Maybery and his furnace at Hirwaun, at the head of the Cynon valley, which may have used charcoal as well as coke in its early years, see Riden, *Gazetteer*, 19–22.

[2] See above, p. 151, for the means of securing exemption from Militia service.

Aaron Wedgwood went to get clear of the Militia & John Edge the same. A rainy day, and no Corn got in but some people cutting corn between the showers.

Wrote to my wife & Mr. Bacon per Postman.

Tuesday Sept. 16th. A quarter after Six o'clock a fair calm Morning. Wind at S.W.

Few hands came & John Edge, Brickmaker was taken out of the List for Militia Men, he having served as a Marine & produced his discharge. Aaron Wedgwood potter was also taken out, as a Labourer & having three children. But James Mason, an Air furnace builder & William Postlethwaite, Carpenter, were continued, as not coming under the Sanction of the Act, had they appealed as Labourers with each three children, they would have been cleared.

Nine o'clock. Breakfast time. Small rain, overcast, has the appearance of more.

About Eleven, came Mr. Williams of Neath[1] & two more Gentlemen to see the Work they went through the whole. I waited upon him at Edward Morgans before as he was a friend of Mr. Rice, Lord Talbots Son in Law, some large showers.

Mr. William is of opinion that Neath will be the best & cheapest Seaport for these works, when the Turnpike is completed, from thence to Pont a Vaun which he thinks may be done in about one year and a half, it is about 9 Mile from Cyfarthfa to Pont ar Dawe,[2] all the iron to that place must be carried upon horseback & from thence to Neath in Carts or Waggons. And when at Neath it may be sent to any part of the Kingdom, there offering vessels ready for that purpose, at Cardiff there are not any vessels but for Bristol which requires double shipping besides other charges attending it.

N.B. By making Memorandum of these hints, one may come to the knowledge of the most convenient & cheapest method of Carriage.

Mr. William with Thomas Guest are gone to view a place in his mountain where there is an appearance of Lead which I am informed lies

[1] Probably Thomas Williams of Court Herbert, Cadoxton juxta Neath, attorney, steward to the lords of Neath Abbey, one of whom was George Rice of Newton, Llandeilo (Carms.), Lord Talbot's son-in-law.

[2] The turnpike road along the Vale of Neath, from the town of Neath to Pont Neath Vaughan (Pont Nedd Fechan), on the Breconshire border, was built under the terms of the Glamorgan Turnpike Act of 1764 (4 Geo. III c. 88). Wood must be wrong about Pontardawe, which is in the Swansea Valley, much more than nine miles away. Perhaps he meant Pont y Ddinas (marked on Yates's map of the county of 1799) or Pont Walby, both of which are near Pont Neath Vaughan.

in hard Lime stone rock by which appearance it will be expensive & difficult trying and must be very rich to answer the Expense of working.[1]

Laid the other frame for hammer gate & Edward Thomas John is walling it up.

About two Mr. Richard from Cardiff came here, viewed all the work and returned to the Village untill Morning.

Masons Joseph Lucas & Benjamin Jones Scabbling stones when fine & building Casting Furnace, when it rained p. days wages.

Edward Thomas John & 2 more upon the hammer hatch upon bargain. David Johns 3 Men upon the Stamp house Gavel End p. bargain. David John himself & Harry Williams were too much tired in going to gett off serving in the Militia, that they could not attend their work. Walter William & Hopkin David upon Pool Wall, upon bargain.

Labourers 4 boring, 2 bearing stones from Quarry to David Thomas, 2 leveling the bank, 1 clearing a place to build a small kiln, to burn the hard stone from Cardiff Lime, 1 serving Walter Williams, 1 at Common Mortar, 2 Serving Jos. Lucas, No 13.

Carpenters. George Ford, his two men at the Clay Mill Wheel fixing it up. William Postlethwaite ¾ & Lewis William a day at the stamper Cheeks.

Sawyers 2 Sawing for Stamper house roof & 2 absent upon Militia Affair.

Horses 8 brought home 3 pieces containin 76½ feet of Timber. 2 carrying Clay to brick kiln. 3 at grass.

Edward Farnels & his 2 Men, Carpenters were framing the Stamphouse roof, p. Bargain.

Evan John, Tyler prepared Slates, or stone Tyles, for one side of the flourishing house, the other side is done.

Two Smiths & a striker constantly employed in making & mending steeling tools & shoeing horses & oxen, althou not every week were still employed.

Thomas David & Edward Harry were leadg Brick from the kiln p. bargain at 5s p. m.[2]

Gave orders to Edward John Carrier to call upon Captain Priest in Cardiff for a Truck & Portmanteau that came to Bristol by the London

[1] W.J. Lewis, *Lead mining in Wales* (1967), 252, notes some unprofitable lead mines in the parish of Penderyn (Brecs.), near Pont Neath Vaughan, and at Cefn Coedycymer (Brecs.), immediately to the north of Merthyr Tydfil.

[2] i.e. per thousand.

Carrier, for me for which Mr. Richards informs me Mr. Priest paid 17s Carriage.

Wednesday Sept. 17th, 1766. Half past Six o'clock a close Morning with small rain. Wind at N.W. The small rain has continued all day. I rode with Mr. Richard & Sam to view Cwm Glo Farm as also a Coal which is near the Brick kiln, 5 feet thick & is the best coal we have yet met with for those kilns, to which there is an old Level opened & drove lower, which will clear it of water and enable them to get Coal to supply the Brick for some years. But to supply the Air furnaces I apprehend a Level should be begun to the N.E. of the present Level which will make it work for many years to supply those furnaces.

Masons Joseph Lucas & James Mason upon one of the shingling furnaces. Benjamin Jones building Lime kiln to burn the stone cover out of the Cardiff Lime.

Walter William & Hopkin David upon Pool Wall p. bargain. Harry William & 3 more upon the hammer hatch upon bargain. David John & 3 more upon the stamping house Gavel End p. bargain.

Labourers 3 sinking the rock for the Shingling furnace Ash pits, 2 bearing stones to hammer hatch, 1 Leveling the bank, 1 at the Cardiff Lime, 1 serving at building the Lime kilns, 1 serving Joseph Lucas, 1 at Common Mortar & 1 Aaron Wedgwood in Clay Mill. No 11 all day wages.

Three making the road from the Quarry under the rock to furnace p. bargain.

Four making the back race to the furnace p. bargain

Six at the Cut, to convey the water to the wheel p. bargain.

Carpenters George Ford & his two men fixing the Clay Mill wheel, William Postlethwaite making a flask to cast brass in & after stokeholes & Lewis Williams upon Stamper frames.

Sawyers 4 Serving for stamp house roof which is 28 ft hollow.

Edward Farnels & 3 more Carpenters framing the stamp house Roof p. bargain.

Evan John preparing Stone Tyles for flourishing house.

Horses 8 brought home 4 pieces of Timber containing 71 feet. 2 My Bror & me had to ride with Mr. Richards. 3 at grass to recruit being very low. 13 being our whole Number.

Particulars of Rhyd y Carr Farm in the Parish of Merthyr Tydfil m for meadow, r rough, a arable, w wood. N for Number of field, A for Acres, R for Rood, P for Perches, Q for Quality

Names of the fields	*N*	*A*	*R*	*P*	*Q*	*Names*	*N*	*A*	*R*	*P*	Q
Wayn Vawr	1	12	1	12	m	Brought forward	27				
	2	3	-	32	m	Gworled	28	3	1	15	m
Coed Car Ycha	3	7	2	18	r	Caer Odin	29	3	-	15	a
	4	9	2	36	r		30	-	3	35	a
Heol Ycha	5	4	2	5	r	Ynis Groes Ycha	31	2	2	24	a
Wain Vach	6	10	1	2	m	Ynis y Pontpren	32	2	2	8	a
Coed Cae Vach	7	13	1	6	r	Ynis Gorove Issa	33	3	2	17	a
Caer Ithon	8	1	2	32	a	Wain Cwm Dae	34	7	2	21	m
Caer Cae	9	16	-	28	w						
Cae Cwm	10	1	3	-	a	Meadow		38	3	36	
	11		2	20	a	Arable		40	2	31	
Caen Cwte Ycha	12	-	2	6	w	Wood		37	3	24	
	13	2	1	12	a	rough		36	2	32	
Cae Cwtair Isha	14	1	1	22	a	House & Garden		1	-	30	
Gworlody Schybor	15	2	-	34	m	Total		155	1	33	
Cae Ychlawr Ty	16	3	2	8	a						
Cae Nessar Ty	17	1	1	18	a	at £ 36 p annum					
Draw Errw	18	1	3	35	a						
Joining thereto	19	1	3	12	a						
	20	-	3	12	a						
Cregwith Bach	21	1	2	7	r						
Ynis Y Vallen	22	2	3	3	a						
Ynis y Cybran	23	3	2	6	a						
Tree-Idwran	24	3	1	32	a						
Joining thereto	25		3	-	a						
House & Garden Yard	26	1	3	30	-						
Coed Isha	27	21	-	30	w						

Carried forward

Particulars of Llwyn Celin in the Parish of Merthyr Tidvil

Names of the fields	*N*	*A*	*R*	*P*	*Q*	*Names*	*N*	*A*	*R*	*P*	*Q*
	1	1	-	16	a	brought forward	35				
	2	-	2	28	m	Cae Isa Lawr Ty	36	-	3	13	a
House & Garden	3	-	1	8	-		37	6	-	-	a
	4	-	3	37	a	Tila Bach	38	1	1	15	a
	6	-	1	28	m	Gwyn Thomas Prees	39	3	-	23	w
Coed Cae Ythel	7	10	1	27	p						
	8	3	2	27	p	Car Rhiw Goch	40	3	2	30	a
	9	-	1	22	w	Gwynled Thomas Prees	41	-	3	15	m
	10	2	-	18	a	Joining the same	42	-	1	30	p
	11	-	2	8	w	Gwerloda Lewis Morgan	43	1	1	29	m
	12	1	-	26	a	Cae Lewis Morgan	44	5	-	33	a
	13	3	3	18	p	Cae Main	45	1	3	34	a
Gord da Bach	14	-	3	14	w	Coed Cae Bach	46	2	0	7	a
	15	-	2	14	a						
Errw	16	2	2	21	a	Pen yr Ynys Vawr	47	3	3	30	a
	17	2	-	18	m	Smith Shop	48	-	17	-	
Ardd Vain	18	-	2	25	a	& Garden					
	19	1	1	16	a	Ynis Pen y Bont	49	3	-	11	a
Cae Draw	20	1	2	34	a	Ynis y Quarr	50	3	3	-	a
A house & Garden	21	-	1	4	-	Wain Vawr	51	24	3	20	m
Cwm Pant Bach	22	1	3	28	r						
Cae Howdu	23	4	3	13	a	Meadow		31	3	1	
Caer Odin	24	3	-	2	a	Pasture		17	2	27	
Gwern Yr Odin	25	2	3	32	p	Arable		76	-	2	
	26	1	-	5	w	Wood		11	2	30	
Caye y ny Coed	27	3	3	2	do	rough		10	2	35	
	28	6	2	23	do	Houses & Gardens		1	2	7	
Gwern Y Coed Ycha	29	6	3	-	do	Total of Area		149	1	22	
Cae Ych lawr Ty	30	5	3	20	a						
House & Garden	31	-	3	18	-	At £31 10s p. Annum					
	32	6	2	38	a	4 10 Advanced by					
Cae Wern Du	33	1	1	8	a	36 - M. Richard					
	34	1	1	23	m						
Cae Thomas Prees	35	3	-	18	a						
carried forward											

Particulars of Cwm Glo Ychaf in the Parish of Merthyr Tydfil

Names of the fields	*N*	*A*	*R*	*P*	*Q*
Coed Cae	1	15	-	-	p
Gwain Cwm Glo	2	19	-	18	m
Pwrcas	3	5	-	31	p
The Cwm	4	-	2	18	w
House, Garden	5	-	3	7	-
Cae Pentwyn	6	-	2	31	a
Coes Cae Canol	7	7	-	22	p
Cae Pwdwr	8	3	1	33	a
Parcas	9	5	-	12	m
Cae Gam	10	13	2	30	p
Gwain y Coed rae	11	4	1	29	m
	12	-	1	23	w
Pedwran	13	1	-	6	a
Joining thereto	14	2	3	-	a
	15	-	3	29	a
	16	1	-	20	a
	17	-	1	35	a
	18	-	2	8	p
	19	2	3	29	p
	20	-	3	3	a
	21	-	3	33	a

Meadow	28	2	19
Pasture	34	2	-
Arable	11	-	37
Wood	1	3	34
House & Garden	-	3	7
Total	77	-	17

Rent not yet fixed

Particulars of the Wern

Names	*N*	*A*	*R*	*P*	*Q*
Cregwith	1	3	3	7	a
Ardd Du	2	-	3	14	a
Cae Tump Issa	3	3	-	-	a
Ynys Thomas Issa	4	2	3	36	a
Ynis Thomas Ycha	5	4	1	27	a
	6	2	1	36	a
Cae Draw	7	2	2	-	a
	8	1	2	5	m
Caer Twyn John	9	2	3	2	a
Cae Glas	10	3	3	14	a
	11	-	-	33	a
Bonmaen	12	-	3	3	p
House,Garden,Yard	13	-	2	5	=
Gworlod	14	2	-	16	m
Caer Lloy	15	1	3	8	a
	16	3	-	35	a
Wayn Vach	17	1	3	25	a
	18	5	1	30	a
	19	1	1	26	w
near the same	20	-	-	23	a
Coed Gwern William	21	5	-	9	r
Gorda Bach	22	1	-	30	a
	23	-	2	30	w
Goetre Cae Wilkin	24	1	3	8	a
Cae William	25	5	2	4	a
Gwern William	26	4	2	12	w
Cae William Bach	27	1	1	33	a
Wayn William	28	-	1	24	w
	29	5	-	5	m
Coed Cae Wern	30	12	3	5	p
	31	11	-	28	w
	32	17	1	-	m
Gwain y Wern	33	2	1	16	w

Wern Tenement

Meadow	25	3	26
Pastures	13	2	8
Arables	43	1	14
Wood	23	0	12
Rough	8	1	4
House & Garden	-	2	5
Total	114	2	29

This is promised when the Lease falls into the Lords.

The several tenements herein mentioned are situated as see underneath in respect to Cyfarthfa where the works are.

Llwyn Kelin continuing		51	149	1	22	p. Annum	36	10	-
Cwm Glo	do	21	77	-	17	do			
Wern	do	33	114	2	29	do			
Rhyd y Carr	do	34	155	1	33		36	-	-
Land from Daniel William & Brn		2					7	-	-
Land from Lewis William John		2					6	15	-
Land from Rd Wm for the Blast furnace		3					6	-	-
Land for the New Road from Wm Lewis								10	-
Rent of the Coal from do							25	-	-
Land on which the Wear is Tyed from Lewis John							1	1	-
Rent for Stone & Coal p. Lease							100	-	-
from John Morgan Tai Mawr		3					5	-	-
1770 Tennement at Tai Mawr							9	-	-

Thursday Sept. 18th. Half past Six o'clock a close moist Morning very little Wind at [*Blank*].

Thomas Guest & Terry came to me this afternoon and informed me that they wanted money to discharge the Plymouth Company Debts and that the Bridgnorth Gentlemen had directed them to sell all the metal in hand and collect the Debts due, for that end. That they were willing to treat with me for 95 Tons of Pig & 9 Ton of Scrap metal, I agreed to give them £3 15s for the Pigs & £2 10s for the Scrap metal the former short & the latter Longweight delivered, here at our Work & a quarter p. Ton for Sand & Cinder in the Pig. I gave them a bill for the Amount £278 15s upon Mr. Bacon at 30 days sight payable to Thomas Guest, furthermore I wrote to Mr. Bacon & advised him of this bill & purchase. Captain Samuel Hughes came here & told me we were welcome to get any fireclay in his Liberty, if we found any suitable.

Masons Joseph Lucas & James Mason at the Shingling Air furnace. Benjamin Jones at the Limekiln.

Walter William & Hopkin David at the Pool Wall upon Bargain David John & 3 more upon the Stamp House Gavel end p. do. Harry William & 3 more upon the Hammer Hatch p. do.

Labourers 2 cutting rock for Ashpit for Airfurnace. 2 bearing stones to Forge Hatch, 1 serving the Pool Wall, 2 with Cardiff Lime, 2 at the Limekiln, 1 digging foundations for drying house, & 1 at Common Mortar. No 11.

Carpenters Geo. Ford & his 2 men fixing the Clay Mill Wheel, William Postlethwaite & Lewis William at the Stamper frame.

Sawyers. 4 sawing roofing for Stamp House & room over forge.

Horses 6 brought 3 pieces of Timber containing 52½ feet. 5 leading manure upon land. 2 at grass. 13 our whole number.

4 Labourers making road from Quarry under the rock to the furnace Stack.

4 at the Cutt for Back race to the furnace.

6 at the Cutt for conveying the water to the furnace wheel all upon Bargain.

Friday September 19th. Six o'clock a close calm morning, no wind to know the point.

This day settled with William Edmund Richards for carriage p. Cardiff Lime

			£ s d
16 dozen & 1 Load @ 2s p. Load is			19 6 -
Turnpike			- 16 -
			20 2 -
June 6th last paid them in part		4 4 -	
July 15 paid p. C. Wood		7 7 -	
Sept 19 paid by S. Wood	7 15 -		
Turnpike	- 16 -	8 11 -	20 2 -

There is to be paid to the burner for 221 Load at 6d p. Load by which it appears that the measure from Cardiff kiln is less than the 2½ bushel per Load of the Carriers by 28 load in the whole.

Masons Joseph Lucas & James Mason at the Shingling Airfurnace, Benjamin Jones at the Limekiln.

Walter Williams & Hopkin David have finished the Pool, in Bargain. Harry William James & 3 more upon the hammer hatch on do. David John & 3 more upon the Stamping house Gavel End & they have began the Drying house.

Labourers 2 clearing rock for Shingling furnace Ash pit, 2 Serving Joseph Lucas 1 with Geo. Ford at Clay Mill Wheel, 1 Serving at Pool Wall, 2 at Lime kiln, 2 bearing stone to the hammer hatch, & 1 at Common Mortar, No 11 days wages. 5 making road from the Quarry under the rock to the furnace p. bargain, 4 cutting the race up to the furnace wheel p. bargain 6 cutting the watercourse to convey the water to the furnace wheel.

Carpenters. George Ford & his 2 men upon the Clay Mill Wheel William Postlethwaite upon a frame for the Gate at the head of the cutt to bring the water to the wheel.

Sawyers 4 sawing for Stamp house roof.

Horses housing Corn, all got in & at Grass.

This has beeen a very fine warm day, as any we have had this Summer.

Lett unto David John, the Building of the Drying Room agreeable to the plan here annexed,[1] he finding Stone from the quarry & having the use of what Cobble in the Pool there is, at the price of 1s 6d p. perch clear of all other charges to the Compy except Lime.

John Edge having had some words with Robert Wilson they parted and the former undertake the Brick himself & the latter work Labouring work here until the furnaces are ready.

[1] Reproduced here as Plate 2.

Saturday Sept 20th. Half past six o'clock a fine Morning, Wind at N.W.

Twelve o'clock there have been several showers of rain since 9 o'clock it is unlike Summer than any we have had.

This day was laid the foundation of the 5th Shingling furnace Ash pit. Evan John began the Drying house yesterday.

Therefore I propsed to abate 1s p. m. in the Common Brick ordered him to close the Brick shade which I have agreed to do and have sent Robert Wilson & Thos. Owen to execute the same therefore brick are made for the future from this time are @ 7s p. m.

Masons Joseph Lucas & James Mason at the Shingling furnace. Benjamin Jones at the Lime kiln. Henry William & 2 more upon the Hammer hatch p. Bargain. David John & 3 more upon Drying house do.

Labourers 2 bearing stone to hammer hatch, 1 clearing for Ashpit at Shingling furnaces, 2 at Lime kiln, 2 at the Brick shade & 1 each at Cardiff and Common Mortar.

Carpenters George Ford his 2 men & William Postlethwaite at Clay Mill Wheel.

Sawyers 4 Sawing roof Timber for Stamp House.

Horses 5 horses & 4 Oxen br't 2 pieces timber 65 feet. 4 carrying manure. 4 at grass. 13 our whole number.

This has been a fine day but showry.

5 Labourers have finished the road from the Quarry to the furnace.

4 at the Cutt for back race from the furnace

6 at do to convey the water to the furnace.

Sunday September 21. Seven o'clock a close foggy Morning. Wind South East.

This has been a fine warm day. Walked after dinner to the race.

Monday September 22nd. Half past Six o'clock a fine warm Morning. Little Wind at South.

After Breakfast went down to Plymouth furnace with my Brother & began to weigh the pigs, but as I found the heaps as weighed before were better weight then I should get by weighing them again I chose to take them as they were there was 99 Ton & it was supposed there would be 10 Ton of Scrap Iron.

Part of the pigs were brought here this day vizt.

by their Waggon	6. Ton	
by our Waggon	6	
by 8 of their horses on back	5 -	
by 5 of our horses	2 10	T cwt
		19 10

Masons Joseph Lucas & James Mason at the Shingling Furnace Stack. Benjamin Jones at the Lime kiln.

Walter William at the Shingling Furnace Ashpit p. bargain.

Harry William & 3 more at the Hammer Hatch p. do.

David John & 3 more at the Drying house p. do.

Labourers 2 Rucking pigs, 2 bearing stones for hatch, 2 serving Josh Lucas 2 clearing the Pool Wall to the rock to ram them with Earth to stop the water, 2 at the Lime kiln, 1 at the Common Mortar and 1 at the Brick shade.

Carpenters George Ford & his 2 men at the Clay Mill Wheel, William Postlethwaite & Lewis William making Doors & Window frames.

Sawyers 4 Sawing Stamper frames & Spars for sills of Stampers.

Horses Six in Waggon fetching pigs from Plymouth Furnace. 5 fetching do upon their backs. 2 at Grass. on whole 13.

4 Labourers cutting the Furnace Rock Race p. Bargain. 3 do cutting the forward section for the furnace p. do. 6 do cutting the race for conveying the water to the furnace p. do.

Evan John, The Tyler covering the flourishing house. Wrote to my wife, Brother Cox & Mr. Thomas Evans, an Attorney in Bristol and sent them in the Letter Case p. Thomas Williams, the Smith to the Postman. This has been a very fine warm day we have now Summer Weather most of the Corn in the Parish is got in, and the crops good, as I am informed except the Wheat and this grain will be short, by a number of deaf ears, among it which I hear is a general complaint.

Tuesday September 23rd. Six o'clock a fine warm Morning little wind at South West.

The Plymouth Company	Waggon brt	Pigs	6 Ton	
do	8 horses		5 Ton	
our own waggon			6 Ton	
our own horses 5			2 10	T cwt
				19 10

Stoped the water & rammed the vacancy behind the Pool Wall with Loam.

Masons Joseph Lucas & James Mason about the Shingling Furnace Stacks. Benjamin Jones at the Limekiln finished this day. Walter William, upon the Shingling furnace Ashpit p. Bargain.

Harry William, Edward Thomas & their two Men have been Scabbling the stone for hammer hatch p. days wages. David John & 3 more were upon the Drying house & the Gavel End of the Stamp house per bargain.

Labourers 3 at Sloping the water & ramming behind the Pool Wall, 2 Rucking Pig Iron & clearing for Scrap Metal, 2 raising stones in the Quarry, 2 serving Joseph Lucas, 2 bearing stones to the Hatch, 2 at Limekiln & 1 at Common Mortar & 2 carrying stones to Wear.

Carpenters George Ford & 2 of his Men at the Claymill wheel William Postlethwaite & Lewis William upon the Sluice for the Level to carry the water to the furnace wheel and the Stamper frames.

Sawyers 4 sawing Spars & Wheel Timber

Horses 6 Carrying pigs from Plymouth Company in Waggon. 5 do on their back. 2 at grass.

4 Labourers at the back race for furnace wheel p. bargain. 3 do at the furnace foundation do. 6 do at the Cut to bring the water to the Fur. wheel do.

This has been a fine day and warm weather.

Wednesday September 24th. Six o'clock a fine Morning but cool West Wind but little of it.

The Plymouth Company Waggon brought	Pigs	6 Ton		
8 of their horses on their backs		3		
our Waggon brought		6		
our 5 horses on their backs		2	10	T cwt
				17 10

Masons Joseph Lucas & James Mason at the Shingling Furnace Stacks. Benjamin Jones Scabbling stones for do. Harry William & 2 more Scabbling stones in the Quarry for hutch in the morning, in the afternoon two of them went to Wain Fair. David John & his 3 men at the Drying house & Stamper Gavel end.

Laborers 2 raising Stones in the Quarry, 2 carrying them out, 2 preparing the Lime kiln, 2 carrying stones to the other side of the Wear, 2 clearing the Clay Mill & making place for Scrap metal, 1 rucking pigs, 1 cutting rock for Ashpit, & 1 at the Common Mortar.

Carpenters. George Ford & Jos. Gibson have finished the Clay Mill Wheel, David Milligan, William Postlethwaite making Box frames for Dryg house, Lewis Williams at the Stamper frames.

Sawyers 4 Sawing roofing for Stamp House & 2 were absent at the Wain fair.

Labourers p. Bargain vizt. 2 a day each at the cutt for back race for furnace & 2¼ day each. 3 at the foundation for the furnace. 6 at the Level to convey the Water to the furnace

All our Moulds for the castings at the Plymouth Furnace were bt. here this day to be ready against we want them.

Wrote to my wife yesterday & sent p. post to Bro. Cox & Mr. Evans of Bristol.

This has been a fine day, the Morning & Evening very cool. This day is the Wain Fair kept upon the Mountain, about 2 Miles from Merthyr Vilage (where there is but one house) for Cattle, Sheep, Geese, hogs & Sundry goods.[1]

Yesterday I delivered Lewis William John, Mr. Bacons Notice, not to cut any more coal at any other place than in one pit, which was alloted him at the time the Lease was agreed upon & a memorandum signed by them two, before Mr. Thomas Morgan & his Clerk, and he then promised that he would not get any more but at that one pit.

Thursday September 25th. Six o'clock a fine Morning Wind cold at South East.

Went to Duffryn in Aberdare with George Ford after Dinner to view some Timber for hammer & Stamper shaft, but the Stewart Mr. Jones was not at home.[2] I left word to come soon to Cyfarthfa, tomorrow or Saturday.

Masons Joseph Lucas, James Mason & Benjamin Jones upon the Shingling furnace Stack upon day wages. David John & three more upon drying house upon Bargain. Harry William & 2 More upon the Hammer Hatch.

Labourers 2 raising stones in the Quarry, 2 bearing Stones out of the Quarry, 2 Serving at the Stack, 2 Serving at the Hatch, 2 rucking pigs & 1 unloading Waggon with broken metal & 1 at the Common Mortar. 4

[1] The Waun Fair, called Twyn y Marchnant or Marchnad y Wayne in Welsh, was well established in Wood's day, although when it was first held is not clear. The site on which it was held, near the road from Merthyr to Abergavenny, was pointed out to John Lloyd in the early 1900s, when he was told that a large fair had been held there recently, with dealers attending from all parts of the adjoining counties of Glamorgan, Monmouthshire and Breconshire (*Early history of the old South Wales ironworks*, 47).

[2] For the Duffryn Aberdare estate see H.M. Thomas, 'Duffryn Aberdare', *Morgannwg*, xxi (1977), 9–41. William Bruce, a London banker and Navy agent, bought the estate in 1750 from James Jones, who was apparently kept on as steward. Timber was the main asset of the estate in the mid eighteenth century.

at the back race cut for furnace wheel upon Bargain. 8 at the furnace foundation, do. 6 at the Level to convey the water to the wheel do.

Carpenters George Ford in the Morning with his 2 Men, Wm Postlethwaite & Lewis Williams upon the Sluice at the head of Level Stamper cheeks & Sills, & George in the afternoon at Aberdair to view Wood.

Sawyers 4, 2 Sawing roof Timbers & 2 Sawing for the Stamper frames.

Horses 6 in Waggon brought broken iron from Plymouth furnace 5 brought of pig from do on their back. 2 at Aberdair with CW, Geo. Ford to view Timber. [*Total*] 13.

The Timber at the Duffryn the Estate of Mr. Bruce (who purchased it of Mr. Jones, who resides there & is a Steward) is very proper for shafts but very steep hill to go up & down with it to Cyfarthfa but as we have not any large enough in Lord Talbots Estate, & if made use of for such purpose four must be put together & bound with Iron hoops which will take more time, & be more expensive therefore those Trees should be obtained if they can and prepared as near the Work as necessary, for the easier and cheaper Carriage. Four Trees put together are not so good, if the Labour & Iron with the Wood was as cheap as the Solid Single piece nor so durable, as it will be difficult to make the joints so close, although Tarred with wool to prevent the water which is continually upon it soaking in & decay it, much sooner than a Solid piece if sound will do.

This has been a fine day, but the Morning & Evening cool, as one may expect at this Season.

Wrote to the Doctor & Mr. Potter, sent to Brecon per John Morgan who is ordered to take a place in the Coach for London for Joseph Lucas & myself.

Received from Plymouth Company		T	cwt
per their Waggon	broken metal	5	18
per our horses	do	6	-
per their horses	Pigs	4	-
per our horses	do	2	10
		18	8

Friday September 26th. Five minutes past Six o'clock, a fine Morning, Wind South East.

			T
Plymouth Company Waggon brought Pig Iron			6
their horses	do	do	5
Our Waggon brought	do	do	6
			17

Masons James Mason & Benjamin Jones at the Shingling furnace stacks. Joseph Lucas viewing the bargains & measuring off David John work. Walter William & Hopkin David upon raising the Wall on the farr End of the Wear 3 feet it being thought, by many, too low for such floods as some times there is in this river. David John & 3 more upon the Drying house p. Bargain. Harry William & 3 more upon the Hammer Hatch p. do.

Labourers 2 raising stones in the Quarry, 2 bearing them out, 2 Serving at the Stacks, 1 clearing the rock opposite the Hammer Hatch to spring an Arch, over for the dwellings above, 1 Tampering Clay, 1 leveling the road, 2 rucking Pigs & 1 at the Common Mortar.

Carpenters George Ford, his two Men, William Postlethwaite & Lewis Williams all upon the Stamper frames.

Sawyers 4, 2 Sawing for Stamper frames & 2 sawing for roof over the Stamp house & Forge.

Horses 6 in Waggon fetching Pig Iron. 4 fetching coal to Smith Shop & Office & Workmen. 3 at grass.

Labourers upon Bargain 5 at the Cut for the Back race for the furnace course to the rock, the blue sill & before they reach the wheel case it will, in my Opinion, be 10 feet deep. 8 at the furnace foundation, continues a Loam or Brick Clay. 6 at the Level to convey water to the furnace wheel.

Edward Farnel & 3 men, framing the roofing for the Stamper house & forge.

This has been a fine day and very little Corn out, all crops good but wheat. John Morgan took 2 places in the Brecon Coach for Joseph Lucas & myself for Monday.

Saturday September 27th. Six o'clock a fine Morning Wind North West.

Upon viewing the cutting of the foundation for the furnace I find that they have begun 20 feet wider than they were ordered. The Stack is to be 36 feet Square & 2 feet more to make room for the Masons to begin the remainder, 20 feet is for the Wheel pit & was to be performed by the hands that cut the back race but as the last part of that digging is already done it is thought that they should proceed at the same rate the cuttings if the back race should have had at 3d p. yard.

Received from Plymouth Company Pig p.	T	
their Waggon & horse	10	
our Waggon & do	6	1
our horses	2	10
	18	11

Masons Joseph Lucas, James Mason, Benjamin Jones and Morgan Jenkins upon the Shingling furnace stack Walter William & Hopkin David upon the Wall at the End of the Wear. Harry William & 3 more upon the Hammer Hatch & Chafery Chimney. David John & 3 more upon Drying house, the last three upon Bargain.

Carpenters George Ford his 2 Men, William Postlethwaite and Lewis Williams all upon the Stamper frames.

Sawyers 4, 2 Sawing roof Timber & 2 Sawing Stamper frames.

Labourers 2 Raising & carrying stones out of the Quarry. 2 bearing stones to the Hammer hatch, 2 Serving at Wear Wall. 2 rucking pigs, 2 at lime kilnn, 2 at the Shingling Stacks & 2 tampering Clay and 1 at Common Mortar.

Labourers p. Bargain vizt. 6 at the Back Race Cut to the furnace wheel. 8 at the furnace foundations. 6 at the Level to convey the Water to the furnace wheel.

Agreed with Henry William, Edward Thomas & David John Mason to Wall & Arch the back race as under vizt. The Wall to be laid in the Mortar & to Quarry & carrying the stone to the Cutt @ 2s p. perch & that part that is to be arched, the Wall to be 6 feet high & the Arch 6 feet wide & 2 feet pitch, they quarrying & carrying stone to the premises, & doing every other requisite relating thereto at the neat price of 6s p. yard in length. The Company to lay Lime & Sand near the place.

This has been a very fine warm day.

Total from Plymouth Furnace

	T	cwt		£	s		£	s	d
Pigs	98	11	@	3	15	p. Ton is	309	11	3
Broken Metal	11	18	@	2	10	p. Ton is	29	15	0
	110	9					£339	6	3

MEMORANDA
1766

Thomas Guest Merthyr Sept. 27 1766

Sir, Upon perusing the letter sent you by Mr. White dated from Bridgenorth Sept 15th 1766 I observe that you are requested to bring over to him to that place all the Books, Papers receipts & Vouchers belonging & relating to the Plymouth Furnace affairs. Therefore in the name of Anthony Bacon & Company Copartners in the said Furnace and Works I thought it proper to declare their dissent, to the delivery of the same. As the publick Accompting house on the premises, is the proper place where they ought to be kept. That the Proprietors on any Exigency may have recourse to them there. These being my Sentiments on behalf of the above Copartners. These we communicate them to you, for your direction herein, that you may not bring on you the displeasure of any of the Partners.

C. Wood for
Anthony Bacon & Co.

A Cylinder Six feet high & four feet & half diameter is equal to a plate of 81 feet. The thickness when cast, one inch & when bored ¾ of an inch. A foot square is 144 inches & 4 solid inches weighs one pound. Therefore One cylinder will weigh vizt.

	ft	in.	cwt	q	lb		cwt	q	lb
81 Square feet × 144 = 11664 Solid inches ÷ 4 = 2916 lb =							26	-	4
							26	-	4
							26	-	4
The weight of the Cylinders							78	-	12
Three bottoms	4	6 diamr & one inch thick	6	1	20	for 3	19	1	4
Three Pistons	do						19	1	4
							116	2	20
The weight of 3 Cylinders with bottoms & Pistons							T5 16	2	20
One crank 17 ft long 28 cwt for two							2 16	-	-
							8 12	2	20

The cylinders when bored are £30 p. Ton & allow 8 cwt 12 the loss in boring

	T	cwt	q	lb		£	s	d
There will then remain	3	10			@ £30 p. Ton	£105	-	-
3 Bottoms & 3 Pistons	1	18	2	8	@ £14 p. Ton	26	10	-
2 Cranks		2	16	-	@ £14 p. Ton	50	8	-
						181	18	-
Freight & other charges to Cardiff suppose						10	-	-
Carriage from Cardiff to Merthyr						10	-	-
						201	18	-

N.B. A pair of Leather Bellows will cost near as much, will often require repairs and renew Leathering every blast, are liable to be frayed & many other accidents which Cylinders are not. The leather Bellows require a larger house and will not provide so strong a Blast as Cylinders as will appear by the calculation made.

A Cylinder 6 feet high and 4 ft 6 in. diameter. To find the quantity of Air pressed out in one Minute, Multiply half the diameter by half the Circumference & that product by the Depth and then by the Number of Strokes, the wheel may Occasion them to make, will give the Answer. Example 6 feet or 72 in. in depth 4 ft 6 in. or 54 in. the Diameter 122 inches the Circumference & to make 10 strokes in the Minute 72 × 27 = 1944 × 86 = 167184 : 1728 = 96.75 × 10 = 967 Cubic feet of Air in one Minute.

Leather Bellows 20 ft long, 7 feet wide at the Breach & 2 feet at the Channel the Medium in breadth will be 4 ft 6 in. allow them to rise 18 inches the Medium, the middle is 9 inches.

240 × 54 = 12960 × 9 = 116640 : 1728 = 67 × 20 for so many Cams in a Minute = 1340 Cubic feet but as it is not possible in the Common Structure of Bellows, to press out the Air contained in them by one third, Nor to make them so close but some Air will escape thro' the Nibbles joints of the threads & other places. One may deduct near one half. Suppose $^{2}/_{5}$ will reduce it 804 Cubic feet of air in one Minute Then the proportion will be as under vizt

One Cylinder will press out 967 & three will press out	2901	Cubic feet
One Bellows will press out 804 & two will press out	2412	
in favour of the Cylinders in one Minute	489	Cubic feet

of Air besides the many other conveniences and advantages attending.

I see Mr. Walker (an Iron Master at Rotherham in Yorkshire)[1] at Mr. Bacons in London and hearing that he made use of Cylinders at his furnace, I asked him how they proved. His answer was, that his Cylinders were but 4 feet Diameter which were too Small. Yet he would not Exchange them for Leather Bellows if any one would give him 500 guineas for so doing. As he seemed to be & had the Character of an honest, Sober minded Man I gave Credit to what he said and upon talking with Isaac Wilkinson & considering & weighing the conveniency and inconveniency of both kinds, One cannot but give the preference to the Cylinders. As the more one I think of them, many more advantages Occur than is already been taken Notice of. One sett of Cylinders will serve an Age, are not so subject to be out of order & will in my opinion require less Water to work them.

In the calculation of the quantity of Air pressed out of Cylinders & Leather Bellows it may be observed that the Bellows are allowed to Cam 20 times in a Minute, & the Cylinders but 10 Stroke but double the Stroke to make them equal to the Leather Bellows & thus proportion them, will be very great in the favour of the Cylinders. These Cylinders, Piston, Bottom & Cranks I propose Casting & Boring upon the Spot at Cyfarthfa which I expect will save two thirds of the price we should give to purchass them at the price sett down in the Estimate.

I see Mr. Watkins an Attorney in Brecon Sunday September 28th on my way to London. He informed me that the Lease for the Lime stone is ready for Mr. Gwinne to execute and that he should be in London on Monday and would wait upon Mr. Bacon with their petition to Parliament for an Act for a Turnpike from Brecon to Neath which would be carryed to Pont Vaun within Nine Miles of our Work, he thought a branch might be added if Mr. Bacon & Company would be at the expence of making that Road they taking the Management & Toll arising from it. However he would wait upon Mr. Bacon & talk further about it.[2]

[1] For Samuel Walker, the Rotherham ironmaster who built an early coke furnace near the town at Masborough, see A.H. John (ed.), *Minutes relating to Samuel Walker & Co., Rotherham, Iron Founders and Steel Refiners, 1741–1829* (1951).

[2] The Breconshire Turnpike Trust Act was passed in 1767 (7 Geo. III c. 60) and renewed with additional powers in 1787 (27 Geo. III c. 75). Roads were built from Brecon to Merthyr Tydfil along the valley of the Tâf Fawr and from Senny Bridge to Hirwaun (W.S.K. Thomas, *Georgian and Victorian Brecon* (1993), 5).

Isaac Wilkinson Queries sent to Mr. Cookson[1]
relating to his Blast furnace with Coke fuel vizt.

			Mr Cooksons Answers
1.	Let me know the Square of the Stack bottom, the hight of it to where you charge.	1.	8 feet 2 inches, 33 feet.
2.	What wideness at the Top of the Boshes and at the Tunnel head.	2.	11 ft 9 by 10½, 2 – 3 Sq.
3.	What length the moving boards of your Bellows and what breadth behind.	3.	17 ft, 5 ft
	How high do they rise every stroke		Leathered 21 deep.
	How many Cams in a minute		38 Cams in a minute.
	The wideness of the Pipes at the Nose.		2 inches $^{5}/_{8}$ wide.
	The thickness of the moving board.		7 inches.
4.	How many charges in 12 hours.	4.	5 charges.
	How many baskets to a charge.		8 baskets.
5.	Weight of a charge of Cokes	5.	9¼ cwt.
	Weight of a charge of Ironstone		9 cwt.
	Weight of a charge of Limestone.		3 cwt.
6.	Do you burn your stone in kiln or on the bank.	6.	On the bank.

[1] John Cookson, who had an early coke-fired furnace at Chester-le-Street (Co. Durham) (Riden, *Gazetteer*, 126–8). His own copy of this letter is in Tyne & Wear Archives, 1512/5571, 21 June 1766.

7.	Does the fire work hot & shining at the Tuère.	7.	Hot & shining.
8.	How many inches do you blow from the bottom of the hearth to the bottom of the Tuère.	8.	22 inches.
9.	Have you fireclay.	9.	Yes.
10.	Are the pigs pretty smooth, on upper-side or a little inclined to be honey-combed.	10.	Sometimes smooth some-times honey-combed.

Low Mill November 21st 1766

I ordered & see done the following Experiment with Cardiff Lime in fine powder from two pieces of stone burnt rapt up close in a leather bag in September 1765 at Merthyr in Glamorganshire and opened when I got here to this place, I found the stones broken into a very fine powder. I put the bag with the powder into a drawer under my Desk & there it remained unnoticed untill this day, when it came into mind to mix it up with Sand about $^1/_3$ & put it between 2 free stones & pressed flatt, & the edges even to make a good joint & laid them in a stand of water to see whether its lying so long in powder had taken any of its binding quality from it. Because various were the opinions of the Masons in Wales relating this. Some particularly William Edwards said that to preserve its strength it might be mixed up immediately upon slacking[1] it, that if it lay any time it would loose it in proportion to the time it lay & they said the laying a time after would not alter it but as the former had, had a great deal of Experience of this Lime I preferred his opinion in the use of it in Wales and This experiment will be a proof of it. This Experiment proves that this Lime ought to be used as soon as can be after slacked under the trial mentioned above was soft & did not bind in water but the stones between whch it was laid separated as soon as taken out of water.

[1] i.e. slaking.

AT LOW MILL
JANUARY 1767

Low Mill January 10th 1767. This day it begun to snow & continued all night. In the Morning the 11th January it was deep continued snowing with a strong cold Wind at N & N.E. Monday the 12th a strong North Wind with Thunder & Lightening continued snowing. Tuesday 13th Wind the same with Hail in some place near us (I am informed as large as Nuts). The Wind drove the Snow in drifts as filled all the roads and made them impassable near a foot deep in the flat ground in our Turnpike road near four feet & in some places 10 & 12 feet as (I am informed) several sheep lost in the Snow the next fields to us & others dug out & brought into our Pot house (p. leave).

Wednesday 14th. The Snow continued with frost but not hard enough to bear. Some of our Men went to Egremont with great difficulty made a road yesterday into the Garden to the necessary house on each side of our Steps before the Walldam the Snow was 6 feet deep. We had not a room free from the Snow. The Wind drove it through the Window frames & several bushels were taken out of our Cellar.

Coal could not be fetched which obliged the Workmen to burn offal lumps which they refused while they could get better.

Thursday 15th. Sent Edward Jolly to Whitehaven with the Letters to the post & to enquire after our friends he got there with great difficulty & was exceeding weary in his return. He brought an Acct that there was four Mails due. The post set forward twice & returned, he could not get to Bransley Brew. Butter @ 11d p. lb, Potato 10d p. Stone But Pork by the joint @ 3d¼ & Mutton @ 3d p. lb which is cheaper than could be expected as few could get to the Market.

Friday 16th the Snow continues on the ground & small snow falls. The Clouds loaded and in my opinion appear like a thaw. Cleared the Cinder heap beyond the flourishing house for riddling to mix with the small offal coal mixed some myself (to set an Example) which make very good fire.

Saturday 17th. More Snow fell last night (3 inches deep.) Little Wind and a very fine day neither Thaw nor frost.

Sunday 18th. A hard frost this last night. Little Wind. a fine Sunny Morning. A very fine Sunny day.

Monday 19th. More Snow fell last night over 3 inches deep A fine Morning Wind North. It froze hard.

I hear that there has been 100 Men employed by the Surveyor of the Turnpike to make a road for Carts as the Communication from County to Towns are stop'd by the Snow. No Post for a Week past. Past twelve o'Clock a fine Sunny day. Just now I hear that most of the sheep are lost.

One Man had 500 & has found no more than 20 alive. Clement Mossing had 2000 and had found no more than 100, his house was covered with Snow for several days which debarred them of Light, they were obliged to burn Candles untill some neighbour came and cleared it away round the house. Six o'clock this day has been a fine Sunny day freeze hard. Mr. Potter, Gale & Josh. Weld dined here & informed me that there was eight Mails due & that Number of hands were employed in clearing the Turnpike Road of Snow which renders it impassable for Men, horse & Cart.

Tuesday 20th. A fine Morning. Wind in East. A hard frost. The Sky loaded with the appearance of more Snow.

Nine o'clock this has been a fine day & a little frost & cold this night is overclouded & has appearance of more snow. I was informed that one Clement Hastley had 3000 Sheep, but could not find more than about 500. It thaws, there is small rain or sleet.

Wednesday 21st. It has thawed all night & Wind N. East. The trees are clear of snow & it melts fast from the houses.

12 o'clock a fine Sunny day. The Snow melts fast.

BACK AT CYFARTHFA
APRIL 1767

Came to Cyfarthfa Saturday April 11th 1767. Afternoon viewed part of the work & found the Stamp house pretty forward the Stacks of the Shingling furnace about as high as the side wall which was as high as there were Bricks. The Clay mill fit for work with one pair of rolls & some clay passed through for a Trial. The drying house roofed ready for slating & 4 kilns ready for use. The Blast furnace Stack about 3 feet high on one side, the other side cannot be proceeded upon until the Rock is taken down for the wheel pit on which there are as many men as can work but will require some time in doing & must retard the going on with that side of the Stack.

Sunday 12th staid within, a fine day.

Monday 13th. Viewed and Leveled for bringing the Water from the natural Wear to Cyfarthfa Rock & found a fall to the Navigation Cut to the top of the Wall 3 ft 5 Inches & 1 ft 5 In. below the Top of the wall which is the bottom of the race from the Natural Wear which makes the whole fall 4 ft 10 in. for Stamper or any other use when occasion should offer. There is a further fall to the bottom of the Navigation cut 18 inches. The distance from this Natural Wear to the Cyfarthfa Rock is from the river to the bank vizt.

River to the Bank	35 yards	9 ft length	4 ft 6 in.	deep &	10 ft wide
Bank to brook	100	do	12, 6	do	12½
from brook to race	92	do	7, -	do	12½
race to rock	48	do	4, -	do	9
	16	do	9, -	do	15

The rock 102 yards to drive through 6 feet high & 5 wide.

Tuesday 14th. Agreed the diging the race from the Natural Wear to the rock to Evan William & partner, from the Navigation cut to that rock at 3d p. solid yard.

Agreed with Isaac William & partner for 40 yards in Length, from the Navigation cut towards the Dingle up the river @ 3d p. Solid Yard.

Agreed with Peter Jones, William Bill & Edward Thomas to cut through the Rock 6 feet high & 5 feet wide 20s p. fathom we finding powder, Tools & Candles which I reckon will be 5s p. fathom more. The Rock is so hard & no pick will stand it.

Harry William Mason in the Ague & Edward Thomas Mason very ill at home, David John & John Richard upon the Arch at the high end of the furnace back race, fine Day.

Wednesday 15th. Gave orders, yesterday, to Edward Farnels to prepare the roof over the middle Shingling Furnace, in order to have it covered, that Jos. Lucas & Jas. Mason may work upon them in Wet weather. The Bargainers to drive through the Rock have begun & find it so hard that it cannot be performed in any reasonable time without Blasting. A fine day, John Morgan & another Man bro't from Cardiff sundry things upon 4 horses that came in the Ship from Liverpool as per Waste book.

Thursday April 16th. A Gloomy cold Morning the Wind at S.E. The carriage with Daniel Williams & David Lewis to fetch plank & Iron from Cardiff & George Ford went to fix the broad wheels to the Carriage. Samuel Wood & John Morgan went to Cowbridge for money. Edward Thomas & Willm Bill begun to drive into the rock in the middle to make room for more men when they have drove 4½ fathom, then 4 sets of hands may work by 8 hour shifts day & night. The rock is exceeding hard and not to brake without Blasting.

About Six o'clock this evening Mr. Isaac Wilkinson came & went with CW to view the Stack & found that the Masons had made a mistake in laying the foundation for the hearth too high & in the Air hole by 4 feet, therefore it must be taken up.

Friday 17th. A cold Frosty morning. Isaac Wilkinson & I went to view the Stack & made some alterations & gave direction for the masonries on the back of the Stack to be cleaned that the water might drain off & to be filled with sound cobble stones that the water might liberty of draining to prevent it getting into the hearth.

Viewed the rock & fixed of a place to take the water in higher up, to obtain a greater fall & less cutting in the race to convey the water. Also viewed the Bank above the rock, for kiln to burn the Mine. The rock proves so hard that I am afraid it will be more Expense than was at first thought. A fine day walked up to Tai Mawr Cut which proves tedious, and more expensive than Estimated.

Walked to the Corn Miln, where on the other side of the bridge from the Miln we see along fine spring of water that produce as much as the river in all dry season & never freeze. And William the Miller informed us that they very seldom wanted water in the dryest Season. Returned home by Tai Mawr & viewed several fine hearth stones upon that Common came home met Thomas William, who came to see Isaac Wilkinson, Brother Sam returned from Cowbridge & Cardiff & George Ford about 8 o'clock at night, he left the Carriage at Caerphilly with 13 planks the 2 fore Narrow wheels. Josh Lucas goods and a bundle with horse Traces.

Saturday 18th. Past five o'clock a Cold Gloomy Morning.

Set out three kilns for burning Mine Stone. The Carriage came about 6 o'clock. The Carpenters about the Stamper wheel. A fine day but very cold with some small snow & rain.

Sunday 19th. A cold Frosty Morning little Wind Northerly. Six in the Evening. Rain with some Hail.

Monday 20th. A fine Morning wind at NE. half past 5. Ordered Evan Jones to get from the several seems of coals a Load each for Isaac Wilkinson to see coked in order to judge which would be most suitable for the Blast Furnace that a Level might be drove to win it for supplying that furnace. Sent the Case with Letters to the postman p. John Morgan.

Tuesday 21st. Past Six a fine calm Morning. Isaac Wilkinson, Sam Wood, Jos. Lucas, George Ford & George Lyndon went with C. Wood to view his proposal for making a Temporary Wear to enable us to work, while the rock driving through, and upon consultation it was thought the most proper method therefore it is resolved to put in execution as soon as stones can be provided and the weather will permit vizt. to erect a Wall to join the end of the Bulwark upon the rock about [*Blank*] feet & from thence to place long boughs of trees under the sand, the branches down the river, so thick as to raise them by gravel and stone, high enough to raise the water into the Pool, from unfinished Head to Stamp Ground Clay & Shingle upon occasion when the forge is ready. And these boughs to join the farr end of the old Wear which is to remain.

This day the corner stone of that part of the Stack next the Wheel was laid upon the blue hard sill. Joseph Lucas took the dimension of the rock that was sent down for a foundation for the Blast furnace stack vizt. 35 feet by 45½ & 23 ft 8 in. which is 1392.16 ft solid yards, The Triangle is 45½ × 37 = 62 yds 9 ft & the soft rock next the corner of the Stack over the wheel 5.5.4 = 3.19.2.4.5 = 1.13.23.4½.4 = 15 yard 9 ft & 3.2.4. = 24 ft - 1392.16 + 62.9 + 3.19 + 1.13 +15.9 + 24 ft = 1476 yards 11 ft @ 8d p. yard £49.4.3.

Four Horse Load of Coal brought from the place under written

No 1. Lyes under Penwain Coalwork below Lewis Williams John Level and the old Scouring work is about 2½ feet thick this seems a dead coal in the house fire, for some time then flame & make a hot fire but in a Smith hearth blown by bellows flames much affords a strong heat & appears to be a tolerable Coal for the Blast is free of Sulphur. There is another about the same thickness below parted by a black sill or Hum called here between them & has some binding quality in it.

The Charges of a Blast at Dowlais Furnace 1764

	Weeks p. week	£	s	d	£	s	d
William Thomas Founder	22 @ 12s	13	4	-			
William Lewis do	57 @ do	34	4	-			
do 3 weeks Play wages[1]	@ 8s week	1	4	-			
William Howel Founder	33 & 3d at 10s week						
		16	5	-			
William Thomas do	4 & 4 @ 12s do	2	9	8½	67	6	8½
Two fillers	57 @ 8s each	45	12	-			
do 3 weeks play wages	@ 5s do	1	10	-			
One Basket filler	59 @ 7s	20	13	-	67	15	-
Gabriel Jones Calciner	57 @ 13s	37	1	-			
do Play wages	3 @ 7s	1	1	-	38	2	-
William Richard Lime stone breaker							
	57 @ 7s				19	19	-
To Sundry Exp. & conting charges p. Book					26	9	4½
William Richard 15 days Labour		-	12	6			
Al at cleaning the Boiler		3	3	-	3	15	6
Cynder Wheeler	57 @ 6s p. week				17	2	-
Jenkin Morgan Coking 1394 doz & 2 @ 10d p. doz					58	1	9½
Oiling the Bellows Engine							
	60 @ 12d p. week	3	-	-			
Engine keeper Total Wages & Sundrys as book							
		71	4	9½			
Expence of Coal to the fire Engine		85	4	-	159	8	9½
1394 doz. 2 Tal of Cokes p. getting @ 4d dz					278	16	8
Coal pit Timber					29	5	4
Blacksmith attendance					44	11	-
Iron used 1 T 4 cwt 2 q 25 lb @ 18/6					22	17	5
	carried forward				833	10	7

[1] Wages paid to retain men during slack periods.

Leather	12	15	-			
Solder	10	17	6			
Oil	4	6	4			
Candles	11	2	9			
Gunpowder	2	4	6	41	6	1
Rent of Coal & Mineral works for 60 weeks				34	3	-
Interest				400	-	-
William Bulls salary for 22 weeks @ £50 p. Annum	21	3	-			
Evan Jones for 57 @ 10s p. week	28	10	-			
John Web for 9 @ £30 p. Annum	5	7	8	55	-	8
Limestone 332 doz 11 bush. at 3s p. dozen				49	18	9
Mine 1354 doz 11 @ 5s p. dozen				338	14	7
Sand in the whole 91 doz 11 b @ 3/6 doz allowd 3 t fur				5	7	4
4 Temp. & dam stones				-	10	-
Carpenters work				23	8	-
				1781	19	-

Pig Iron & Castings 732 T, 1 cwt, 3 q, 8 lb

One doz of Mine is about 1 T, 17 cwt, 2 q, & 3 ½ lb make a Ton of metal.
About 21 sacks or Tubs to 1 Ton of Iron metal.
Limestone about ¼ in proportion to the Mine.
The charge upon the Engine is about 5s 6d p. Ton.
Wages including Smith & Carpenter 8s 2¼d p. Ton.
Clerk, Coal pits, rent & Sundry Expenses 4½ p. Ton
Mine for the Blast 2562 T cost about 2s 8d p. Ton of Mine.

No. 2. A Coal from Cwmy Glo, a 9 feet band in three lifts. A parting about the thickness of half Crown a Good Roof burns well by Blast is a clean sweet coal but dull in a house fire.

No 3. Coal in the Mountain above Cwmy Mine, this Band or vein lyes in two lifts about 2 feet 6 inches deep, dull in a house fire, but burns well in a Smith fire a sweet coal.

No 4. in the bottom of Lewis William Johns Old race burns the best of any in an House fire but not so well in the Smith fire before a blast. This seems the best for an Air Furnace.

No 5. Coal from Brick kiln between 6 & 7 feet thick about 7 yd from the Surface is found the best Coal for burning Brick, hitherto found but I do not think it better than No 4 as it appears to me by tryal upon the house fire.

No 6. Lyes at the bottom of Cwmy Mine about 2 feet thick.

No 7. Lyes at the Top of Cwm y Mine about 3 feet thick where the Level was begun under it. This coal burns in a Smith fire very well affords much flame, is sweet & free of Sulphur & I think will coke for a Blast Furnace. Isaac Wilkinson was present when this was try'd &

approved of them fit for the Blast Furnace & that they would do without coking but this in my opinion is a whim.

No 8. Lyes at the new race where they cut the Lime Coal about 3 feet thick this in the Smith fire burn sweet offer as much flame & I think will make a good Coke. Isaac Wilkinson is of opinion that this coal will be unusable for a blast furnace.

No 9. Lyes over No 4 about 6 feet thick and about 5 yards of ground below.

No 10. Lyes within 4½ feet of No 9 about 9 feet thick

No 11. Lyes 9 feet above No 10 and 6 feet thick

No 11. Lyes next to No 10 and about 4 feet thick.

No 12. Lyes next to No 11 about 6 feet thick where Clifton was cutting Coal. There are supposed to be more Veins not yet discovered. This coal was tryed the 28th & proved a good Coke but heavy, by Iron mine & lying in it as per Acct that day.

From Tuesday April 21st. Past Six o'clock rains hard.

Wednesday 22nd. Six o'clock, a cloudy morning, a deal of rain fell last night. Wind in East.

Called in Harry Williams & David John two of the head Masons at the Stack and gave them positive orders not to put any Cobble stones into the outer pillars next the wheel pit & race, as it is the support of near half of the stack. The cobbles having a smooth Service & round when a weight is upon them they press upon such other as wedges & consquently must open & separate and force the flatt outward stones, which are as a case from the foundation and the fabrick must fall. And the higher such a building is, the greater the weight & pressure & the more danger. A Blast Furnace having a large hollow, a pipe filled with Ironstone, Coal & Lime stone, layer upon layer, of a great many Tons weight, pressing upon each other to descend to the bottom, reaching of the force of the fire excited by a strong Blast, have a great force upon the outward Wall, therefore it ought to be well bound, with Iron, to keep it from opening and falling. Instance an Air furnace (a low building) & nothing within of weight to press against the sides, as in the Blast, if not well bound, the heat & force of the fire would rend it to pieces, was it not well bound together in every part. The Blue Sill or slaty rock in the Back race from the river to the furnace about 30 yards from the river & rises until it is 9 feet at the Stack.

Nine o'clock, rains hard, Masons & Labourers off work the river freshening & prevent us going on with the Bulwark walls.

7 o'clock rain continues, the river high.

Thursday 23rd. Six o'clock a rainy Morning. Wind S.W.

A Consultation about securing the Masons from the rain at the Stack resolved to erect a shade with Poles & Dales.[1] I gave order to prepare for the same & it is the opinion of Isaac Wilkinson that it will be of more advantage to the Company to make a gravel road, to the Coal & stone, than a rail or waggon way, & that we should have taken up this waggon road, to make gravel & to employ the Country in the Carriage.

Six o'clock rain most of the day. Joseph Lucas, James Mason & 2 more were about the granulating cistern in the flourishing house. The river is high.

One of the Stamper wheels is now finished & the floor began to be flagged at odd times.

Friday 24th. Half past five a cold cloudy Morning the appearance of more rain. Wind in N.W.

The pillar of the stack next the race & wheel pit, is laid upon the hard blue Sill; the opposite corner & the back were laid before I came & upon the shivery rock but I do not apprehend it can fail.

Isaac Wilkinson informs me that he has tryed Mine & stone unburnt which made as good iron but no more then two thirds in quantity. As the stone looses one third in weight in burning there can be no advantage in puting it into the furnace unburnt, but the reduce as it takes more fuel & lime then when burnt.

This has been a fine day & work gone well. The granulating Cistern is now finished, Stones begun to be brought from Lewenkelly for the foundation of the Bulwark Wall to turn the water into the Pool. One of the Stamper Wheels shrouded & bucketed.

Saturday 25th. A quarter past 5 o'clock.Wind at East. A fine fair morning. Mr. Wilkinson walked with me to the Brick kiln and to view the Coal & Mine at Penywain, Cwm y Mine & from thence up the Mountain as farr as Lewis William John's old work. By washing it has laid bear several veins of Coal & Mine; to all appearances that will serve several generations. The Coal of different thickness & the Mine the same. The Coal under the Brick kiln represented to the fine coal of about 7 or 8 feet thick. John Edge the Brickmaker, informs me that about 4 feet at the bottom of this Coal is but very indifferent, & therabout three feet at the top is a good Coal & fit burning of Brick and consquently for Air furnaces, which I shall farther try. There is a vein of coal called the

[1] i.e. deal boards.

Lime Coal, laid bear which to appearance is as clean & sweet fine Coal as one would wish to see, but it is not having a sufficient depth of Earth or cover upon it, is tender & not fit for any work that requires a flame but when got further into the Dip I cannot help being of opinion that that coal will be of much better quality. A Level brought up from the low part of the Common under their several veins will lay them all dry and they may be got with that Level very commodiously.

This day being Merthyr Wake, which they call a Revell,[1] all the Masons & most the Labourers were absent and the work of a fine day lost in the Erecting our Stack & a loss to their families. George Ford, his two Men Postlethwaite worked as did Joseph Lucas, James Mason, Ben. Hopkin Masons.

The Sawyers half a day & 4 of the Labourers for supplying the Stack with Stone, these were all that worked this day.

Sunday 26th. Past Six o'clock a rainy Morning W at SW. About 12 o'clock it took up & proved a fine day.

Monday 27th. Half past five, a fine warm Morning, Wind at North East. Four more Masons came this Morning to the Stack. After Breakfast, set on four Labourers to lower the far side of the river to turn the Course of the water on the opposite side, in order to lay the foundation of the Bulwark wall, to the Turn it must have to the rock & will secure in the meantime to part of the temporary Wear.

Sent Evan Jones with a letter to Abergwythen to Mr. Joshua Glover[2] about some Timber that he has to dispose of about 5 Miles from Cyfarthfa.

The Carriage & 2 horses are gone to Cardiff to fetch part of the Treeplank and Iron that came in the Liverpool vessel. Since Dinner fourteen of the Labourers that got & carried stone to the Stack have left off, because they could raise their wages, & have not left one to serve the Masons, they insisted upon 14d per day, but the Masons who had them would not consent, as their agreement (as I am informed) was to give them 13d p. Perch. After the same measure, they the Masons were to have to raise them in the quarry & to deliver them convenient to their work. And to pay them 1s per day untill the Building was completed & if the measurement was more than 1s per day to pay the surplus to them.

[1] The annual parish revel, perhaps originally a patronal festival. Known locally in Welsh as a 'mabsant'; 'wake' would be the northern equivalent familiar to Wood.

[2] Joshua Glover had succeeded his father at the ironworks at Abercarn in Ebbw Vale (Mon.): Riden, *Gazetteer*, 12.

Their Names are Wm Moses, Harry Moses, Howel Powel, John Howel, Thos Watkins, Walter Rees, Howel Rees, Richard Edward, Wm Jon William, Wm David, Wm Thos., David Herbert, John William & Morgan Robert. These are not to be employed at this work unless they repent & return to their bargain tomorrow morning. William Bill, one of the men that took driving through the rock (with Ned Thos. and Peter Jones) refuses to proceed thereon, unless he has insured to him one shilling and sixpence each shift, which is but 8 hours this is refused therefore he is I suppose gone off. This has been a fine warm day.

Tuesday 28th. Six o'clock a fine warm morning but cool the Wind at East. Half past five, this has been a fine warm day. This day we tryed four different sort of coal, a load of each put on a heap on the bank above the house vizt. No 1 the top part of the Brick kiln Land which is about three feet thick it burned well & clear no visible difference between this & Dowlass Coal the Coke is heavier then Dowlass & upon examination it was found that there is Iron Mine mixed with it, which I discovered by the magnet, the reason of my trying was a piece of heavy (like a rotten) Coal was brought me that was found in this coal, as a bad sign and as I generaly try all heavy bodys I meet with in the fire, I put a piece of this into the fire & upon applying the Magnet I found it to be very rich Mine & conclude that much of this Coal is loaded with this Mine. This is No 12 in my former Acct.[1]

No 2 was a load of Dowlas Coal procured from Dowlas Furnace as a pattern to try ours by; I tryed this coal coked in the dust with the Magnet, but not the least appearence of Iron in it, it is light fine Coke, much like No 1 but lighter for the reasons given before.

No 3. The coal from Cwm y Mine, between the rock (No 2 in my former Acct) this is a dull burning Coal & will not coke, what it may do when got farther into the coal time must discover.

(No 4. Is the No 3 in my former Acct.) the 2 foot band under the Lime Coal. It burns well & full as good as Dowlas, a light Coke & thought by Wilkinson to be the best Coke for a Blast furnace it produced the whitest Ash of any.

Wednesday 29th. Half past five a fine warm Morning Wind at N.W. The Masons have taken several of their Labourers in again this morning. Began to lay the foundation of the Bulwark wall joining it to the Wall to be carried with an Angle to the rock, with the Wern stones in Cardiff

[1] See above, pp. 179–81, for Wood's previous list of local coal seams.

Lime. George Ford sent two Carpenters & two Sawyers to Gethligaer to cut and prepare a piece of Wood there belonging to Lord Talbot, for an hammer beam & followed them himself.

Isaac Wilkinson left us this Morning for Bristol & London lent him a Horse to the Passage[1] & sent the horse keeper with him to bring it back. Carriage brot 21 fine planks, the Till broke, therefore was obliged to wait a day longer to procure a new one. They left 15 plank short (4 miles from Cardiff), returned there to get the Carriage repaired & then brot the 21 planks.

The horsekeeper returned at night, he went no further than Newport, where Mr. Wilkinson waited to go in a Vessel to Bristol.

Thursday 30th. Half past five o'clock a fine warm calm Morning. This has been a fine warm day, walked with Brother Sam, Geo. Ford & Joseph Lucas to view the Tai mawr cut & dertermine whether to drive this work for near one hundred yards in length, or build a wall next the river and in my opinion, it will be as useful, and sooner executed & will not cost so much by 3/5 therefore I chose, as my Brother differs in opinion with me he is for driving thro' the rock and his reason is from a doubt of the permanency of the wall. Joseph Lucas our furnace builder thinks as I do that a wall will not fail & George Ford the same.

They go on well with the Stack all the pillars are near Level. The Bulwark wall is near three feet high next to the grate, & I think will answer the end it was built. George Ford begun to put the other Stamper wheel together in its place. The water post Sill, are Mortising in order to be hard down for laying out the wash.

Friday May 1st. Half past five a fine Morning, Wind at N.W. begun to lay the foundations of the sloping side of the wall joining the rock, two men laded water to find the rock which was in holes & occasioned trouble, but it was cleared to & leveled with small stones & Cardiff Lime and the Wern stones laid, headers from 2 to 3 ft long for the foundations All in Cardiff Lime.

I had a consultation with Sam Wood, George Lyndon, George Ford and Joseph Lucas whether it would be the best & safest method to leave a vacancy in the Bevel wall next the rock to allow the river come into the Pool by the Temporary Wear, & how high. S.W. & G.L. that it should be lower than the river in its present low state & I joined them. Joseph Lucas thought the wall should be as high as the river, as he

[1] i.e. the New Passage on the Severn.

imagined that would not work when the water was lower. And George Ford was of opinion that the Wall should be quite finished and after fixed in it, to let the river come onto the Pool as we thought proper. Upon weighing the several opinions & arguments it was thought the most desirable to follow George Fords opinion and as there is a gate already made that will answer for this purpose, it would not retard the going on to finish it while the weather continues fair. We Leveled from the top of the farr end of the Wear now standing to the bottom of the cut in the rock now cutting, by Peter Jones (which I thought was too high) & it was found 19 inches lower as it was intended. And from the Surface of the river, as it now is, their will be 19 inches head for the Stamper & Clay Mill. the Troughs of which are laid upon a Level, and by making a Wear by Bushes, Stone & Gravel an addition of 2 feet may be easily obtained, which will be sufficient for both the stampers, Clay Mill & hammer. the latter I think will shingle at all times, when the others can work, but may be longer about a charge than when the Pool is full. Therefore I am in great hopes, making such a temporary Wear as will enable me to work up all metal we have, before the Blast furnace is ready for Blowing & the rock & other cutts are completed to convey the water through the rock.

The water that is proposed to be brought from the land of Tai Vawr for an Overshot wheel may be too little in a dry summer. Isaac Wilkinson proposed that the water from the two branches might be brought first to the Furnace wheel, in aid to the other as an undershot, which would make the quantity of water more certain for the furnace at all seasons & be as equally as cheap as by conveying it through the rock in the method I proposed, this was so visible an advantage as could not be objected to & therefore assented up accordingly.

The Furnace is this day brought up to a Level in every part & is carried on in a workmanlike manner by Harry William & David John, two of the contracting Masons, the third Edward Thomas is ill & has not been at work upon it since I came.

George Ford & his Men with Wm. Postlethwaite were fixing the other stamper wheel.

There being a dispute over the damage done by a Trespass upon the Land of Mr. Jenkins farmer, Lewis Evans wrote to me that he was willing to refer it to any reputable person, my Brother sent John Morgan to Mr Daniel William requesting his viewing the premises & this day the said Mr. Daniel William went with Samuel Wood & John Morgan to Lewis Evans (agreeable to my promise) and offered him five guineas for the damage by bringing Timber thro' his land although the said Daniel Wm said it was more than the damage was done, but the said Lewis

Evans refused taking the same, & to referr it to Daniel Wm although he acknowledged him a reputable person but said he would referr it to his Landlord Mr. Jenkins.

This day I agreed with John Morgan from Tai Mawr for the fields we are to drive cuts through for conveying the water to the furnace wheel for the farm he holds it, at four pounds four shillings p. Annum & five guineas in hand with the approbation of Lord Talbot & Michael Richards Esq. Lords of the same. This prevents disputes about damages we being obliged by our Lease to pay the Tennants reasonable damages & their field I suppose may rent to a Workman for the money we pay or more being near the work and as Land will increase in value as the work do, it is right to secure all we can & rent it again to such persons as are most servicable to the Company.

Saturday May 2nd. Half past six a fine Mild morning. Wind N.E. got near above the river as it now is & laid 2 are laid for the Sluice and they have gone on very well this day as also the Stack. George Ford & his men were about the other Stamper wheel.

The Carriage brought 15 Firr plank, the same left 4 miles from Cardiff and a Grindstone p. the Cargo from Liverpool. The Stack has gone on well near high enough for Lintels & Springing the Arches.

Agreed with John Morgan of Tai Mawr for three of his fields, one more than yesterday, where the cut comes through at £5 10s p. Annum to prevent any dispute about Trespass which I find very difficult, without pay. An exorbitant rate. These fields I imagine may let for the same to a Workman, it laying contiguous to the furnace. This has been a fine warm day.

Sunday May 3rd. A quarter of Six a fine calm morning Wind at North. After breakfast I took a walk with Bro. Sam & George Lyndon, George Ford & Joseph Lucas to the furnace & cut, Viewed the fields we took from John Morgan. Returned home to dine. A Warm forenoon. About three o'clock the Wind was brisk at North West, whistled & the Clouds have the appearence of rain. The air much altered, the wind being cold & sharp which occasioned my ordering a fire in the Office, wnich we suffered to go out in the Morning, it being very warm and needed none.

Put some of the Cinder from the Brick kiln Coal (that was made to try with the Dowlas Coal) upon the Office fire, which burned exceeding clear I reckon will serve a Blast furnace very well.

A piece of the rock through which they are now driving was put into the fire by Isaac Wilkinson to see what effect it would have upon it as he thought kindling a fire against it would soften it & make more easy to work, but it came out after being red hot, near the same. This piece I put again into a hot fire, at the first, it not crack & burst, as is generally the case with most rock and enduced the heat seemingly as well as Stourbridge or any other fire clay or Sill. After the first fire it came so soft as to be cut by my knife, much the same as those Sill, after the second fire it appeared brown & hard like a Tinder rock & not any appearence of a Clay.

Monday May 4th. Half past five o'clock cold cloudy morning Wind at North.

Two o'clock. There has been showers, but not to hinder any work. George Ford, his two men & Farnel men about the other Stamper wheel. Postlethwaite making hoops for the furnace stack, Air holes & Cox mortising the Water post sills.

Joseph Lucas, Sam Mason & Hopkin David, Masons with 6 Labourers upon the Bulwark wall whch is now above the water in the river. The Furnace Stack goes on well.

William Davis, Labourer, was sent to clear the Land belonging to Thomas Lewis, of the stones that fell from the rock in making the Taimawr cut. The men in driving thro' this rock, find it hard & go on but slowly. This day I sent George Lyndon to Dowlas Furnace, to Richard Davies, the keeper there, to know if he would let me have his son, who is a Moulder, to cast the Lintels for the Stack & His answer was that John Guest, was to have the management of that furnace & as he was certain they could not agree, he would come down & speak to me, & if we could agree he & his son would cast for us and if we could not agree upon terms, he & his son would go to Neath. Isaac Wilkinson gave this Richard Davies a good character as a keeper therefore if he is at Liberty & is determined to leave that furnace, we are at Liberty to hire him as well as any other person.

Agreed for 20 Oak Loads (p. Geo. Ford) from Morgan John Robert, that are 14 year seasoning some of them inch & other ¾ thick at 2½s p. foot.

Wrote to Mr. Richards the 2d about Gwm Glae Land to send by Robert Thomas who goes with the Carriage.

Tuesday May 5th. Six o'clock. A cold cloudy Morning. Wind N.

Carriage gone this Morning to Cardiff to fetch Daleplanks, part of the Liverpool cargo.

This has been a cold day and it snowed about Eleven o'clock and a brisk wind at North East. David, one of George Fords Apprentices, has the ague & shaked much. There are Number of people as I am informed ill with this disorder. George Ford, his apprentice, Joseph Gibson & Cox, Carpenters were making Centres for the blast furnace & William Postlthwaite finished four boxes for keeping open the Airholes in the Stack, pursuant to Isaac Wilkinsons directions.

Sawyers Two sawing Dale plank for flooring boards & two more sawed Timber for forge.

Joseph Lucas, James Mason & Hopkin David, Masons with two Labourers bearing stones & two making Cardiff Mortar & serving it at the Bulwark Wall.

I am just now informed that John Guest is at Dowlais furnace and has undertaken the Management for 14 years; but upon what terms I do not know.

Two Smiths vizt. Thomas Williams & William Black are employed in mending & making Tools & shoeing horses etc.

Wednesday May 6th[1] Half past five a cold frosty Morning. Wind N.W.

Agreed with Richard Davis his son a founder to cast Lintels for the Blast furnace Stack, Standard & Anvil Block for the forge etc. at £11 [per] Ton. This is a very high price but as we cannot get any other person are obliged to submit to give it. Richard Davis the Father who was keeper at the Dowlais furnace & who sent me the answer by George Lyndon on Monday has agreed to wish John Guest to remain there in that station.

Preparing the casting furnace for use against to Morrow Joseph Lucas is altering the door cases as there was a Stone put where the Tap hole ought to have been.

Worked up all our Iron in bars & wanting boring tools, sent Thos. William, one of the Smith to purchase some Squrs at [*Blank*] He bought 29 lb (all that he had except one small bit at 20 p. cwt.)

Ordered Patterns for the Arches Lintels as p. plan of Blast Furnace Stack, to be made the first over the Timp to be 8 feet in length supposing it in a Line & 4 inches by 3 thick & 9 inches deep

8ft = 96 inches & 3½ the medium = 336 + 9 the depth = 3024 : 4 the number of inches in the pound = 756 lb or 6 cwt 3 q - .

[1] Incorrectly given as 'Wednesday 5th' in the MS.

(Error)[1]

The larger Lintel is ordered to be 11 ft 4 In. in Length supposing it a line = 136 Inches + 4 the medium the thickness = 544 + 9 the depth = 4896 Inches : 4 the number of inches in a pound weight

1224 lb wt or 10 cwt 3 q 20 lb. Error.

Mr. John Guest & his Brother Thomas were here this day the former informed me that he had taken the Management of Dowlas furnace for the term of 14 years, but he did not inform me of the Terms only that he was to deliver the Pigs in the bank at a certain price & to be paid Monthly for them. And he said he would be glad to be upon good Terms with me & do all we each of us could for the benefit of both which I told him was my desire.

The Centres for the Twere & front Arches of the Blast furnace are made. The Pattern for the Lintels also made and the Air furnace Nealing for use. The coals from the Brick kiln will prove as good for fire Air furnace.

The Bulwark wall goes on well & every other branch. This has been cold but fair, and a good working day.

The Carriage has brought 18 fir plank & Isaac Wilkinson Modell for Blowing by a fall of water.

Thursday May 7th.[2] Six o'clock a rainy Morning the Wind at West. George Ford has made a mistake in giving me the dimension of the pattern for the Lintel by informing me of the diameter when it is half a Circle, or near it. Therefore when reduced to a line they will be as follows vizt. The small one 10 feet long = 120 in + 3.5 In the medium thickness 420 In + 9, the depth = 3780 Inch : 4 as 4 inches weighs a pound vizt. 945 lb = 8 cwt 1 q 21 lb.

The larger Lintel will be 17 feet in Line = 204 In : 4 the medium thickness = 816 In + 9, the depth = 7344 In : as 4 Solid inches of cast Iron weighs a pound = 1836 lb = 16 cwt 1 q 16 lb.

The patterns are made half an inch thicker then at first intended which will add to the weight for the small one 1 cwt 0 q 23 Tot = 9 cwt 2 q 16 lb.

For the large one do 2 cwt, 0 q, 3 lb Total vizt. 18.1.19.

[1] *Sic* MS.

[2] Given incorrectly as the 6th in the MS.

Ordered William Lewis, who was one of the keepers at Plymouth furnace, to attend Thomas Davis the founder, in working the furnace for casting the Lintels etc.

This day we began with Casting furnace we charged 12 cwt of the Motley Pig & the Brick kiln coal & although the furnace was never used before it melted that quantity in 3 hours the metal run thin & well & we cast 3 Stamper heads 7 furnace bars & a stoke hole very good ones, I observe that this small coal does as well in their furnace as larger, the latter were broke small by the furnace man. Thomas Davies seems to be a very good moulder.

George Ford, Josh Lucas & Cox were fixing the Center for the front Arch. Jos. & 2 men at the Stamper wheel. James Mason, Hopkin David & Benjamin, Masons with 3 Labourers were at the Bulwark wall.

Friday May 8th.[1] Halfpast Six, a Cloudy close Morning but fair, Wind South East.

The Dimensions of the Pattern for the Anvil Block to be cast in Iron, vizt. The top 29½ In. sq., the bottom 33½ In., in length 23 In. The medium 32½ + 32½ = 1056 + 23 = 24288 Inches : 4. the number of cubic inches in a pound = 6072 lb the hole in the Anvil will be 18 in. sq. & 11 deep. 18 + 18 = 324 + 11 = 3564 : 4 = 891 lb deducted from 6072 lb - 5181 lb = 2 T, 6 cwt, 1 lb the four feet each a cubic of 4 inches, will be 16 lb and allow for Scull & a large head to prevent it being hollow etc. for waste 2 cwt & then there ought to be put into the furnace 56 cwt of pigs & 28 cwt in each furnace.

Two o'clock weighted and charged the Air furnace with 16 cwt of pigs to cast the small Lintel & two plates for it to stand upon as a precaution in case the stones shd fly by the heat as is often the case. The plates to be each three feet long & 1 foot broad & one inch thick.

It rains moderately very seasonable for the grass & Corn.

Agreed with William David & [*Blank*] to make a Wear cross the river near from the Bulwark wall to the part of the old Wear now standing by a Course of Stakes the first course as high as shall be thought necessary by George Ford & Joseph Lucas the second course lower & the third course the lowest to be well raddled or Wattled & filled with slurry & gravel, as also the front and back to be well supported by stone & gravel to make it substantial and to finish the same in fourteen days from this day the Company to make what Stakes they can spare from old pieces of Slabs, & what shall be wanted more than we can spare they are to

[1] 7th in MS.

pursue & fetch all to the spot. The Company to be at no further Expenses except finding them 2 Wooden Mallet & a Crow or an armed Stake & 8d p. yard in length for each of the two first courses & 7d p. yard in length for the last course. To be completed in such a manner as the aforesaid George Ford & Joseph Lucas shall direct.

William Lewis the person appointed to attend Thomas Davies, Moulder, does not understand the management of an Air furnace, if a person that has been accustomed to the care of a casting furnace, a charge of metal of 62 cwt might be melted in about 2½ hours. The coal is swift in burning, but very hot, and I believe will do well for flourishing & Shingling, but the quantity a furnace will consume is not yet tryed.

Measured the work of Peter Jones in driving into the rock he has been [illegible] weeks at work & has done three yards used 8¼ of powder Edward Thomas & Wm Bill have been 2 weeks & have done a fathom and used 22 lb of powder.

Six o'clock this has been a fine moderate rainy day good for grass & Corn. The Bulwark wall goes well, with James Mason, Hopkin David & Benj. Jones Masons & two Labourers. The Masons & Labourers at the furnace Stack left off about three o'clock, it being pay day, & went to the Vilage to settle with each other. George Ford, his 2 Men & 4 more Carpenters were upon the Stamp wheel & making a Pattern for an Anvil Block, Morticing the Waterpost & jointing together wheel case frames.

We have cast the smallest Lintel & one plate for it.

Saturday Morning, May 9th. It rains hard, Wind in South. Six o'clock, fine weather for the Lands.

This has been day of rain. No Masons work out of doors. The Masons at the Stack are preparing stones for the Arch under cover. Joseph Lucas & James Mason underpining Wall plates, over Mixing Room & Benj. Wedgwood serving them.

George Ford his two Men & two more finish the Stamper wheel & planking before the Stamper boxes. William Postlethwaite, Cox, Thomas John making patterns for Anvil Block.

Weighted 14 cwt of Pigs for casting plates to bind the furnaces, but Wm Lewis not managing the fire as it ought, he kept the metal in five hours which made it so thick near one half would not run & was drawn out with the shell which will occasion a great waste, there was only 2 plates & a stoke hole that would be fit for the use intended and the plate miscarried.

Received 14 Load of Cardiff Lime the Carriers Measure but 16 Load from the kiln @ 2s p. Load for Carriage & 6d p. Load at the kiln.

J.W. to T. Jones Sept. 1761.

I apprehend & dare venture to assure you that your Merthyr Stones are not so much in fault, as your Blast has been with respect to the waste your Hearth has suffered. This supposition will be more clearly established when you blow out, if you find the Twire side only gone, which I presume will be the case. And this circumstance will happen with a weak Blast or Velocity whatever Stones you have and to be at the trouble if making a Tryal, with any from this Country will be as expensive as it will prove dissatisfactory. I have given it as my opinion to Thomas Bousner, that your Twire side only has suffered and that your Hearth may be repaired to be as good as quite New with fresh stones in that Side. I asked him his opinion of your Stones which he thinks are very good ones. He shall send you Dimensions of the Hearth put in & instructions for the preparing such stones as may be wanted.

The Section of the Hearth that was laid in Merthyr Furnace

	ft	in.
The Length of the Hearth	5	6
The Width at the Backstaff	1	8
Ditto at the Back Wall	1	6
The height of Ditto	6	-
From the bottom stone to the top of the Twire plate	1	6
The width of the Twire hole	-	4
By	-	4
To run	-	6
From back wall to Twire plate	2	4
From the bottom stone to the bottom of the Twireplate	1	8

The Twire wall & Wind wall to Batter off one inch & half each wall

BW	Twr	WW	3 ft 6 in.
1,8	1,7	1,7	
1,6	2,-	1,7	
1,4	1,4	1,4	
1,6	1,1	1,6	
1,-	1,-	1,-	
7,-	7,-	7,-	

Thomas Bourns Dimensions etc.
Dimension of Hearth of Merthyr Furnace

Bottom stone to be in three pieces each stone to be 4 ft 6 in. long 2 ft 4 in. broad & 14 inch heigh. Backwall stones, two, to be 3 ft 6 in. long & 2 ft 9 in. broad & 1 ft 8 in. thick each stone.

Two stones to be 2 feet long, 2 ft 9 in. broad & 1 ft 6 in. thick each stone.

The stones to be 3 ft long 2 ft 9 in. broad & 1 ft 4 in. thick, each stone.

Three stones to be 2 ft long, 2 ft 9 in. broad & 1 ft 6 in. thick each stone.

Two stones to be 3 ft long 2 ft 9 in. broad & 1 in. thick, each stone.

The Twire Wall[1] one Stone 5 ft 6 in. long, 2 ft 9 in. broad, & 19 inches thick.

Two Stones to be 2 ft 6 in. long, & 2 ft 9 in. broad and 2 feet thick, each stone.

Two Stones to be 1 ft 8 in. long, 2 ft 9 in. broad & 1 inch thick each Stone.

Stones 2 ft 6 in. long, 2 ft 9 in. broad, and 8 feet 1 inch thick, each stone.

Three stones 1 ft 8 in. long, 2 ft 9 in. broad and 1 foot thick each stone.

End Wall one Stone to be 2 ft 6 in. long, 2 ft 9 in. broad & 1 ft 7 in. thick each stone.

Two stones to be 2 ft 6 in. long, 2 ft 9 in. broad & 1 ft 7 in. thick each Stone.

Three stones 1 ft 8 in. long, 2 ft 9 in. broad & 1 ft 4 in. thick each stone.

Two Stones 2 ft 6 in. long, 2 ft 9 in. broad & 1 ft 6 in. thick each stone.

Three stones 1 ft 8 in. long, 2 ft 9 in. broad & 1 ft thick each stone.

The Timp stone[2] 3 ft 6 in. long 3 ft broad at one End by 1 ft 8 in. broad, at the other end and two feet 2 inches thick.

Two Squinchins[3] to be 3 ft 8 in. long, 2 ft 3 in. broad & 10 inches thick each stone.

[1] i.e. the wall containing the tuyere through which air is admitted to the furnace.

[2] The stone forming the base of the tapping arch of a furnace.

[3] A squinchin is an arch across an internal angle.

8 feet of Bosh stones, from 2 feet long, to 3 ft 6 Inches, from 2ft 4 In. to 2 feet do from 10 inches thick to 8 inches thick.

Sunday May 10th. Six o'clock a Windy but fair Morning Wind at West. Wrote to my wife & Mr. Bacon.

This has been a fine day & fair, except a shower of hail about Eleven o'clock. Mr. Powel Minister of this Parish called upon me this Evening and upon my informing him what Lewis Evans threatened me with upon sending for the Tithe from his Land which was a suit for a Trespass he promised me the Tariff[1] which I am informed, sets forth the Custom of the Parish, in conveying the Tithe from their several fields, in order to prevent any dispute upon such cases. This Lewis Evan seems to be a Litigious troublesome Man and because we did not comply with his exorbitant demand for going through his Land with Timber as is before mentioned, He seems determined to do all the ill natured behaviour in his power.

Evan Jones his Account of the expence
in making Pigs, at Machen Furnace,
late Mr. Morgan of Tredegar
Now Mr. Mabury[2]

				£	s	d
Wood 10s 6d p. Cord 2 cord p. doz				1	1	-
Cutting off cord 3s	do			-	6	-
record 1s 4d & Coaling 4				-	5	4
Carriage 7s Cabin hurdles				-	9	8
1 dozen of Coal				2	2	-
Stone getting	6	-				
Carriage	3	-				
Royalty	2	-				
			1. dz	-	-	11
Lime at the furnace p. doz.						3

Rent for furnace & three forges 200 p. annum
26 weeks of Blast 20 p. week 520 Ton

[1] *Sic* MS, although 'terrier' would seem to fit the sense better.

[2] The ironworks at Machen, near Newport (Mon.) was a forge, rather than a blast furnace, worked in conjunction with the furnace at Caerphilly (Glam.) for much of the eighteenth century (Riden, *Gazetteer*, 15–17). It is probably the latter furnace that is referred to here, then in the hands of John Maybery, the Brecon ironmaster.

Coals 22 sacks @ 3/6 p. Sack								3	17	-
Stone 2 dz								1	2	--
Lime 1 doz								-	3	-
2 keepers					1	4	-			
2 fitters						14	-			
Stokers at bridge						12	-			
Burners of Mine						7	-			
Breakers of Limestone						7	-			
Stackers of Coal 2 p. m.						13	-	-	5	-
					3	17	-			
rent of furnace					-	2	-	-	2	-
per Ton of Pigs								5	9	-

Pigs at Hirwaun p. Evan Jones						
2 dozen on furnace Bank					14	-
stone 1 doz					3	-
To do doz 1						
do 1 p. doz						
Sacks of Coke s p. doz					16	8
for 1 doz pigs	2	-				
Stones do	1	6				
Stones broken	1	2				
burner	1	2				
wheeler & Smith p. person	1	2				
for coal work		6				
Baskets in p. yard	1	2			8	8
Stocktaker					3	-
& Iron					2	-
				£2	7	4

Forge Account vizt.						
held at forge Long wt 28 cwt @ £6 8s p. Ton				8	16	6
Coal 18 sacks @ 3s 6d @ sack				3	3	-
for 11s Hammerman 10s				1	1	-
Common Charge				2	-	-
for 1 ton of barrs				15	0	6
Ditto half Coke & half charcoal Pig						
Coke at £3 5s dd at his forge	2	5	6			
Charcoal	4	9	3	6	14	9
£3 3s Workmen £1 1s				4	4	-
Common charge				2	-	3
				12	19	-

An Account of Cardiff Lime used at Cyfarthfa vizt.

1765					
August 24	p. Carriage of 42. Load @ 2s p. Load		£4	4	-
Nov. 1	p. do 12. do		1	4	-
1766					
Sept. 19	p. do 193. do		19	6	-
	p. Turnpike			16	-
	p. burning in Cardiff for 283 Load at 6d		7	1	6
			£32	11	6

Dowlais Blast 1764 for 60 weeks

Mine 1355 doz at 5s a doz = 1 T 17 cwt 2 q 2 dz			
about 3½ T to T of pigs			£338 14 7
Coke 1394 at 4s 10d do			
is about 21 sacks or Tubs to the Ton do			336 18 6
Limestone 333 doz at 3d			
about ¼ in proportion to the Mine			49 18 9
Wages at the Furnace		£210 4 8½	
Do for Smiths Work	44 11 -	-	
Iron used	22 17 5	67 8 5	
Do Carpenters work		23 8 -	
Engine Expenses		204 10 5	
Clerks		55 0 8	
Coalpits		29 5 4	
Sand £5 17s 4d			
& sundry Expenses £26 9s 4½d		32 6 8½	
Rent of Coal etc.		34 3 -	
add		- - 11	656 8 2
Pigs 732 T at about £1 17s 9s p. Ton			1382 - -
Mine 3½ at 2s 8d p. Ton		9s 4d	
Coke 21 Tubs at 4s 10d p. doz		8 6	
Limestone		2 2	
Engine		5 6	
Wages & Expenses in smalls		8 2½	
Clerks		4 -½	£1 17 9

The measure of Land in the Parish of Merthyr Tidvil within the Hundred of Caerfilly in Glamorganshire[1]

23 feet square is one Yard, 48 of these yards is one Cover & 4 Covers is one Acre.

23 × 23 = 529 × 48 = 25392 × 4 = 101568 : 9 = 11285 : 4840 = 2 a. 1 r. 13 p. To English Statute measure.

The measure for Grain in Caerphilly, Cardiff, Cowbridge & Llantrissant 10 Gallons to the bushel three pecks makes the bushel, Eight pecks the Lestra. The wheat is streaked & the Oats heaped as high as it will go. In Brecon 8 gallons is their bushel for wheat & Oats, but for Oats there is two bushel for one or 16 Gallons, both streaked.

One peck is 13¼ quart three pecks is 1 Bushel Eight Pecks is a Lestra }	At Cardiff, Caerphilly, Cowbridge & Llantrissant which are the Chief Market Towns

The wheat streaked & the Oats heaped as high as it will go. A Lestra is three Winchester bushels, 2 gallons, 2 quarts ²⁄₃ but the heaped will make the Oats nearly 36 galllons the Lestra streaked measure therefore Oats are at 6s a Lestra (here at the present price) it is equal to 4s for 24 Gallons a Cumberland bushel or three Winchester.

[1] The best account of traditional weights and measures in South Wales in this period is given by Walter Davies in his report to the Board of Agriculture (*General view of the agriculture and domestic economy of South Wales* (1815), ii. 499–506). A 'cover' (from the Welsh *cyfair* or *cyfer*) at Merthyr was a land measure of 2 roods 13 perches statute; there were four *cyfairs* to the *erw* ('acre'), which was equal to 2a. 1r. 13p. statute. The 'lestra' (i.e. *llestraid*) was a corn measure which varied from market to market and is a term peculiar to Glamorgan, varying from 2½ to 3 Winchester bushels. To streak or streek is a North of England term, meaning to level corn to the rum of a bushel or measure by passing a piece of straight wood over it (J. Wright, *English Dialect Dictionary*).

CHARLES WOOD 1766
NOTE BOOK

Dec 4th 1759. Ground a basket heaped of Clay & mixed with Dung. made 18 Potts with lids & Cakes.

Mr. John Watkins at the Copper Furnace in Warrington, his account of fire brick[1]

I buy my brick at Hardwin about four Miles from Flint in Chester river but put on board about 37s p. m. burnt ready for use & the Boatage to Liverpool is about 3s p. Ton Longweight. I have just now had a parcell and you may have, by sending a Wood Mould any weight & Size in proportion what I have is the same dimention of a Common Brick. The largest size And they endure any fire if you would deal there I will send you the makers Name & direction where to write to him, he can send them to Liverpool & there you must order an Agent to look after them, or a small Boat may be hired to take 15 or 20 Ton to you directly would be much the safest way.

Steel Furnace will cost Building £400
Coals used in one heat 7 ton
Workmen £1 11s 6d a heat with Meat, this Account was given to Joseph Wild at Sheffield by William Mekin at Durnal.

Dartford Air Furnace built by Samuel Wood for heating Iron slitting & rolling Iron for hoops his charges in Coal, wages etc vizt.

If the Furnaces are worked all day long, and kept to a constant heat, they consume 9 bushels of coals & will cutt 7, 8, 9 or 10 furnaces of Iron according, as the water comes.

[1] Cf. J.R. Harris, *The Copper King. A Biography of Thomas Williams of Llanidan* (1964), 16, 22–3, 52.

So reckoning one time with another 2 Bushel & 1 peck is used in cutting 1 Ton

2 bushels & 1 peck of coal at 1s p. bushel	£0 2 3
Charltons wages (at furnace) ¼ of a day	- - 5
Charches	- - 4
Foremans 6d, Boy 2d & Provis. 4½	- 10½
	- 40½
Burning 1 Ton of Coals	- 1 -
Wear & Tear 5s p. Ton	- 5 -
	- 10 -

For Streightening of hoops	5s p. Ton
Plates	6s p. Ton
Vat hoops	6s p. Ton

Weilding hoops rods	7d p. cwt
Plate rods	10d p. cwt.

William Wood Letter to C. Wood

Laleham, May 18 1753

Dear Bro,

I have your Lr by Mr G. who called on me here, in his way to Windsor. I very rarely go to London above twice a year, having no business there but to receive my Interest. Mr. Wilkinson is the only person I know that can supply you with Scraps, & Mr. G. has been with him.

Your 2 bills are in Mr. Beaches hand, so that I cannot send them to you till I go to London. I am glad to hear that you succeeded so well in your business & hope by degrees you will find out a method to make your bottoms durable & free of Iron from your Slag. In our bottoms we used of river Thames sand, after the glass grinders have made use of it, & when the bottoms opened, we filled up the Cracks with fresh Sand and after a firing it incorporated with the other part & became firm & Smooth.

It is not practicable to cast large slitting rolls in Brass Moulds, for of quantity of metal required for them will melt the Brass. The Moulds which we used were made of Loam, divided into two parts, after they are dryed upon the Wooden Module, & when taken off are bound together with Iron Wire. When they are well sealed, they are buried in sand, well pressed down to keep the metal from bursting the Mould, and placed perpendicular with the Mouth open for the receiving the metal and there must be a vacancy made in the Sand for a head of metal of about ¾ of a hundred weight for a supply as the metal Sinks away, & it must be filled up as long as it will receive any, otherwise the rolls will prove hollow. Great care must be taken to skim off all this slag from the metal when it is pouring out of the Ladles into the Moulds.

The Iron used for rolls must be of strong body inclinable to be harder. We used about 4 cwt of Shott in Bomb shells of a light strong Cold short grain & 2 cwt of the strongest toughest grey metal we could get which made a good Temperature for rolls; If they proved to hard, we put them into the furnace after the castings were over & covered them about 2 inches thick with Sand to keep the Air from them, & let them continue there all night, by which means they were made softer, but where ever the Air comes, it makes that part much harder.

The Cores we used for Scale weights ore made of highgate Sand in wooden Moulds, divided exactly in two equal parts & fitted together with three Iron pins on one part to go into the same number of holes on the other side, thus the Cores being made to taper and dryed in the furnace gradually, which makes them strong enough for use; The Cores used for small holes, are made of Loam about 1²/₃ & ¹/₃ of horse dung well tempered & mixed together, with a small Iron wire through them, without which the force of the metal would break them. The waste was very uncertain in the Iron we made use of, because the soots were so various. In the Potomack & Principia pigs,[1] it wasted sometimes 3 or 4 cwt or more in a Ton as it was more or less fluxed & free from slag. Clear cuttings or pieces of Dutch backs that have not been used in the fire mixed with Shott or Bomb shells, make very good rolls. If you make use of Guns, you cant be acquainted with their goodness till the Tummel are broke off, by which means you may see the grain, if it breaks of a bright white grain or Motley white, it is hard & unfit for any Castings if of a bright grey, then it generaly proves strong & middling tough. If of a close grey, then it will prove soft & tough, but if it be not well fluxed will wast much & have no body or strength. It is very difficult to know the goodness of the metal in Guns, unless you try Tummel first in a small furnace, & then you may come to a certainty & have such metal as is required for different goods. All cast Iron that has been used in the fire, or is the least burnt proves rotten when melted, besides the extra ordinary waste.

[1] i.e. pig iron from the American colonies.

Potomack pigs are now made very bad, being not half fluxed, & prove both white & rotten when made into castings. The overseer or Clerks at the Furnace have no fixed Salarys, but are paid by the Ton & therefore overburden their furnace for a quantity & so the pigs are all white & suffer a great Waste. I know not how to give you any more particular direction in this business, nothing but Experience can make you come to a tolerable certainty in the knowledge of these things.

The Expense of making fire Brick at Lowmill

One bushel of Clay, when ground heaped measure make 40 Bricks

30 Bushel to one thousand at 1s p. m.	£1	10	-
Labour in grinding for one thousand agreed for	-	2	6
Wear & Tear of the Mill	-	1	3
Making & burning agreed for p. m.	-	12	-
Coals to burn them			
6 Ton for one kiln 4 m. 500 for 1 m.	-	8	-
Wear & Tear of kiln p. m.	-	-	3
p. m.	£2	14	-

	lb
1 box of Longnor Mine weighed when ground	34
1 box of Bigrigg Mine weight	37
1 box of Cleetor Moor Mine weighed	37

The box is Long
Wide
Deep[1]

[1] The dimensions of the box have not been inserted; the three sources of ore mentioned are all in Cumberland.

A Tub to measure 3 sacks of Coals taken from the Tub at Backbarrow & Leighton Furnace in Lancashire.

53 Inches & half square within
23 inches do
One Sack Tub at ditto
39 Inches & ¼ within
17 Inches deep

N.B. The cleats at the boxes about 2 inches square cutt into two are included in the said dimensions the measure to be level with the wood.

Sept. 12, 1757. Weighed two loop load of round coal of the best sort Top Coal from Wingill or 8 Load four load on each Cost as sold at the Pitt whch weighed

1 loop	6 cwt	0 q	19 lb	12, 0, 27 the Ton
1 loop	6 cwt	0 q	8 lb	

Weighed at the same time a Bushell out of our Meer small & middling together water measure

1 cwt 2 q 12 lb, the 8 load or Ton is 12 cwt 3 q 12 lb.

Operations with Pitt Coal in an Air Furnace

August 7th, 1752. No 1, 2, 3, 4 Worked
5 boxes of Coal Pulverized
7 boxes of Longnor Mine
1 box of Lime

This did not gather into a loop being fluxed too high but then went in pieces

No 5 4 boxes of raw coals pulverized
5 boxes of Longnor Mine
$^{2}/_{3}$ box of Lime

Turned up well put in Loops (not weighed) shingled well.

No 6 — 3 boxes of raw coals
4 boxes of Longnor mine
1 box of Lime

Turned up well put in Scraps at guess shingled well

No 7 & 8 — 4 boxes of raw coal
8 boxes of Mine
with ½ bag of scraps
2 boxes of Lime

Divided into two operations they were too small for the bottom did not gather & were very red short.

Tuesday August 11th 1752.

		T	q	lb
No 1 Operation	Bigrig Open Cast Mine 5	1	2	17
	Raven Scale Gill Coal			4
	Lime Slacked	1	0	0
	Scraps	0	1	14
		T 2	0	3

Turned up exceeding Mellow & shingle in a New bellows which was not usual with Longnor, Frizington & other ore. Tryed a piece of the Loop free from scraps, in the Smiths hearth, hollow fire worked well into Nail, and not red short. This Mine is a rich Coldshort of the best kind.

The Half bloom after Shingling

	cwt	q	lb
weighed	0	2	8
Scraps broke off	0	0	12

No 2 Operation.
Was part of the first 4 Operations ground & mixed as follows
7 boxes of Metal
3 boxes of ground coal
1 box of lime

It did not gather in the furnace nor come into nature, therefore conclude it was burnt by the body of Iron destroyed.

Tuesday August 11th, 1752. No 3 Operation.

		cwt	q	lb
Bigrig Mine	5 boxes	1	2	17
raw pit coal	4 boxes			
Slacked Lime	1 box			
Scraps		0	2	0
	cwt	2	0	17

Turned up very well & shingled close the Solid and the half bloom weighed with two pieces broke off (one of which was heated in a hollow fire in the Smith hearth & drawn under the forge hammer into a bar part half flat & part a small square without the least Crack 1 cwt 0 q 7 lb.

This iron free from the red short quality & fitt for most use & may be as easily worked by a bad Smith as most other Iron, as fine a grain as any Iron of equal in goodness to forge Iron from the Pig with Charcoal fuels.

Tuesday August 11th, 1752. No 4 Operation.

		cwt	q	lb
Cleator Moor Mine	5 boxes	1	2	17
Coal	4 boxes			
Lime	1 box			
Scraps		0	1	0
		1	3	17

Turned up a little short, therefore let it remain in the furnace one fire, after which it wielded better if more Solid, took it out & shingled it with Wooden Manl & put it again into the furnace for two fires, took it out under the hammer but it being not of a good heat it cracked, put it again in the furnace & gave it three fires then it shingled under the forge Hammer round & solid. Half bloom weighed 0 cwt 2q 1 lb.

I observe that the Iron become more solid & fitter for the Hammer by remaining in the furnace after turning up one or two fires therefore a furnace should be made for that purpose besides a heating furnace for the Loops which would drain them of the superfluous Slag or Cinder & make them shingle under the hammer as Solid as finery Loops. It is the too great a quantity of Cinder that makes them soft & spongy. Therefore will not bear the shock of a heavy Forge Hammer.

Fryday August 14th, 1752. Operation No. 1 Big Rig Mine 185 lb weight without Scraps produced upon a New Bottom an Half Bloom weighing 30 lb Redshort.

No 2. Big Rig Mine 185 lb weight without Scraps produced an Half Bloom of 39 lb weight drew it at several heats under the forge hammer into a Barr of 27 lb weight, very Red short.

No. 3. Operation. Big rig Mine 185 lb weight Scraps 12 lb. Produced an Half Bloom of 65 lb weight Drew it at several Heats (in the Chafery with Brags) many more than usual, with good tough Iron into a Barr weighing 53 lb.

Fryday August 14th, 1752. No 4 Operation. Big rig Mine 185 lb weight. Scraps 20 lb produced an Half Bloom of 68 lb weight Which drew into a Barr in the Chafery with Brags at several Heats weighing 52 lb.

No 5 Operation. Big rig Mine 185 lb weight produced without Scraps an Half Bloom weighing 77 lb. Broke into two pieces when it near Shingled Solid.

Monday August 17th 1752. Sent to Whitehaven in order to be sent by way of Liverpool to Mr. Cockshutt to take off the Red Short.

No 1. Two pieces of the Half Bloom made of Big Rig Mine the 14th Instant weighing 2 cwt 7 lb.

No 2. five pieces of Frizington half Blooms, made 20 pieces weighing 9 lbs.

Two pieces Square Barr drawn from No 2 Operation made the 14 Instant.

In a Cask Broken Loops only Shingled with a Wooden Moul weighed 2 cwt.

Tuesday August 18th 1752. [*No entry]*

Oct. 24th 1752. Sent to Whitehaven in order to be sent to Liverpool for Mr. Cockshut Ten hundredweight of Metal prepared from Big Rig, & Longnor Iron Mines mixed, made in an Air Furnace with Pit Coal in the Proportion before mentioned. It was brought well into Nature and if Mr. Cockshutt method of sinking with Pit Coal makes good Iron from Redshort Cast or Pig Metal. I am of opinion the above Metal will produce the same. I reckon tho' no regular Acct was kept that the above Ten Hundredweight might be the Produce of Twenty Operations. Each Operation having 96 pound weight of Iron Mine which is 17 cwt 0 q 18 lb.

Several Operations that were made in Order to be sent to Mr. Cockhutt not being thoroughly brought into Nature. I put them into a furnace to see if a Second heating would perfect them in some degree better them, for as they was, they were of no use, that I knew. I gave them two good fires & found a large quantity of Slag flow from them, brought them well into Nature & near as Solid as Finery Iron and found them incline to stick or wield together into a Lump that they might have been brot out of the Furnace in a good Loop. But I brought them out in pieces One of which I gave to Nicol, a Smith to draw into a small barr, to try its nature and quality. It drew very well & made two good sound Spike Nails not inferior to those made of any other Iron. I broke one of these to see if the Black Grain was anything altered by this Method which I found much better & did not break short as before, but of a beef grain. Upon this Iron alode that as good Iron might be made in this method as in the old with Charcoal & Sinking in a Finery and this must be affected by a Method to drain it of its Superfluous Slag or Cinder as the finery does, the Pigs for the Mine wants nothing but a Sufficient Quantity of Slag, Cinder or Dross to be purged from it, in order to be brought into a malleable useful state & could this be done at one heat it would ensure the Good as well as at two, as is done with the Metals such as Lead, Tin etc. But as is found by Experience in the Common Method with a Blast Furnace that the First running is short of the malleable state, required. The Firing is Calculated for perfecting it, and the forming of this Hearth to drain, or purge, the Pigs of the Superfluous Slag depends on the goodness of the Iron, if it makes the heat sufficiently intense to leave the slag thin in a Tough Pig the Iron will be good, if thick the reverse. A Cold short Pig does not require so intense a heat as the Tough by reason that the Slag in it is more fusible and more inclined to be thin and the management of the Workmen in the Fining will also alter the quality. If he is not astute and take great care to keep the pieces of Metal that is broke from the Pig, continuously in Motion with his Forging in order to drain from it the Superfluous Slag, the Iron when sunk will be what the Workmen call raw & not bro't into Nature that is not drained of so much Slag as is necessary to bring it into a Malleable State. For to the piece of the last refined Iron in file dust mixed in a Crucible with a quantity of Cynder or Slag give them an intense heat & that perfect Metal shall be reduced into the former state of Bar or Pig Metal in the proportion to the quantity of Slag reduced with it. This I think plainly demonstrates what is wanting to make the Iron Tough & usefull.

I do not think that the Charcoal fuel makes the Iron better than Pit Coal provided the latter was as free from Sulphur or as agreeable to iron as that former but the separation of that Matter that prevents the Iron becoming Malleable is the thing wanted & that is an intense heat with a mixture of what is generally called a flux but is of no other use but to prevent the particles of Metal joining with the dross when near becoming into a fluid state in an Air furnace. In a Blast Furnace the Gravity of the metals causes the separation when the heat is sufficient, to flow the ore, because the dross is lighter, and consequently must be uppermost, but the Bottom of an Air furnace being flatt, unless something was mixed minutely with the Mine to prevent, or rather separate the Particles of Iron Metal from mixing with Slag & Dross when in a fluid state there would be no separation for the Nature of Iron when brought into a malleable state is not inclined to fluidity, when in that degree of heat which would make other Metal so, but is of a Waxy Nature so as to collect many particles into one body, by that Glutinous quality it then has which is called wielding.

By the mixtures made use of with the Ore or Mine in an Air furnace there must necessarily (when the heat is sufficiently intense) be a Separation of the metal from the Mine and in proportion to this heat the quantity & quality of the Iron will be, but as the form of the Furnace is only calculated for bringing the Metal in the Mine to a degree of Malleability there will be wanting a furnace of another form to finish it, by draining it of so much more Slag as to make it Tough & fitt for use. Too much Cynder may be taken from it so as to render it as short as Pig Metal.

The form of this refining Furnace should be within That is the bottom of a Flatt surface with a little Sloop no more than will suffer the Slag or Cinder, to run from the Metal as it melts; and Experience must show the time that it will require to drain a sufficient quantity of the Slag from it, which when discovered I do not see why the Iron should not be equally good with the Finery Iron in the Common method with charcoal Provided the Pit Coal be clean & free from sulphur. It being well known that sulphur is the greatest Enemy to that metal as may be seen by mixing a small quantity with the best Tough Iron which will alter its Nature so that it may be beat in a Mortar to a powder. Upon this bottom the Metal prepared in the first furnace should be put on in Small pieces that the Slag may sooner be drained from it, for experience shows in the Heating Furnace that when an Operation is turned up into the form of a Loop & beat together by a Wooden Mall, & in that shape put onto an heating furnace before the Slag can be drained from the heart or middle of it, the outside would be burnt and reduced to a Slag with what goes from it which will be prevented by putting the Metal into the refining Furnace in Small pieces, as a fire will have more power upon and more effectualy drain the slag fm it. When the Slag is drained sufficiently from it it will be in that Glutinous state as to be gathered & stuck together in the Lump, as large as the furnace will allow & carryed under the

Hammer for Shingling into an half bloom. If this Method of Working answers many advantages are obtained which could not be had in the former way both in the time & quantity & quality as follows. In the former method the furnace were obliged to be made so large within that is the Crown so high from the bottom as to allow the operations to be shapt up into a Loop and the larger the operation the higher the roof from the bottom which allows more room for the flame and consequently a less degree of heat in proportion and the operation must be longer in coming and not so well brought into Nature nor the Iron so good. By this New Method the Crown may be made so low as only to allow the operation to be spread when ready raked out by which a greater degree of heat is obtained and the Operation sooner brought into Nature a larger quantity of metal got from the Ore & brought out much sooner. The Bottoms in this new method may be of Sand which if they last a Week as I believe they may, a new one may be put in on Saturday & glazed ready for working on Monday and so go on in as regular method as in the old way. The refining Furnace should be made no larger than to drain the quantity of about three Operations at one time which I suppose may, when thoroughly Purged be about the size of a Large Finery Loop & produce about Six stone of Iron so that one refinery may serve three Preparing Furnaces. And brought out nearly one an hour.

The furnace built with a good fire stone I take to be as good as Brick and the reason that those built with stone have not so great an heat is that with Brick I conceive is from the Flues being at a greater distance from the Stack than that built with Brick. For the Furnace near the Chafery tho' of stone when it was Built close to the Stack, as the Brick one is, Was brought to as intense an heat if not greater than the Brick one But after it was pulled down & rebuilt at a distance from the Stack to admitt of a Passage to wheel Coal etc to the Ignifying hole which is about 4 feet wide it does not heat sufficien to bring off an operation in reasonable time. (Not room in the flue to allow a free passage for the fire.)

Therefore I think one may reasonably conclude it is not the Matter the furnace is made of but the Manner of Building it that makes the difference of the Drawing. The Stacks of the furnaces should be high which occasions the Drafts to be stronger as it stakes off the pillar of Air which impedes the draft in proportion to height. I doubt not but a furnace may be built to afford a sufficient heat to run the Iron into Pig Metals and in my opinion to great advantage as such works may be erected near the Ore & Coals, and if there was no other Profit but the saving of Carriage which is generally given it would be great.

May 9th 1753. Put into the Scrap Scouring Tub 9 cwt of Scrap Iron taken promiscuously from the Heap and cleaned them from the rust until bright wasted 22 lb, put the remainder 8 cwt 6 lb into Thirteen Potts which Produced

Put into Thirteen Potts 9 cwt of Scrap Iron not Scoured taken as above from the heap which produced

July 1753 made the following Tryals of Clay made into Potts

No 1. Bransay Clay ground 15/16 with 1/16 of fire Clay & some cracked in burning in a kiln about 1 in 6 but in an Air furnace put in when cool & fired gradualy not one break or cracks in the Air furnace with Scraps. leave the scraps soon & become soft which the Loops when bro't out of the furnace therefore not to be used.

No 2. Bransey Clay ground 5/6 with 1/6 of Clay got in the Road opposite to Hollins belonging Mrs. Steel. These cracked much in the Kiln not fit for use.

No 4. Bransey Clay ground 2/3 with 1/3 of a Broken pott from Wm Sons these Cracked in the Kiln about one half of them.

No 5. Bransey Clay ¾ with ¼ of Stourbridge pulverized Fire clay Brick, it came from Brick Kiln. All those were whole when taken out of the Kiln stood lower than those of Brownrigg Fire clay but not long enough to presereve the Iron from wasting too much.

No 6. Bransay Clay ground & sifted through finest Wire Sieve. Most of these cracked in the Kiln. No good.

No X. 3 boxes of Stourbridge weighing 1 cwt 2 q 0 lb Longweight & 6 boxes of Bransay weighing 2 cwt 0 q 18 lb Longweight made 16 Potts which burnt well in furnace as before No 1 stand the fire with Scraps and do not stick to the Loop wch occasions the Iron to be better had more yield from the Scrap.

One Half of Bransay Clay & the other Half Clay got upon Willi Moor Most of them whole when taken out of the Kiln No X, in Left, these did not stick to the Loop & stood untill near ready.

No 1. One part of a yellow tough Clay got at Silly Bank on Willimoor & two parts Bransay in one Potte. Nil.

No 2. Three parts Bransay Clay, & one part Silly Bank Clay three potts. Nil.

No 3. 5 parts Bransay & 1 part Silly Bank Clay Three potts bad.

No X1. 2½ Boxes of Stourbridge & 4 Boxes of Bransay Clay made

Stourbridge	1 cwt 1 q 0 lb
Bransay	1 cwt 3 q 22 lb long weight made 11 Potts

Stood the fire well & left the iron clean

No P. One part Clay from Willimoor near Castle Rigg & one part Bransay made into Potts. Burnt very well in an Air furnace and stood the fire better than any except the Stourbridge but stuck to the Iron too much Bransay in.

No 10. parts Bransay and one part Pipe made into melted & stuck to the Loop very bad.

Four Potts brought by Andrew Wedgwood made of his own Clay at Harke in Parish of Durham put into the furnace with one Pott marked x with Stourbridge & Bransay Clay withstood the fire.

Half Bloom 3 2 19.

No 2. Potts of Clay got at Brick kiln near Harris above John Jacksons House One of these two potts broke in falling into the furnace as it was not laid upon the Grate before.

No 6. Potts made of 2 parts of bottom & 1 part of the Top Willimoor Clay stood about half the time but as they were thin & unequal turned that might be the reason they did not stand longer.

No II. Potts $^1/_3$ Willimor Top $^1/_3$ bottom & $^1/_3$ Racoe stood but about half their time.

No IIIII. Potts $^1/_6$, $^1/_6$ Durham, $^1/_3$ Willimor Top, $^1/_3$ Bottom.

stood about half their time.

No VIII. $^1/_6$, $^1/_6$ Durham, $^1/_3$ Willimor Top & $^1/_3$ Willimor Bottom. Stood as above.

VII. $^1/_3$ Durham, $^1/_3$ Willimor, $^1/_3$ Bransay.

stood as above.

No VI. 2 parts Willimor Top & Bottom & 1 part of Bransay stood about 2 hours did not stick to the Iron the Half Blooms clean & good.

No VIII. 3 Parts Willimor Top & Bottom with Bransay, dropt soon.

No XVI. 3 Parts Willimor Top & Bottom & 1 part Bransay, stood the fire about 1 hour & half & left in the Loop partly clean, tho' not well as if there had not been any Bransay.

No I. 5 Potts 2 parts Top Willimor & 1 part Big rig Stone. Burnt & ground not good.

No II. 4 Potts Willimor Bottom not ground, stood as well as most.

No III. 4 Potts Whitehaven Rock Sill ground & sifted. not good.

No IIII. Potts one part Wingill Sill one Rurse Clay bad almost melted in burning.

No IIIII. Potts of 3 parts Racoe Clay and 2 parts Big Rig Stone burnt & ground fine.

No X. 2 Potts of Racoe alone. Bad.

No – . 1 Pott of 2 parts Bransey & 1 part Racoe. Bad.

No I. Six Potts of Willimor bottom ground & not sifted. stood as before.

No II. Three Potts of Keekle Gill Clay. Bad.

No I. 7 Potts of one part Whitehaven Rock Sill ground & sifted and one part Willimor Top Clay.

Fly to pieces in burning.

No II. Five Potts of one part Stourbridge from Friz[ington] and one part Whitehaven Rock Sill, craked.

No – . 10 Potts of 5 boxes of Willimor bottom & 2 boxes of Whitehaven Rock Sill. stood about 3 parts of the time.

No – . 4 Potts of all Willimor bottom not ground made stronger than formerly stood but took more fire.

A Furnace Erected

The Clays for the Potts are Whitehaven Rock Sill & Clay got upon Willimor Castlerigg in the following proportions viz. 5 Parts Sill, 4 parts Clay & 5 of horse dung laid in a heap, layer upon layer, then cut down & mixed well together ready for passing to the Iron rolls, placed horizontally three times, the first time wide enough to break the lumps small of an equal size, the second time the rolls closer to grind it smaller, or rather scourge & temper them altogether and lastly the third time to squeeze & tamper it more to the stiff consistency of Tough Clay. After these several Operations, the clay is moulded & worked with the hands ready for rolling with rolling pin on a board with ledges on either side about 5/8 of an Inch higher than the board to make the Clay of an equal thickness for the potts which are as follows. The Mould of Wood made round about twelve inches deep within Eleven wide & the bottom to increase gradually to Twelve inches at the Top to make the Clay with the Iron leave the mould when turned out upon the Paddle ready for the furnace. The Clay is rolled into flat pieces & put into the mould each piece carefully joined together form the Pott, the bottom & sides, but first there is put pieces of old Coal sacks at the bottom & sides of the Mould, before the clay goes in that it may prevent its sticking to it & leaving it. These moulds when clayed are carefully filled with clean scraps free of rust cast metal and all other foreign matter and weighed then a Cake of the same Clay put upon the Top & closed & joined to the other Clay. When they are charged they are turned upside down before the Clay is dry upon an Iron Paddle slung on a hook & chain upon a Crane for the more conveniently conveying them into the furnace but before they are put into the furnace & while on the paddle rolled pieces of Clay are put on the Top & Sides of those potts wch are put next the Bridge and in the hottest part of the furnace. After the sheets of clay are joined to the clay that forms the pott, there is a pricker about half an inch diameter of Iron to make a number of holes thro' the Clay on the sides & Top & a larger one on the Center on the Top & the Clay lifted up to lye hollow on the Top in order to give the Air and moisture liberty to come out, otherwise the Clay would burst & the Scraps scatter about the furnace with a loss it being difficult to gather all the small Nails out of the furnace bottom from among the Coal Cinders of which its made. Experience must direct that part of the furnace, that requires the potts to be lined with fresh Clay besides those next the bridge wch are always to be Lined, althou' you may build several furnaces as near the dimension of each other as possibly there will be a difference in their workking and heating.

The working up of Iron Scraps in Potts is an Expeditious & profitable way, & makes the best of Iron as the small pieces are always of the best kind of Iron & if there should be any among them of a Cold short, or red short quality, yet the greater quantity being of the best they do not alter the Nature of the whole Mass but the contrary gives it a stronger body without destroying its Toughness & consequently makes it more useful especially for all large works but then great care must be had to the cleanness of these Scraps and that no cast Iron, brass Lead or Pewter be put in the Potts with the Scraps, which prevent the pieces welding or uniting together and make the Iron in the barr hollow and not so fitt for use. Rust occasions a sharp Cinder, prays upon the Iron & makes a greater Waste. Therefore the scraps should be clean & free from all foreign matter and if the pieces are placed close together in the Pott, the Nail heads & other longer pieces next the Clay with the smaller to fill up all the vacancies, & large ones in the middle, the Iron will be good, the Waste little, not so liable to burn if the clay should fall off at the latter end, in the furnace and a greater quantity made in the same time & fuel. When we first began this branch, we were not so carefull as we found afterwards was necessary we put the Scraps in by hand full and shaked them down to settle themselves, in this method we would not separate the Cast Metal, Lead, Copper Brass Pewter and rusty pieces nor were the potts Solid & heavy which made great waste in the furnace and the Iron not so good as other ways it would have been. When care is taken to place the pieces of Iron regular and closely by each other, one by one, no piece of any other kind can escape the filler by which means, the pott is closely & well filled. of clean Iron, that ward the Clay off, would stand firm in the furnace & being solid the fire would not have that power to melt and wast the Iron as when open & Spongy to admit the flame into the body of Loop besides when the several pieces are not complete & close together and laid cross each other to support them, when put into the furnace off the paddle they settle & break the Clay, which, when beginning to heat, falls off and expose the bar Iron to the flame, which must waste on the outside before the heat of the Potts is of Welding heat but if the Clay remains whole, it preserves the Iron from the flame untill the whole is ready for the hammer. At first the filler had three farthings a pott and would fill Twelve in one day, these were badly filled, hollow & fixing the metal mixed, now we give three half pence a pott & get them well filled a greater quantity of Iron put into a Pott, all clean & good so that from the three & four Ton made in one furnace in a week (4 Ton we tho't extraordinary) we now make Eight, Nine or Ten Ton a week. When the Loops are shingled the Shingler should Nick away one in the middle down about one third that they may be sooner hot. for the Quickening which occasions less waste in that operation in a Chafery with Pitt Coal we had used under 2 cwt in the Ton in the hollow fire and since they have been nicked in the middle & care taken in heating in the Chafery the waste is but about 46 lb weight a charge or 17/18 lb in the Ton from the half bloom after shingling, to the Blooms for the Hammerman.

The Furnaces are made to hold eighteen or 20 potts at one time, each Pott if well filled will contain from 3 q 20 lb to 1 cwt 0 q 20 lb of Scraps in the general run the eighteen potts contain 17 cwt of Scraps to 19 cwt. The Wooden Moulds are 12 inches deep & 11 wide at bottom to 12 at the Top within. Great care shouds be observed in Erecting the furnaces first the Stack or Chimney should be upwards of 40 feet high, the Tunnel or hollow part 13 or 15 Inches square or any other form for the more convenience of the place its erected upon for it matters not what form it is of, so that it contains the hollow space required to contain the quantity of flame from the body of fire from the furnace; the Number of solid inches contained in the hollow of 13 or 15 or 22 in square diameter round rather than Square we find sufficient for our present purposes but this size form & manner of building any furnace must be adapted to the use its intended for, or the person who erected it will be disappointed of his erection. The higher the Stack or chimney is the stronger the draft it takes off or lessens the Column of Air from the pressure of the flame and the hollow of the Tunnel should be of good fire brick laid with Clay of the same, the joints within & close as possible for although the Clay may be very good and in body as large as bricks will endure a long intense heat yet the clay will as it acquires body and not burnt and in time will choke the Tunnel so much as to take off the strength of the draft & oblige you to take the whole Stack down to rebuild which will be troublesome & expensive besides the disappointment of stopping your work. The hole left for the joining of the flue to the Stack should be left long & wide to allow a free admittion of the flame if it be hindred there you can not expect a good heat. in the body of the furnace, it will indeed occasion a smarter draft, but too much to keep the flame to heat the metal in the furnace, it draws the flame too suddenly & before it can execute its office up the chimney. The same care should be observed in the flue to give it room before and at joining the Stack for the same reason. The bricks for the body of the furnace should be laid with as little clay as possible and especially the Arched roof otherways when the fire dry the Clay the joints are open & let the bricks fall down & shrink, which alters the form of your furnace and disappoints you, both of the size you intended it, & the smoothness of it. The closer & smoother the Arch is, the fire has less power upon it, as there is less resistance for comparatively speaking, it is like water the greater resistance the stronger the power, if there is Brick better then other they should be used in the fire place & bridge which sooner burn down as it is the hottest part of the furnace. And as Brick is an Expensive Article it should be observed that the bricks from the roof not being burnt through will serve to lay the sides of the furnace about two feet from the bridge towards the Mouth, which will serve New ones for the roofs & hottest parts.

Dimensions of a furnace for Cold short metal

Tuères about 1½ or 1¾ of an inch below the base to leave a little at the Top into the work. The base to leave a little into the work è to leave a little to the firespit so much as water will but just run off at the Edge.

The firespit to be as high, or near it as the base.

The bottom to be about 5½ or 5¾ Inch deep, under the Tuère, & the Tuere to be placed 8 inches from the base. The bottom to be laid to the Cinder hole so that water may just run to grove next the Cinder hole of the firespit but not to run to the firespit.

The finery should be formed to the quality of the metal to be refined. Cold short metal requires a less degree of heat then tough or redshort, the Cinders, of the latter requiring a thinner fusion, to drain it of a sufficient quantity if it bring the super body of the cinder left in the body of the Iron that gives it that quality so that if a Finery is formed to have a heat sufficient to thin the cinder, that it may be discharged at proper times, any red short metal may be in part mended, but very few workmen have the knowledge but go on in their old method & are often at a loss when they meet with a metal different in quality from that they have.

Nov. 17. 1761. Try charcoal made of firewood and ground small with Iron Ore mixed with kelp[1] and waste and if it does not mend the red short quality try the prepared metal in a pit coal Finery with a little kelp put in at different times to stand the cinder.Also try the Slag or Cinder from the ores made in the method above mentioned with cast metal instead of Finery, or the cinder with a little kelp and waste and let it stand in the potts or moulds a week before used that the alkaline salts may have time to penetrate the metal.

Try also the prepared metal after made solid by the hammer in potts with cinder and kelp & waste & without and by itself with cinder & the same fluxes which may answer a second refining.

These acids joined to may sometime with the same metal of Finery happen to be out of order & require taking down to alter, for not knowing the first principle stricken through it upset them at the least alteration in their plates alter the quality of the Iron confounds them whereas if they were well acquainted with these good iron goods with less degree of heat, so the nature of the metal requires, which is obtained by observation & experience & by known by some it would save Fuel, Iron & Labour.

Isaac Wilkinson form of a founders furnace

The inside at the bridge 4 ft wider in order to contain the metal, singly and the pieces not to lye upon each other, that the fire may have its full force by whch means the same quantity of metal usualy put at one charge and is two hours in melting, may be performed with less Iron in one hour or less and in order to obtain a heat sufficient, the flue should be large & the Stack high, the higher it is the less will the column of Air be, to obstruct the draft. The fireplace he would have, near the whole breadth of the shingling furnace, and narrow in the length, in order to have liberty the better to dross the grates. The cleanest Coals should be used in these furnaces, to facilitate the metals melting & prevent the grates clinkering up, and stop the free passage of the air & cleaning the grate of the clinkers or vitrified Dirt that is raised with the Coal, at all the Colleries in Cumberland when the Coal is not clean the bars are

[1] A seaweed; its ash, after calcining, contains soda.

frequently opened, to get the Clinkers out the coals come out with them, the furnace is cooled, the melting of the metal retarded, & time lost, besides the loss of Coal used in bringing the furnace up the same degree of heat, it was in before the grate was daused.

Isaac Wilkinson's opinion of making iron, from the ore, in an Air furnace.

I am not against making Iron in an Air furnace using your ore for making the Iron in the Air furnace but the difficulties that I thought of was in giving it a regular heat, without running the top into a regular, & leaving the middle raw. In as I apprehend you put the Ore with the flux, three inches thick into a flatt bottomed furnace the uppermost inch, must be made regular before the middle is hot enough, or brought into nature. And then when you have turned it the underside is liable to the same fate, so I think the upper and underside when turned loose, a good quantity of the metal will be in a regular, and if it be taken sooner, before so much is withdrawing then the middle is not brought into nature & when you roll it up into a loop, the top is inside up of the two insides, which is enough in some parts, and since too much, and the middle that is not enough which makes the Iron bad, notwithstanding your puting it into another furnace to heat more regular. The way that I thought to remedy was that I build an oven like unto a kiln for Earthen Ware with usual bellows in it, one above another, so that one might have four or five bellows seven or eight feet diameter & heated with the same fires so that a fifth part of the fuel would heat the same quantity of Coal, with a more equal intense heat, yet not such a draft as an Air furnace hath, for I think that it is too quick a heat upon it, for I look upon Iron to require a long & intense heat, quick heat, turning it into a regular. A kiln, for which ore are a float, is not enough. I have always been of opinion that it might be brought to do very well. For when I was at Clifton Furnace I got a little Ore & pounded it, mixed it with Coal dust and put it into the foot of an Air furnace when we thought it to be enough, we took it out and Mr Bowes (who was your great surveyor at that time) hammered it upon an Anvil, and was convinced that it might be made to serve very well & it was but a small quantity, as a pint, or the like. I think I did not burn it. It may be that I may try some little more of it again when I have built a furnace which I expect to do shortly. If I could be of any service at any time to you I should be very willing to do it.

I am with best respects to you
and yours
Your very humble Servt
Isaac Wilkinson

Wilson House, Dec 18th 1751

In flourishing or bringing squared metal or granulated or stumped small equal to granulating in potts the finery cinder into nature the difficulty arises bringing the heart of the potts into nature for although they shingle well under the hammer and make seemingly good half bloom yet when anchored & drawn into a barr it being raw in the middle it is hollow & will not draw, sound which in my opinion may be remedied by metal thoroughly brought into Nature being put in the middle, of the pott to be about six inches diameter, about two inches in the middle with metals in nature, and granulated or stamped cast metal round at the sides whch will then be only about 2 inches thick round the metal in nature that is put in the middle should be within two or three inches of the top of the pot, as that part is most exposed to the fire & is better brought into nature & seldom is raw but the bottom of the pot should be covered with metals in nature, near two inches deep as that part does not partake of the greatest heat, is generally most raw. These pots of about six inches hollow with the metal in nature in the middle as before should be put in the middle of a large pot instead of scraps, and granulated or Stamped metal round the sides & about 2 inches deep on the Top but the bottom must have Scraps of metal in nature small an inch or two thick, round the sides at bottom. This method in my opinion will answer to make good Iron if rightly managed in the furnace. The smaller the metal & cinder is the sooner & better it is brought into nature & will answer the end proposed. In all those methods of making Iron in pots it is supposed that the Clay the pots are made of will stand the fire until the metal is thoroughly brought into nature & ready for the hammer otherwise it will fall to the bottom of the furnace, spread flatt mix with the bad cinder & coal the bottom is made of & consequently be of little worth, but if the potts do stand the time required care must be taken when the loops or part are brought out of the furnace, that they do not take up any dirt, or coal cinder as they fall from the furnace for as they are generally open and not so solid as a finery loop, would receive that dirt into the hollow which would be shingled in the half bloom & when Anchored & drawn would be hollow in that part where the dirt or cinder was. To prevent this, they should be taken from the furnace mouth with the Tongs &

carryed to the hammer the floor laid with old cast plates or swepped clean before the furnace is drawn, for the loops to fall on. These methods observed will, prevent a deal of Iron from being hollow and Labour & charge besides the waste of Iron, in doubling up the hollow bars which must be done before they can be slitt or otherways useful.

Some observations on my Journey with
Gabriel Griffiths into Yorkshire etc.
September 1754

Called at Burgh Forge belonging to Mr. Thomas Chadwick. They draw their finery Iron out with Pit Coal and have 2 q yield in a Ton of Iron They put a bar of Iron about 4 inches broad, 1 inch thick & about 4 feet long, fixed upon the helve, & it comes through under the pole of the hammer which they say prevents their breaking. They also make use of a water Tuiren, so that two are wielded together at the nose & heel to contain water, with two pipes or tubes screwed in, the one to convey water in, the other to discharge it, which keeps it always cool.

Their coal appears to be very indifferent as bad as at Low Mill Charles Taylor, Hammerman tells me that he draws weekly 4 Ton single hand. Their pit coal costs 2d p. cwt at their forge Charcoal 30s per doz. Mr Stock Clerk. Mr. Chadwick informed me that before he used the barr upon the helve one did not serve a week but since the use of it it lasts a Month or more. Likewise the double Tuiren in the Chafery will serve 6 months.

Sorts of Iron used at Warrington are Rolled plates 12 inches broad, thickness of a shilling, for plate Locks and about ³/₈ thick & 2½ & 3 inches broad for Cart Wheels that carry dung on Land.

Narrow flat about 1½ & ¾ for Hinges these are sold at 18s p. cwt Long weight Rod Iron slitt from Toula bar iron for small nails at £18 10s per Ton Long weight. Ditto made from Sable, for Horse Nails & small Spikes at £21 10s per Ton Long weight.

Pig hogs for Lockware used here.

Sept. 3. Tuesday called at Mere Heath Furnace (Mr. Smith Clerk) which makes all cold short pigs with charcoal.[1] They use Lancashire Mine when they cast uses. They make 18 ton weekly thro' the blast, as

[1] A large, charcoal-fired furnace in North Staffordshire, near Newcastle-under-Lyme (Riden, *Gazetteer*, pp. 83–4).

they say, The Charcoal costs them 38s p. dozen. But the stone lyes near which makes amends for dearness of Coal. This furnace is 5 miles from Newcastle & 4 miles from Stone. At Taulk upon the Hill Coal is sold at their pits at at 1d p. cwt or 2½ cwt which is the Horse Load for 2½d.

Fryday 6th. Morning we left Woosley Bridge for Cankwood forge Mr. Hopkins Manager a Single work, which makes double hand 3 ton weekly, Mill Iron from Cold short pigs; draws out with pit coal. They tell me that they have about 10 cwt in the year more than 2 q in the hundred over yield. But when they draw with Brays they have 1½ cwt & ¾ over yield. Distant from Woosley bridge 5 miles and from Woverhampton 9 computed Miles, got to the Latter about 12.

Saturday Sept. 7th. We went from Wolverhampton to Stourbridge called upon Mr. Bowyer, who informed us, that there was not any probability, of Iron falling there because the Woodowners had raised their Cordwood, in proportion to the advance of iron prices. He went with us to view their clay, the best which is in solid hard lumps if picked clean from of any other matter. It goes to Glass houses pots & is ground & sifted fine. The smaller sort wch is not picked, is ground by a stone, & made into Brick. This Clay lyes 20 yards under the Surface. Observation—Low mill clay if clean picked seems to be much better for use in bricks than theirs. But not as good as that seperated for Glass house pots. The Low Mill method of grinding their clay & preparing it is in my opinion much better & more expeditious than theirs. The best picked Clay would make excellent Brick, but it is too dear for that use.

10th. At Wednesbury with my brother John. He makes but 4 Ton weekly in one furnace & draws out with pit coal, in a close Chafery fire & makes 2 cwt 2 q from 22 cwt half blooms, which is more than I can do at Lowmill. The closer the Scraps are placed in the pots the less the Waste will be.

12th Thursday. Called at Heath Forge belonging to Mr. Jordan, a Single Work they tell me that they make from 3 ton 15 cwt to four ton weekly of Mill Iron draw out with Pit Coal have ¾ over yield, use 12 cwt of Coal to draw out 1 Ton of Iron. The finer informs me that their making that quantity is from their diligence that he could make 3½ Ton from any pig. They use Grange[1] pig made from Stone alone it is a very driving pig.

Breakfasted this Morning with Mr. Bowyer. He went with us to the forge underwritten, vizt.

Called at Stourton Mill upon Stour belonging to Mr. Cooke. He slitts 1000 tons yearly, as we are informed he has 15 p Ton free of waste. The Iron Masters send him 21 cwt. Longweight in the Bar & he sends back 20 cwt Longweight. There is not more than 6½ ft head & fall.

About one mile from this lyes Hide Mill which slitts the same quantity. And near this is Kinver Corn Mills.

We then came to Whittington forge belonging to Mr. Knight.[2] This is a double work & refinery & a Chafery which make from English Pigs from 7 to 8 Ton weekly if they have water but never less than 300 T p. Annum. They draw out with Pitcoal and get ½ cwt yield.

The next place was Cookly forge belonging to the same person, works the same works & make the same quantity, draw with pit coal yield ½ cwt. Their hammer about 6 cwt goes but slow yet draws 10 Ton weekly when they have Water. Below there is a hammer mans forge it was not at Work the Hammer wheel is but 8½ feet diameter, head & a fall about 6 feet.

The next forge was Wolverley, a double work belonging to the same person. They work all Foreign[3] Pigs one finery with Tubal & Cardiff pigs for Mill Iron the other with Bush River pigs for Mill best Tough which they say makes the best Iron in England. I know it to be a good pig. They make of Blend of 3½ and of B.B. 3 Ton Weekly. They draw with Pit Coal & have ½ cwt in the Ton thro' the year. Their Blooms or Anconys go at 20 to the Ton. Their barrs are full inch thick. They give 11s p. Ton for Anconys Doublehand if they make 3 Ton if less but 10/6. For drawing 9d & 1s p. cwt overyield. But to keep up the quantity I am informed that if the finer cannot keep to 3 Ton per week Mr. Knight will not keep him but this does not often happen. There is not any Clerk at any of these forges. The stocktaker keeps an Account & delivers it once a week to one of Mr. Knight's Sons. They use 11 sack of Coals for 1 Ton of Bloom, 8 sack to the dozen. A sack is 2½ yards long & 4 feet wide. The coals Mr. Knight lays in cost 55 to 60s for 8 Sacks.

[1] Another of the North Staffordshire furnaces: ibid. 78.

[2] For the Knights' forges in the Stour valley see L. Ince, *The Knight Family and the British Iron Industry, 1697–1902* (1991).

[3] i.e. American.

Saturday Sept. 14th. Called at Sutton forge near Shrewsbury. A Double Work. One finery makes Osburn[1] Iron for Wire the other Merchant. They say that they make Single hand Merchant Iron from 2–2½ Ton weekly they have not more than 3 hours sleep in the 24. The whole length of their helve before husted is 8 feet. Their Anvil is 6 inches lower than the centre of the helve & hust.

Their Arms take about 6 inches above the Center. The Anvil is high in the heel so that it may bear upon the Pin. At Tearn they use a barr of Iron above & under the the helve, which they say preserves it much. Their hammer about 6 cwt.

William Hazeldene is Carpenter at Tearn & John Robinson at Sutton. They do all the new and old work for 8s p. week house & fire.

Richard Jones is the finer & hammerman. They say they make 3 Ton of blooms from 4 Ton of Pigs & have 10 cwt over yield in the year. They work Bersham Pig[2] sell their Iron @ 22s p. cwt Longweight. They have their uses from the Dale[3] & make good Iron from the flourished hammer & Anvils.

The Carpenters business is as follows. To prepare keys & Wedges etc. but if a key or Wedge & any small thing is to be done in the night, or at any other time, the hammerman, is not to wait to call the Carpenter but to do it himself. This is the Custom in all these parts.

The Iron on the Top & bottom of the helve, is lett into the holes & a thin board put upon the Iron between it & the Brag; Likewise a Thin wedge next to the pole of the hammer & the Iron. The Iron to be 6 or 8 inches long, behind the Brag. The Iron not to be thicker than ¼ of an inch thick, and to be rolled.

At Tearn, the boards upon the Wear are fixed with a hinge, like the wire hinge upon a dale box, with Iron & a weight to keep them up when little water & when a deal of water, the weight of water being heavier than the Iron, it forces it down flatt, to allow the water a passage over it.

I am informed that at Upton & Withiford Forges they make use of their Brays in the Chafery without washing & produce the same yield. The Stocktaker is not allowed the use of a rake, when he fills the Brays, in order that the good and bad may be used together.

[1] i.e. Osmund.

[2] i.e. pig made at Bersham furnace (Denbighs.).

[3] i.e. Coalbrookdale (Shropshire).

Monday Sept. 16th. Called at the Dale.[1] The first Forge belongs to Mr. Tho. Allen which is employed in plating for Frying pans, fire shovels etc. all their damaged plates are made into chafing dishes, as the small pieces will serve for some part of them.

The next Water Work is a Mill for Boring their large Fire Engine Cylinders.

The next above, is a forge with 2 finerys & a Chafery. The finerys are employed in Sinking pit coal pigs, & they say, they make 1½ Ton Weekly by Single hand.

The next Work above is a Furnace for castings, they say they make 12 Ton Weekly, and can make the Pigs of any grain they please. They have made Mill Iron from Coke pigs, with Charcoal, for 30 years. And the Scarcity and great demand for those pigs induced them to Erect more furnaces as they bear a good price. The vein of Coal, that they make use of, for Coking is not more than 2 feet thick. Their Ironstone measure is thick. But Mr. Ford thinks that both Coal & Stone will fail in 20 years so that it will not be worth any ones while to continue or Erect other works there. He informs me that [they] have made Stamper heads & Shanks for the Stamper houses in Cornwall of wrought Iron made in a finery with the small coke that they could not use in their furnace from their Coke metal & he let me see some of them which appeared clean & good.

Above this Furnace there is another which makes the same quantity of Castings with Coke. Mr. Ford says that they employ about 250 hands, besides Carriers etc. The castings are taken by the Workmen at a certain price p. Ton. Their Bellows are 20 feet long. Blow hard & have a good blast. The Coal they use to Coke is called Clod Coal & is a weak Coal for the strong & hot will not do. The coke made of it is near as light as Wood Coal.

Their Stack is nearly the same Dimension as other furnaces, as Mr. Ford informs us.

Layton Furnace lyes about 2 Miles from Buildways Bridge.[2] Blows with Charcoal, belongs to Mr. Ford. They make 20 Ton weekly through the Blast, this he says is from an improvement he has made, in the Structure of it. The water is raised by a fire Engine & runs into the pool again in the same manner they do at the Dale otherways they would not have water sufficient. There is the most work done at these places with

[1] i.e. Coalbrookdale.

[2] Leighton (Shropshire), near Buildwas, not to be confused with a furnace of the same name in Cumberland (Riden, *Gazetteer*, 62, 114).

the least water, of any place in England. All their Castings are undertaken by the Ton in Companys, and are made from the Blast & Air Furnaces to aid it when any large p[iece] is to be cast.

Wednesday Sept. 18th. Called at Bersham Furnace[1] which was blowing with Coke, they made 10 Ton weekly. They say, that they blow with Coke & Charcoal a Month alternately. Isaac Wilkinson informed us, that he had good coal which will be raised easily, when a Bob Engine is erected, to draw the water, which is near finished. They have Kennel coal which he proposes to Coke, & try in this furnace. He says this furnace is 9 feet wide at the boshes. But if he was to build another he would make 12 feet. That the wider the pipe you blow through the better. His, that he now blows with are 2½ & the next shall be 4 inches.

He has made this a compleat work, Air furnaces on each side of the Blast Furnace, with the three, he says he can cast 5 Ton at one casting. And can run in his Air furnace Metal in three quarters of an hour which I believe, is from the height of his Stack, which appears very high.

He says Millstones beat small & made into the bottom for Air furnaces, will be servisable.

He says he uses 60 Ton of Raw coal made into Coke weekly, which at 10 Ton of Metal is 6 Ton of Coal to the Ton of metal.

[1] Ibid., 65–8.

INDEX OF PERSONS AND PLACES

There is no wholly satisfactory way of indexing within a reasonable space a text of this period in which a large proportion (but not all) of persons mentioned appear to be using Welsh patronymics (but without the insertion of *ap* or *ferch* between their first and second names), rather than hereditable surnames. Occasionally Wood names a father and son in such a way as to make the use of a patronymic obvious, or he gives someone three names, which at this period, among craftsmen and labourers, clearly points to the use of patronymics, rather than surnames. At the same time, the Englishmen who appear here are of course using surnames. It would be possible to index everyone who appears to be using a patronymic twice over, under both their first and second names, but this would lengthen the index enormously without making the identification of individuals any easier. Instead, an arbitrary decision has been made to treat second names as surnames throughout and to index everyone in the usual inverted form.

Another problem concerns the indifferent inclusion or omission of a terminal 's' in common names such as William. Again an arbitrary decision has been made to standardise all first names without an 's' and to group second names under single headings, e.g. 'William(s)', irrespective of how the name is spelt in the text. Other minor variations in the spelling of personal names have been silently rationalised under the usual modern form; more substantial variants have been cross-referenced.

As far as possible, all place-names have been indexed under parishes and parishes given geographical county suffixes. Place-names in Wales (by far the majority) have generally been spelt in the form in which they appear on the latest Ordnance Survey map or, if they are no longer current, in what appears to be a standard modern Welsh form.

INDEX OF SUBJECTS

Since many topics, such as the weather or the more commonly used building materials, recur almost daily throughout the diary, only the most important occurrences have been indexed here.